Serial Killers

Louise Gerdes, *Book Editor*

David L. Bender, *Publisher*
Bruno Leone, *Executive Editor*
Bonnie Szumski, *Editorial Director*
David M. Haugen, *Managing Editor*
Brenda Stalcup, *Series Editor*

Contemporary Issues
Companion

Greenhaven Press, Inc., San Diego, CA

Every effort has been made to trace the owners of copyrighted material. The articles in this volume may have been edited for content, length, and/or reading level. The titles have been changed to enhance the editorial purpose. Those interested in locating the original source will find the complete citation on the first page of each article.

Library of Congress Cataloging-in-Publication Data

Serial killers / Louise Gerdes, book editor.
     p.   cm. — (Contemporary issues companion)
   Includes bibliographical references and index.
   ISBN 0-7377-0167-6 (lib. : alk. paper). —
ISBN 0-7377-0166-8 (pbk. : alk. paper)
   1. Serial murderers. 2. Serial murders. I. Gerdes, Louise. II. Series.
HV6515.S47 2000
364.15'23—dc21   99-23601
                                                  CIP

©2000 by Greenhaven Press, Inc.
P.O. Box 289009, San Diego, CA 92198-9009

Printed in the U.S.A.

CONTENTS

FOREWORD

In the news, on the streets, and in neighborhoods, individuals are confronted with a variety of social problems. Such problems may affect people directly: A young woman may struggle with depression, suspect a friend of having bulimia, or watch a loved one battle cancer. And even the issues that do not directly affect her private life—such as religious cults, domestic violence, or legalized gambling—still impact the larger society in which she lives. Discovering and analyzing the complexities of issues that encompass communal and societal realms as well as the world of personal experience is a valuable educational goal in the modern world.

Effectively addressing social problems requires familiarity with a constantly changing stream of data. Becoming well informed about today's controversies is an intricate process that often involves reading myriad primary and secondary sources, analyzing political debates, weighing various experts' opinions—even listening to firsthand accounts of those directly affected by the issue. For students and general observers, this can be a daunting task because of the sheer volume of information available in books, periodicals, on the evening news, and on the Internet. Researching the consequences of legalized gambling, for example, might entail sifting through congressional testimony on gambling's societal effects, examining private studies on Indian gaming, perusing numerous websites devoted to Internet betting, and reading essays written by lottery winners as well as interviews with recovering compulsive gamblers. Obtaining valuable information can be time-consuming—since it often requires researchers to pore over numerous documents and commentaries before discovering a source relevant to their particular investigation.

Greenhaven's Contemporary Issues Companion series seeks to assist this process of research by providing readers with useful and pertinent information about today's complex issues. Each volume in this anthology series focuses on a topic of current interest, presenting informative and thought-provoking selections written from a wide variety of viewpoints. The readings selected by the editors include such diverse sources as personal accounts and case studies, pertinent factual and statistical articles, and relevant commentaries and overviews. This diversity of sources and views, found in every Contemporary Issues Companion, offers readers a broad perspective in one convenient volume.

In addition, each title in the Contemporary Issues Companion series is designed especially for young adults. The selections included in every volume are chosen for their accessibility and are expertly edited in consideration of both the reading and comprehension levels of the audience. The structure of the anthologies also enhances accessibility. An introductory essay places each issue in context and provides helpful facts such as historical background or current statistics and legislation that pertain to the topic. The chapters that follow organize the material and focus on specific aspects of the book's topic. Every essay is introduced by a brief summary of its main points and biographical information about the author. These summaries aid in comprehension and can also serve to direct readers to material of immediate interest and need. Finally, a comprehensive index allows readers to efficiently scan and locate content.

The Contemporary Issues Companion series is an ideal launching point for research on a particular topic. Each anthology in the series is composed of readings taken from an extensive gamut of resources, including periodicals, newspapers, books, government documents, the publications of private and public organizations, and Internet websites. In these volumes, readers will find factual support suitable for use in reports, debates, speeches, and research papers. The anthologies also facilitate further research, featuring a book and periodical bibliography and a list of organizations to contact for additional information.

A perfect resource for both students and the general reader, Greenhaven's Contemporary Issues Companion series is sure to be a valued source of current, readable information on social problems that interest young adults. It is the editors' hope that readers will find the Contemporary Issues Companion series useful as a starting point to formulate their own opinions about and answers to the complex issues of the present day.

INTRODUCTION

Although serial murder accounts for less than 1 percent of the total homicides in the United States each year, the phenomenon receives significant attention in the media. The public obtains most of its information about serial killers from television, newspapers, novels, and movies. According to criminologist Steven A. Egger, "this media information is frequently in the form of hype and unfortunately contains a number of myths, inaccuracies, and outright falsehoods." However, even the experts disagree on a number of issues concerning the topic, including the exact definition of serial murder. One point on which they do agree is that serial murder involves the killing of three or more victims over time, with a "cooling off" period in between each murder that can last from days to years. This general definition distinguishes serial killers from mass murderers, who kill three or more victims at one point in time.

Experts also agree that identifying and apprehending serial killers can be extremely difficult. Many police agencies have unsolved serial murder cases in their records. For instance, authorities in King County, Washington, have never caught or even identified the Green River killer, whom they blame for the deaths of forty-nine women in Washington and Oregon. The killings stopped in 1984, and some officials believe the killer moved on to continue killing elsewhere. Others theorize that the killer may have been incarcerated for unrelated criminal activity, and still others think the killer may be dead. After so many years have passed, many believe that it is unlikely that the case of the Green River killer will ever be solved.

One reason it is difficult to catch serial killers is that they frequently blend in so well that community members and police officials never suspect them. For example, John Wayne Gacy, who was convicted of killing thirty-three young men and boys, was widely considered to be a friendly man who often dressed as a clown to entertain children for charitable events. His neighbors had never seen the dark side of his personality and were stunned to realize that he was a serial killer. Other serial murderers are able to disappear into the background, either through their nondescript appearance or their use of disguises. Authorities claimed that serial killer Ted Bundy "never looked the same from photograph to photograph." Furthermore, people often hold the misconception that serial killers must look monstrous or evil, which causes them to overlook the pleasant, normal-looking murderer next door.

The type of victims that many serial killers choose can also complicate matters. Serial killers often select victims from a powerless or marginalized section of the population. The most frequent serial murder victim is the female prostitute, whose lifestyle makes her easy prey. Serial killers select prostitutes because they are easy to control and are not likely to be reported missing. Their remains may not be found until long after the murder and then are typically difficult to identify because of the victim's lack of close ties to family and the community. Due to the marginalized status of these victims, the public places little pressure on the police to solve such cases and apprehend the killers.

Serial murder investigations also present law enforcement officials with problems that do not occur in other types of murder cases, which is another reason serial killers are difficult to apprehend. One of the most significant problems these officials confront is known as "linkage blindness," the failure to link one killing to another or to find patterns among homicides. Because policing in the United States is decentralized and control remains in the hands of local police agencies, law enforcement agencies in different jurisdictions do not often communicate with one another or coordinate their investigations. Therefore, officers in one jurisdiction may not be aware that similar murders are taking place elsewhere.

Another problem encountered by law enforcement agencies is the sheer volume of information that accumulates in a serial murder investigation. Typically, the police are inundated with leads, tips, evidence, and good suspects. While investigating the Yorkshire Ripper, British investigators accumulated twenty-four tons of paper records. Without the aid of computers, this information is difficult to manage, yet many police agencies do not take advantage of or are not adept at using complex computer programs.

Some authorities believe that to determine whether several murders have been committed by the same killer, police agencies must verify that the murders share similar patterns, or modus operandi. This requires a network that processes information from various jurisdictions, collects the data at a central point, and redistributes its findings to the different agencies. One such network is the Violent Criminal Apprehension Program (VICAP), located at the FBI National Academy in Quantico, Virginia, as a component of the National Center for the Analysis of Violent Crime. Pierce Brooks, credited as VICAP's creator, described it as a "nationwide clearinghouse . . . to provide all law enforcement agencies reporting similar pattern violent crimes with the information necessary to initiate a coordinated multi-agency investigation." After years of planning, in 1984 VICAP developed a sixteen-page form on which police agencies can report any solved or unsolved homicides, missing persons, or unidentified dead bodies. However, as of this writing, VICAP's effectiveness in apprehending serial killers is still uncertain.

Finally, police agencies are often reluctant to commit to serial murder investigations because they place the police in the public eye, and since serial killers are notoriously difficult to apprehend, the police may face a great deal of negative publicity. Egger remarks, "Serial killers make the police look bad. To commit to trying to catch one makes the hunters look inept, at the very least." Moreover, once the police open a serial murder investigation, the media attention can be detrimental to solving the case. For instance, when Danny Rolling viciously butchered five people in Gainesville, Florida, within seventy-two hours during 1990, the sensationalistic media coverage significantly contributed to the state of public hysteria in the community. Journalist Michael Reynolds described the scene as a "media carnival" and characterized his peers as "rats on Methedrine" in their frenzy to report the gruesome details of the murders. When the public hears that a serial killer is on the loose, they become hungry for news, and the media is eager to give the public what it wants, even if the information is inaccurate, inflammatory, or damaging to the law enforcement investigation.

How then are serial killers apprehended? Surprisingly, often by pure chance. For instance, in what began as a routine driving violation, two New York state troopers tried to pull over a pickup that had no license plates. The driver, Joel Rifkin, led the troopers on a chase that ended when his pickup crashed. The troopers discovered a decomposed female body in the truck bed—the last of Rifkin's seventeen victims. In other cases, a suspect in one murder may confess to other homicides that police had not previously classified as serial murders. Perhaps the most infamous example is Henry Lee Lucas, who, while under arrest for one killing, began to confess to hundreds of murders throughout the United States. In these situations, law enforcement officials were not actively looking for a serial killer but ended up apprehending one.

Sometimes the media, politicians, victims' rights groups, or relatives of homicide victims put pressure on law enforcement agencies to pursue a serial murder investigation. For example, after Donald Harvey had confessed to causing one death at the hospital where he worked in Cincinnati, Ohio, a local TV station pressured the police into reexamining twenty-three other suspicious deaths at the hospital. Further police investigation resulted in Harvey's confession and his conviction for thirty-seven murders in Ohio and Kentucky.

The most controversial technique for identifying and apprehending serial killers is psychological profiling. Former FBI agent Robert Ressler defines psychological profiling as "the process of identifying the gross psychological characteristics of an individual based upon an analysis of the crimes he or she committed and providing a general description of the person, utilizing those traits." Ressler and his colleagues at the Behavioral Science Unit at the FBI studied and interviewed many incarcerated serial killers to develop the following technique: First, the profiler must conduct a thorough inspection of the specific crime scene in the case. The profiler must then conduct an in-depth examination of the background and activities of the victims and any known suspects. Next, the profiler must formulate the probable motivating factors of all parties involved. Finally, the profiler develops a description of the perpetrator based on the overt characteristics associated with his or her psychological makeup. Ideally, this profile will help police agencies to narrow their pool of suspects.

In most fictional accounts, serial killers are identified and apprehended through the profile provided by either an FBI agent or a local psychiatrist. In reality, profilers may not be called in to assist investigators until late in the investigation, and the profile may or may not help identify the serial killer. John Godwin, a critic of the profiling technique, claims that profilers "play a blindman's bluff, groping in all directions in the hope of touching a sleeve. Occasionally they do, but not firmly enough to seize it, for the behaviorists producing them must necessarily deal in generalities and types. But policemen can't arrest a type, they require hard data: names, faces, fingerprints, locations, times, dates. None of which the psychiatrists can offer." Even FBI agents like Robert Ressler, Roy Hazelwood, and John Douglas admit that profiles rarely lead directly to the solution of a case. However, they argue that profiles are intended instead to provide assistance to the investigators by directing the investigation toward suspects possessing certain characteristics.

Although law enforcement officials, criminologists, and psychiatrists disagree over how to best identify and apprehend serial killers, they do agree that investigating serial murder is anything but an exact science. While academics continue to study serial killer behavior to better define and understand this phenomenon, law enforcement agencies keep exploring new investigative technologies and learning from shared experiences and information. The authors in *Serial Killers: Contemporary Issues Companion* look at the various sides of this issue while exploring the nature of serial killers, examining possible causes for their behavior, and evaluating the impact serial killers have on society as a whole.

CHAPTER 1

THE NATURE OF SERIAL MURDER

Serial Homicide: An Overview

Jan Scott

Much of what the public knows about serial killers is based on speculation and stereotypes, writes Jan Scott, Professor of Psychiatry at the University of Glascow, Scotland. In the following selection, Scott summarizes the research available on serial homicide. The author explains that most of the research describes and classifies serial killers, identifying the methods they use, the victims they choose, and the locations they select. In particular, Scott looks at research that reveals the differences between male and female serial killers: For example, women tend to use poison and kill for personal gain, while men often have sexual motives and are more likely to torture and mutilate their victims. Although serial killers often suffered traumatic childhoods and tend to have violent sexual fantasies, Scott asserts that these factors alone do not indicate potential involvement in serial homicide. To prevent serial murder, Scott concludes, more research on its causes is necessary.

The British media's preoccupation with Myra Hindley and Rosemary West, two now infamous convicted female serial killers, both reflects and reinforces the public's fascination with such crimes. Myra Hindley was jailed in 1966 for the murder of five children and has made a public plea for understanding and forgiveness. Rosemary West was convicted in 1995 of the murder over a period of 16 years of 10 young women, including her 16-year-old daughter. The press reports express our anxiety that such a person could have lived undetected in the community for so long, our abhorrence at the nature of the crimes, and our confusion about how anyone, particularly a woman, could commit them. It is easy to condemn serial killers as monsters. However, it is important to explore beyond the stereotypes and consider what we can learn from the research literature about women and men who kill repeatedly.

E. Hickey defines a serial killer as "someone who, through premeditation, kills three or more people over a period of time." His descriptive study of over 200 serial killers, identified over a period of more

Reprinted from Jan Scott, "Serial Homicide," *British Medical Journal*, January 6, 1996, by permission of the author. (Endnotes in the original have been omitted in this reprint.)

than 100 years, found that offenders tended to be about 30 years old and that 90% were white. On average, the murderers killed between eight and 14 victims over a period of four to eight years. As with single homicides, 12–17% of offenders were women. Women tended to commit the murders over a longer period than men, probably because they escaped suspicion during the early stages of police investigation.

Because of the rarity of serial killings, there are few empirical studies examining their aetiology. Speculation outweighs valid and reliable research data. The media stereotype of a serial killer is of a male psychopathic sexual sadist. However, descriptive classifications identify four subgroups: serial sexual killers, team killers, family killers, and institutional killers. Recent typologies have systematically assessed killers' geographic mobility, the methods they used to kill their victims, and patterns of attack. Three patterns of mobility are recognised: travelling killers, local killers, and killers whose attacks are limited to a specific place. From reviews of the methods of murder and patterns of victimisation, four combinations have been identified, from killers who select specific victims and use specific methods (such as ritualised torture then strangulation of young women) to killers who murder a variety of victims using a variety of methods.

Compared with female serial killers, male serial killers are more geographically mobile (50% are local killers), show a greater tendency to include torture or mutilation as part of the process of killing, and more often report a sexual motive (50%). Female serial killers are more likely to report personal gain as a motive, carry out place-specific murders (60%), and poison their victims (60%). While most male serial murderers kill strangers, women mainly kill their husbands or relatives. Consecutive filicide (murder of one's own children) is usually associated with mental disturbance. A fifth of female serial killers murder people in hospitals or nursing homes where they are employed. When women are implicated in sadistic sexual homicides, they have usually acted in partnership with a man. About 35% of all serial killers have accomplices. In two thirds of mixed couples involved in "team killings," the man is the dominant partner. The extent to which the woman is involved may range from awareness of the murderer's behaviour through to active participation in the abduction, torture, and killing of victims.

The Fantasy Life of Serial Killers

One of the most disturbing aspects of these crimes is the individualised nature of the killings. While most serial killers have severe personality dysfunction (usually psychopathic disorder) this alone cannot explain their behaviour. On the basis of information from interviews, A. Burgess and other researchers suggest that serial killers tend to have experienced impaired childhood attachments, formative traumatic experiences, and a private internal world of violent thoughts and fantasies. This combination leaves the individual isolated, preoccupied, and lacking awareness of socially accepted constraints on behaviour. Support for this model comes from studies of male sexual killers and sadistic offenders. In a retrospective comparison with 17 killers who had committed single sexual murders, 25 male serial killers showed an intrusive fantasy life as evidenced by higher rates of paraphilias [a dependence on unusual, narrowly focused, or forbidden stimuli to achieve arousal] and violent fantasies. The scenes of their crimes were also more likely to be organised, suggesting more premeditation and planning.

However, intrusive violent or sexual fantasies are poor indicators of potential involvement in serial homicide. Other factors must be involved to translate fantasy into actual behaviour. Pornography, alcohol, and drugs may act as facilitators, but in many cases the factors that contribute to initial disinhibition are unclear. Once restraints are removed, serial killers frequently engage in increasingly more accurate behavioural rehearsals of the fantasised murder. After the first homicide has been committed, the subjective experience of domination and control of a victim becomes a powerful reinforcer of the behaviour. Also, the reality never perfectly fits the fantasy, so the murderer may repeat the activity to try to achieve a match between real and fantasised outcomes.

We do not know whether this model of fantasy-driven behaviour, derived from interviews with male serial killers, can be applied to female serial killers. Interview data give tentative evidence linking female serial killers with high rates of severe parental deprivation, childhood abuse, personality disorder, low self-esteem, and a sense of personal inadequacy. The lower prevalence of sexual killings by women is compatible with the notion that women tend to experience power and control through other methods. Women who commit consecutive filicide and some who commit murder in institutions may be labelled as suffering from Munchausen syndrome by proxy [a condition in which offenders injure or induce illness in children or other dependents in order to gain attention and sympathy for themselves]. However, little research is available.

The low prevalence of multiple homicides means that current theories will take many years to test. Epidemiological principles exploring time, place, person, and individual risk factors have been used successfully in investigating serial killings in hospital settings. This model could provide a useful framework for examining multiple homicides occurring in other settings. Retrospective analysis cannot prove cause and effect. However, this research is important in developing profiles of a group of offenders who are more heterogeneous than previously realised. If we are even to contemplate preventing serial homicide we must move beyond rhetoric and try to understand why such crimes occur.

DEFINING SERIAL MURDER

Belea T. Keeney and Kathleen M. Heide

Because the way killers are classified influences how criminologists and law enforcement agencies examine and draw conclusions in murder cases, write criminologists Belea T. Keeney and Kathleen M. Heide, a carefully crafted definition of serial murder is necessary. Much of the research conducted assumes that serial killers are male and that serial murder is a type of "lust murder," the authors reveal. However, Keeney and Heide argue that these assumptions ignore other types of serial murder behavior. In order to develop a satisfactory definition, the authors summarize the research conducted on serial murder and conclude with a definition they believe encompasses all types of serial murder, including female serial killers and those who have relationships with their victims. Keeney is a criminologist who has consulted with several Florida law enforcement agencies. Heide is a licensed psychotherapist and a professor of criminology at the University of South Florida in Tampa.

Dorothea Puentes, 59, was charged in 1989 with the murders of nine of her tenants in a Sacramento, California boarding house. The murders occurred over a four-year period and were alleged to have been overdose poisonings of legal substances.

Brian Rosenfeld was charged in 1992 with the murders of three nursing home patients in St. Petersburg, Florida. The murders occurred over a five-year period and were alleged to have been overdose poisonings by injection of legal substances. Rosenfeld was suspected by law enforcement officials of murdering over 20 other patients.

Christine Falling, 19, was charged in 1982 with the murder of three children she was babysitting. The murders occurred over a three-year period and were alleged to have been strangulations or smotherings. Law enforcement officials also suspected Falling of two other child murders.

Classifying Offenders

Three murderers, three types of victims, three methods of killing with common elements: the murders were multiple and spaced over time.

From Belea T. Keeney and Kathleen M. Heide, "Serial Murder: A More Accurate and Inclusive Definition," *International Journal of Offender Therapy and Comparative Criminology*, vol. 39, no. 4 (December 1995), pp. 299–306. Copyright ©1995 by Sage Publications, Inc. Reprinted by permission of Sage Publications, Inc. (References in the original have been omitted in this reprint.)

Despite evidence of having killed several people over an extended period of time, these offenders would not have been classified under traditional definitions of serial murder. With few and isolated exceptions,
the professional literature on serial murder published before 1990 would
not have considered these individuals to fit within its parameters.

Since the early 1970s, serial murder has received increased attention from both law enforcement agencies and the popular media. A
series of highly publicized multiple murders committed by men
prompted predictions of what J. Norris called an "epidemic of serial
homicide." Research on this topic has been extremely limited, however, due to the relatively rare occurrence of this phenomenon and the
difficulty in obtaining access to these offenders. Basic research in this
area is literally in its infancy; to date, little traditional, academic, or
empirical research has been attempted.

One frequently encounters two implicit assumptions in the psychiatric literature on serial murder: (1) the serial murderer is male, and
(2) serial murder is a type of "lust murder," perpetrated by a "sexual
sadist." All too often writers fail to define the phenomenon of serial
murder in their manuscripts, preferring on occasion to defer to law
enforcement and criminology experts to do so in another forum. Others, such as D.J. Sears, appear to assume that the phenomenon is so
obvious that the operationalization of the term is unnecessary at this
point in time.

The failure of others to examine their implicit criteria for classify-
ing a killer as a serial murderer affects the cases examined and the
conclusions drawn. In his recent chapter on serial killers, G.B. Paler-
mo, a forensic psychiatrist whose cases included Jeff Dahmer, cited
more than 20 cases of serial murder. These cases extended back into
the nineteenth century, crossed continents, and included cases in
Europe and Great Britain as well as the United States. Interestingly, all
the serial murderers he referenced were male and all appear to have
been motivated by "lust."

Definitions of serial murder, when provided, have typically been so
narrow and exclusionary that they have not adequately represented
the totality of multiple murder behavior. This article reviews the evolution of the definition in professional literature and proposes a more
complete definition for future use. In order to understand and prevent serial murder, social scientists need an accurate definition of the
phenomenon; one that encompasses *all* of the multiple murderers
who kill in separate incidents over time.

Serial Murder Distinguished

Prior to 1980, serial murder was grouped into the more general classi-
fication of mass murder. Scholars have since agreed that multiple
murder can be grouped into one of three classifications: mass, spree,
and serial murder.

The killing of three or more victims in one event has been defined as *mass murder*. For example, George Hennard opened fire on diners at the Luby's cafeteria in Killeen, Texas in October of 1991 and killed 23 people before he committed suicide. Because he remained in the same location and only a short amount of time elapsed overall, his crime was categorized as a mass murder. Another example of mass murder was the case of James Huberty. In July of 1984, he killed 21 people in what was dubbed the "McDonald's Massacre."

The killing of three or more victims in different locations but within the context of one event has been termed *spree murder*. William Cruse of Palm Bay, Florida killed a total of six people at different locations without ceasing criminal activity in April of 1987. Because there was no "cooling off" period between the murders, the locations changed and his homicidal activities continued, his crimes were categorized as spree murders.

The killings of multiple victims spaced over time was a core element in the definitions of *serial murder* frequently cited in the professional literature. The killings have occurred over a period of days or weeks to months or years. Well-known examples included Ted Bundy, John Gacy, and Albert DeSalvo. Ted Bundy, after conviction, confessed to the murder of over three dozen women in Washington, Utah, and Florida over an estimated four-year period. John Gacy was believed to have killed and buried over 30 teenage boys under his home near Chicago over six years. Albert DeSalvo, "The Boston Strangler," murdered 13 women in 1962 and 1963.

B.M. Cormier, C.C.J. Anglicker, R. Boyer, and G. Mersereav were the first researchers to attempt clarification of this crime. They used the term multicide to refer to a number of murders committed by one perpetrator and spread over a significant period of time. Cormier and associates stated that the motivation was primarily pathological. They maintained that the murderer consistently selected a certain type of victim and was likely to continue killing until arrest.

Summarizing the Dimensions of Serial Murder

Table 1 summarizes six dimensions of serial murder typically considered by Cormier and colleagues and the nine authors that followed them: motive, victim type, relationship with victim, sex specific, time period, and psychological state of the murderer. Two observations are apparent following perusal of this table. First, some authors did not address one or more dimensions in their definitions. Second, often the authors narrowly restricted the range of variability on specific dimensions.

Nine of the ten authors cited an internal, nonrational motive as a factor in defining serial murder. Eight definitions included a similar victim type as another factor in their definitions.

Of the eight authors who examined the killer's relationship with the victim, seven concluded that the relationship was typically either nonexistent or limited. Of the seven authors who specifically addressed gender, six stated or implied that participation in serial murder was limited to men or an almost exclusively male phenomenon.

Nine of the ten definitions of serial murder have emphasized repetitiveness and a specific time frame (e.g., months or years) between homicides. Furthermore, nine of these definitions held that an abnormal psychological state existed in the murderer.

Limitations of Existing Definitions

In reviewing existing definitions, it became apparent that some researchers have defined serial murder very narrowly; others, too broadly. For example, Steven A. Egger (1990) included numerous indicators as to motive, victim type, relationship with victim, sex of offender, time period, psychological state, and geographical base. He stated that a homicide is a serial murder when "a second murder and/or subsequent murder" is committed by one or more people

Table 1: Dimensions of Serial Homicide Considered by Author

Definition Elements *Author*	Motive	Victim Type	Relationship with Victim	Sex Specific	Time Period	Psychological State
B.M. Cormier et al., 1972		yes, usually type selected			months or years	deep-seated psychopathology
Steven A. Egger, 1990	power over victims	powerless, symbolic value to killer	none	usually male	over time	compulsive behavior
Eric Hickey, 1991	pleasure and/or gain	victims have common factors	any	males and females	over time	"Jekyll and Hyde" aspect
R.M. Holmes & S.T. DeBurger, 1988	intrinsic and nonrational from within killer		none or little		months or years	nihilistic and often sociopathic
Jack Levin & James Alan Fox, 1985	excessive need for domination & control	usually similar victims	none	usually male	over time	typically sociopathic
E. Leyton, 1986	destruction of established societal order, sex secondary	usually special social class		male	over time	"lustmord," enjoyment from killing
C. Linedecker, 1990	power, domination and control	helpless, vulnerable	none	usually male	over time	usually sadistic, sexual psychopathic
J. Norris, 1988	no apparent rational motive		fragile			"addicted" to murder
Robert Ressler, A. Burgess, & J. Douglas, 1988	sexual maladjustment with violent fantasies	yes, peculiar to offender	usually none	male	months or years	
A. Rule, 1980	no apparent motive	yes, vulnerable	none	usually male	over time	psychopathic and egotistical

whose killings share certain characteristics. Egger indicated that the killers, who are typically men, have no prior relationship with their victims. The second or subsequent killing occurs at a different time and has "no apparent connection" to the first murder and is typically committed in a separate geographical site. The murderer in these types of cases is motivated to kill to achieve power over his victim rather than material gain. Victims may be selected for their "symbolic value," and are perceived as lacking status in society. Those killed are generally not capable of fighting back or alerting other people to the mortal situation in which they find themselves. Egger gave examples of "vagrants, prostitutes, migrant workers, homosexuals, missing children, and single and often elderly women" as classes of people who are viewed as powerless "given their situation in time, place or status within their immediate surroundings."

K.M. Heide (1991) noted that "Egger's definition may exclude some 'killers' who would fit under this general rubric, were the phenomenon not so over-defined." In Heide's view, Egger's definition limited further exploration by narrowing the definition "to capture a specific type of serial murder, rather than serial murder in general."

In sharp contrast to the extensive definition provided by Egger, the definition used by the FBI was brief. Serial homicide was indicated by the murder of at least three victims with a cooling off period between them. This period could be as brief as two days or it could be longer, such as weeks or months.

One of the more broad definitions was offered by Eric Hickey. He maintained that serial murderers should include men or women who kill "a minimum of three to four victims" over time. He noted that there is typically a pattern evident in their homicides. Hickey's definition was an important step forward for several reasons. One, it shifted the focus of serial homicide research away from the current and almost exclusive perspective on the male serial "lust" murderer. Two, it explicitly acknowledged the participation of women in this crime. Third, it allowed for the inclusion of offenders who had a relationship with their victims (such as landlords, health care workers, etc.) as part of this phenomenon.

Belea T. Keeney developed the following definition in an attempt to refine this concept and further scientific investigation:

> Serial murder is the premeditated murder of three or more victims committed over time, in separate incidents, in a civilian context, with the murder activity being chosen by the offender.

This definition obviously excludes killings performed by military functionaries as part of their job duties and political assassinations by terrorist groups. It does include health care workers who murder their patients, parents who murder their children, professional assassins who operate under the confines of organized crime syndicates, and persons who kill multiple spouses/lovers. The minimum number of murder victims is set at three, which coincides with the FBI designation.

The Advantages of a New Definition

The proposed definition has several benefits. It appears to encompass all types of serial murder,not only those committed by roaming males who act out of lust. It is premature at this time, given the empirical knowledge available on serial murder, to equate serial murder with sexual sadism. It is currently unknown whether the incidence of multiple murders perpetrated by sexual sadists over time is the most prevalent type of serial murder because the phenomenon of serial murder has not been operationalized by many investigators. Hence, samples of "serial murderers" have often been generated by the investigators' unstated conception of which multiple murderers do and do not qualify as serial murderers.

The traditional exclusion of women from consideration as sample subjects by many investigators is an excellent example of how prevailing beliefs can limit science when not subjected to scrutiny. In a sample of serial murderers who killed from 1795 through 1988, Hickey found that 34 of the 203 individuals who killed multiple victims in separate incidents over time were female. These data suggest that over the last two centuries, approximately one of six serial murderers has been female.

In the last several years, other authors have examined the participation of women in serial murder and illustrated the ways in which women kill. In contrast to their pioneering work on *Mass Murder* published in 1985, the analysis and discussion of serial murder by James Alan Fox and Jack Levin in *Overkill* included several examples of women who killed multiple victims over time. Philip Jenkins argued that feminist writers have obscured the real participation of women in serial murder to advance their ideological platform that women are exclusively victims in this regard.

Keeney and Heide's 1994 study compared male and female serial murderers on 14 variables. Gender differences were found on nine variables: damage to the victim, torture of the victim, weapon/method used, stalking vs. luring behaviors, crime scene organization, reasons for the murders, substance abuse history, psychiatric diagnosis, and household composition at the time of the murder. Similarities between male and female serial murderers were found on the remaining five variables: broken homes, race, educational level, childhood abuse, and occupation.

The FBI typology of serial murderers (disorganized asocial type vs. organized non-social type), which was based on male serial murderers, may need to be expanded when cases of females are entered into the data analysis pool. In addition, the commonly held position by

European criminologists that multiple murderers are either paranoid schizophrenics or sexual sadists may bear re-examination when women are included in the sample.

In contrast to many earlier definitions, the proposed definition includes murders committed by those who do have a relationship with their victims such as spouses, parents, or caretakers. In addition, unlike the definition proposed by Jenkins, it does not exclude multiple killings committed over time for presumed financial gain. Instead, the definition seeks to focus attention on those who murder serially for instrumental as well as expressive reasons. Given the paucity of scientific knowledge, those who kill repeatedly need to be studied to further understanding of this phenomenon. Finally, by being more inclusive and broad, the proposed definition opens up areas for future exploration in the field of homicidal behavior.

UNDERSTANDING SERIAL KILLERS

Michael D. Kelleher and C.L. Kelleher

Michael D. Kelleher specializes in threat assessment and human resource management for public and private organizations. C.L. Kelleher is a volunteer counselor and human rights advocate. Together they authored *Murder Most Rare: The Female Serial Killer*, from which the following selection is taken. The authors define serial murder as the murder of three or more individuals, with each murder separated by a discrete cooling-off period. The media often portray serial killers as white male sexual predators, note the authors, but serial killers are actually a diverse group of both men and women who have complex and varied motivations. Although male serial killers surpass female serial killers in number, the authors assert that the women typically commit their crimes over a longer time period. Furthermore, male serial killers are often sexual predators, but female serial killers select victims who are easily dominated and made dependent on them, the authors write. The diversity and complexity of serial killers make this type of crime difficult to solve, the authors explain.

The terms *serial murder* and *serial killer* have become deeply woven into the fabric of the American popular media and press since they were first introduced more than twenty years ago. Understandably, these concepts have now been transformed into compelling elements in a mosaic of collective fear, which constitutes a significant part of the American psyche. In particular, over the past two decades, the serial killer has become a fundamental and easily recognized protagonist in the most popular products of the American entertainment industry. Television and the film industry have imbued our citizens with an irresistible visual and visceral link to the popularized—and often inaccurate—image of this inscrutable criminal. The pervasive and relentless reporting of the gruesome exploits of the sexual serial killer has fostered a remarkable national intimacy with this crime and its perpetrator. In essence, the media-created image of the sexual serial killer of the late twentieth century has become a symbolic national nemesis whose violent activities have been lionized in print, on television, and in the movies to a level that is unprecedented among other categories of crime. Because of this phenomenon, terms such as *serial murder* and *serial killer* have been endowed with a common understanding that has made them an integral part of our collective cultural awareness. However, this common understanding is fundamentally incomplete and misleading, although its power is undeniable.

Popular Definitions Are Inaccurate

In truth, there is little about the crime of serial murder that is simple or easily understood. In fact, it is one of the most perplexing and least understood categories of violent crime to plague our society. The very definition of serial murder remains uncertain and constitutes a point of controversy among the most eminent criminologists and behaviorists in this country. Although the general public embraces a prosaic definition of serial murder that has been inferred by the popular media and the entertainment industry, the definition is grossly inaccurate for at least one fundamental reason—it is unacceptably limiting in its representation of the true breadth and diversity of this crime and its perpetrators. In reality, the perpetrator of serial murder who has been so successfully popularized in the entertainment industry is but one of a rather large number of types of serial killers who have been active for many centuries and in many countries throughout the world.

The covert world of the serial killer is populated with a diverse array of characters who cannot be genuinely represented by the single contemporary legend of the sexual serial predator. Furthermore, the crimes of the serial killer extend far into the history of the United States and other countries. This criminal has been active in virtually all industrial societies for centuries—particularly in areas of dense urbanization. It is a common mistake to overlook entire categories of serial murderers, such as the Nazi perpetrators of the Holocaust in World War II, for reasons that remain inexplicable and invalid.

In the contemporary understanding of the term, serial killing is often considered to be the act of narrowly defined individuals who undertake crimes that are heinous, but also narrowly defined. In fact, serial killers may operate alone or in teams; the killer may join others in a highly organized group whose fundamental purpose is to commit murder or may be a woefully disorganized individual with little or no awareness of his or her actions, who operates alone. The perpetrators may be male or female, and they may be motivated by any number of perplexing reasons that defy common understanding. Serial killers may wreak vengeance on those who are completely unknown, acquaintances, friends, coworkers, men, women, adolescents, family members, or children. Their compulsions to kill are surprisingly diverse and frequently convoluted. Their motivations range across the wide plain of human emotions, from the perverse obsession of a sexual predator, to the desire for profit, an obsession with control and domination, or because of psychological impairments that are little understood and, sometimes, completely unrecognized.

Awareness of Serial Murder Is Increasing

Because the crime of serial murder has received far more popularization than serious research, it is understandable that misunderstanding and myth surround the activities of the perpetrator. We are only now beginning to learn something of the dark motivations that lie behind the gruesome crimes of the serial killer. Furthermore, we have yet to understand enough about this crime to even reach a consensus about how to properly categorize the perpetrator or adequately comprehend his or her actions. In part, this dilemma exists because the crime of serial murder is still a relatively rare event in this country. Even though the exploits of the serial murderer capture the attention of the public in a unique and compelling way, this is not a crime that threatens a significant number of citizens. Relative to other violent felonies, serial murder remains a generally impersonal and non-threatening type of crime to the majority of Americans. It has become an issue in the consciousness of our citizenry because of the horrifying nature of the crime itself, not because of its personal impact in terms of the number of victims claimed each year. However, in recent decades, this situation has begun changing as the number of active serial killers in America increases.

The crime of serial murder has been increasing in recent years. In fact, the average number of serial murders that occur each decade has steadily increased since 1960. However, these statistics may not be as alarming as they seem on their surface. The crime of serial murder has only received the abiding attention of researchers, criminologists, and law enforcement personnel for approximately three decades. Although law enforcement personnel have long recognized the pattern of related felonies that we now define as serial murder, this crime has only recently benefited from serious and intensive research. In other words, researchers, criminologists and law enforcement personnel are now acutely aware of a category of crime that has finally been defined and recognized as unique. In addition, law enforcement personnel have recently developed a variety of sophisticated techniques to identify the activities of a serial killer and somewhat understand his or her motivations, methods of operation, and possible future activities. Because of the rapidly increasing knowledge of this crime and its perpetrator, it is likely that criminologists and law enforcement personnel are now able to recognize and identify serial murders in situations that were overlooked a few decades ago. This increased sophistication in recognizing and categorizing the crime may, in part, account for the apparently steady increase in serial murders in recent decades.

However, it is unlikely that improvements in law enforcement strategies or research techniques could solely explain the dramatic increase in serial murders over the past few decades. Thus, it is also necessary to recognize that there are probably more serial killers active in society today than were active in the past. Considering the imperatives that are known to be associated with the commission of this crime, it seems likely that the increasing average number of serial murders each decade is due, in significant measure, to the simple fact that there are more serial killers among us today than in previous decades.

Defining Serial Murder

In order to understand the motivations and nature of the serial killer, it is obvious that we must have some common point of understanding in defining the crime itself. However, this is not a simple matter. A variety of questions naturally arise concerning when to define multiple murders as serial killings. The answers to such questions are numerous and, in the final analysis, completely subjective. For example, how many murders are required to define a crime as the actions of a serial murderer? Must there be a specific minimum period of time between murders to fulfill the criteria? Are the types of murders or method of operation of the murderer important to an accurate definition? Is it significant whether the murderer acted alone or in conjunction with one or more other perpetrators? Each of these questions is valid, and each fosters significant contention among those who seriously study the crimes of the serial killer.

The number of murders traditionally considered necessary to constitute the crime of serial murder ranges from the obvious minimum of two to as high as ten. However, most researchers and criminologists have settled on a minimum of three or four murders to fulfill the definition. A more contentious question involves the minimum period of time required between murders to define the criminal pattern as serial murder. Researchers and criminologists often use a period of thirty days to define a number of murders as serial in nature. Therefore, one common definition of serial murder has become *the act of murdering three or more individuals in a period of thirty days or more*. Using this definition, if a perpetrator murders three or more individuals in less than thirty days, the crime is usually defined as a *murder spree*.

Some researchers point to the perpetrator's method of operation or the qualitative nature of the crime itself as crucial elements in defining an act of serial murder. However, using these constraints tends to classify serial murders in a minimalist fashion by eliminating those perpetrators who slay their victims in diverse and inconsistent ways. In general, the use of the perpetrator's method of operation in defining serial murder is not as widely accepted as the more traditional criteria of a minimum number of victims murdered over a minimum period of time.

Our research into the issue leads to a somewhat broader view of the crime of serial murder. There is no question that the definition of the crime must encompass a minimum number of victims, even in cases where law enforcement officials are fortunate enough to apprehend a perpetrator before he or she reaches that minimum. It is perfectly reasonable to expect that an *intended* serial murderer may injure his or her victims in significant numbers yet fail to murder sufficient numbers to meet the arbitrary minimum of any definition. In this sense, the intent to commit serial murder is a significant element to consider. However, intent is not something that can be easily measured or quantified. For this reason, we agree with the concept that a minimum number of victims must be slain in order to constitute an act of serial murder. We believe that three is a reasonable number of victims to define such a crime.

The Period Between Serial Murders

In considering the minimum period of time that should be used to define an act of serial murder, we were troubled by the constraints of arbitrarily selecting some number of days, weeks, or months to qualify a crime pattern as serial in nature. Rather, our research indicated that there exists a related and crucial element that was often overlooked in attempting to establish this part of the definition of serial murder. The missing element is the *cooling-off period,* which always constitutes a recognizable component in a genuine pattern of serial murder.

By any reasonable definition, the serial killer attacks his or her victims over some period of time. In other words, serial murder is a series of crimes that take place over time. Whereas the crime of mass murder implies the slaying of a number of victims in a single event, the crime of serial murder is, at its root, a composite of lethal crimes that take place over a protracted period. It is this period of time between murders—the cooling-off period—that truly defines the nature of serial murder.

The cooling-off period is a time of quiescence during which the perpetrator does not engage in lethal activities. Rather, this is a time when he or she will engage in a variety of different activities that are intimately related to an ongoing criminal pattern but do not, in themselves, involve murderous actions. Typically, this cooling-off period involves activities such as fantasizing about a crime that has already been perpetrated or planning for the next violent attack. In effect, this is a time during which the perpetrator considers what he or she has done and will do in the future. It may also be a period during which the perpetrator searches out or stalks his or her next victim. In any event, the cooling-off period is crucial to the activities of the perpetrator and, in our opinion, clearly differentiates the crime of serial murder from other violent felonies.

Therefore, our definition of serial murder incorporates the two crucial elements of number of victims and time in a way that allows for a broader definition of the crime: *the murder of at least three individuals in which each lethal act was separated from the next by a discrete cooling-off period.* In this sense, we have disregarded such elements as the perpetrator's method of operation, the qualitative nature of the crime itself, and the need for any fixed minimum period of time between murders. Rather, the focus of this definition is on the pattern of the criminal activity itself, as it occurs over time. This pattern must clearly demonstrate discrete acts of lethal violence that have been separated by discrete periods of quiescence. To the extent that the perpetrator's activities during the cooling-off periods are known, any indication of fantasy about the crimes committed or any demonstrated efforts to plan a future crime would provide compelling evidence to further support the conclusion that this was truly a crime of serial murder.

Characteristics of Serial Killers

Although the majority of serial killers are male, the history of this crime abounds with a number of female perpetrators who have engaged in a wide variety of heinous murders. In fact, female serial murderers are often highly successful in their crimes and present a challenge to law enforcement personnel that frequently surpasses that of the typical male serial killer. In general, it is difficult for law enforcement personnel to solve most cases of serial murder. By its nature, this crime is complex, covert, and often well planned. The majority of serial killers take pride in their ability to avoid apprehension and make every possible effort to continue their murderous ways for as long as possible. The average serial killer (of either sex) is typically able to extend his or her period of lethal activity to over four years before he or she is apprehended or the crimes are brought to a halt by some other means. This is also the median period of lethal activity for the male serial killer who acts alone. Because the number of male serial murderers far surpasses the number of female, the median killing period for *all* serial murderers closely approximates that for males.

However, female serial killers are able to carry out their crimes for a median duration of over eight years before the killing is stopped—double that of the male serial killer. For a variety of reasons, the female serial murderer is much more successful at avoiding apprehension than her male counterpart. Her choice of weapons, generally careful selection of victims, and methodical planning of the crime, combined with a strong social bias that denies the likelihood of a female serial killer, make this criminal significantly more successful than the male serial murderer. The female-serial killer who does not operate as part of a killing team is typically very careful in planning and carrying out her crimes; also, she is often eminently successful at avoiding apprehension for a surprisingly long period of time.

Female serial killers are rarely involved in sexual homicides—the overwhelming motivation for most male serial killers. The motivations inherent in serial murder committed by women are usually much different than for men and, for this reason, their crimes tend to exhibit a different victim typology. In general, male serial killers range widely in their choice of victims. Because male serial murderers far outnumber their female counterparts, statistics relating to the victims of all serial killers indicate that adults of either sex are at approximately equal risk for attack.

Victims of Serial Killers

Male serial killers, acting as sexual predators, tend to target adult female victims; however, in the final analysis, this perpetrator is usually more than willing to slay an individual of either sex. On the other hand, female serial murderers are more likely to select their victims for reasons that do not involve the sex of their prey.

The female serial killer who operates alone (as contrasted with the perpetrator who operates as a member of a killing team) exhibits a decided preference for victims who are children, the elderly, a lover, or a spouse. It is rare for a female serial killer to attack an adult stranger—the most likely victim of a male serial killer. When a female serial murderer does attack a person unknown to her, it will almost always be a very young child or an elderly individual; in other words, individuals who are easily dominated and who will be naturally dependent on the murderer.

When a woman carries out her crimes in conjunction with one or more partners, she will sometimes engage in serial killing that is sexual in nature. Even though she will rarely commit such crimes alone, the female serial murderer can become a monstrous sexual predator when partnered with one or more individuals who are themselves active sexual predators. In such a situation, the female perpetrator is considered a team killer and is most often associated with a male who is himself a sexual serial killer. On occasion, two or more women join together to form a killing team; however, their motives for murder are rarely sexual in nature.

IDENTIFYING SERIAL KILLERS

James Alan Fox and Jack Levin

James Alan Fox and Jack Levin are the authors of *Overkill: Mass Murder and Serial Killing Exposed,* from which the following selection is taken. One explanation for the American fascination with serial murder, the authors write, is that people hope to protect themselves by being able to identify the typical serial killer. Unfortunately, Fox and Levin explain, serial killers vary widely in appearance, socioeconomic status, and personality. However, they state, serial killers do conform to certain profiles: Some kill for thrills and sexual satisfaction; some kill out of greed, in order to obtain money from their victims; some prey on the vulnerable to gain a sense of power; some suffer from serious mental illness. Fox is the dean of the College of Criminal Justice and Levin is a professor of sociology and criminology, both at Northeastern University in Boston.

Andrei Chikatilo of Russia, serial killer extraordinaire, was arguably more power hungry and control minded than Ted Bundy and John Wayne Gacy put together. Between 1978 and 1990, Chikatilo killed, dismembered, and occasionally devoured 21 boys, 14 girls, and 18 women in and around Rostov while he worked as an office clerk and part-time teacher. The 54-year-old father of two didn't particularly care about the age or gender of his prey, as long as they were naive and willing to follow him from a bus or rail station, café, or other public meeting place. Some of his victims were too young to know better, and others were mentally retarded or homeless drifters, but many of those whom Chikatilo destroyed were bright youngsters from middle-class families.

What all his victims shared in common was a trusting nature; any twinge of caution that they may have felt easily dissolved because of the killer's kind and assuring manner, what Chikatilo himself termed his "magnetic personality." Once he had them alone, however, his demeanor would change instantly and dramatically. "I was like a crazed wolf," explained the predator. "I just turned into a beast, a wild animal." Sometimes he tore out and ate their hearts, lips, or tongues;

sometimes he cut off their fingers, eyes, or genitals—whatever suited his passion at the moment.

Chikatilo's sexual problems dated back years before his first murder. Chronically impotent (although he did manage to father two children), he found some degree of pleasure and comfort from molesting young boys and girls. This was nothing, however, like the arousal he discovered when he first committed murder (after abducting a 9-year-old girl). He soon learned what pleased him, what atrocities made him feel whole. "When I used my knife," he explained, "it brought psychological relief."

Serial Murder in America

In recent years, Americans have been fascinated but at the same time shocked by serial killers operating here and abroad. While they occasionally surface in other countries, including Russia, these killers are much more common in the United States. Destroying some 200 Americans per year in total, serial murderers kill repeatedly over a period of weeks, months, or even years, generally not stopping until they are caught.

With each new discovery of another serial killer, the level of brutality and gore seems to sink even deeper into the abyss of inhumanity. In the 1970s we became acquainted with the term *serial murder* in the context of the hideous rapes and murders committed by Ted Bundy. In the 1980s we were introduced to new and even more grotesque atrocities—a Philadelphia man who kept sex slaves shackled to a post in his basement, and a gruesome twosome who operated a torture chamber at their Northern California hideout. The 1990s produced even more chilling abominations, such as the crimes of Milwaukee's Jeffrey Dahmer, who cannibalized and engaged in postmortem sex with at least 17 young men.

Perhaps because they do not fit the popular stereotype of a crazed lunatic, serial killers who seem like "the boy next door" have become household names. It certainly would be comforting if real-life serial killers acted like those in classic horror movies. If they looked like Jason from the *Friday the 13th* film series, we would beware whenever they approached. If they were introverted loners like Norman Bates from Alfred Hitchcock's classic film *Psycho,* they could not charm victims so easily into their deadly clutches. But the frightening truth is that serial killers like Ted Bundy and Jeffrey Dahmer are incredibly credible and, therefore, so very dangerous. Underneath the trustworthy and smooth veneer often glorified by the media lies the heart of a monster whose supreme passion is stalking his prey.

Even when it is known that a serial killer is on the loose, the precautions that worried citizens take may be inadequate. Many serial killers are clever and inventive. Some will pose as police officers or as stranded motorists in need of assistance. Others will answer classified newspaper ads in order to get into the homes of unsuspecting victims eager to sell a television set. Still others simply grab victims off the street by force. If they really want to get someone, they will likely find a way.

This does not mean that all or even most serial killers are handsome and smooth geniuses. Many people consider Ted Bundy a prototype serial killer in large part because of his attractiveness, charm, and intelligence. While these qualities are important in understanding his keen ability to lure his victims and elude the police, Bundy is more the exception than the rule. At the other end of the spectrum are some serial killers who are high school dropouts and some who might even be called ugly. Most, however, are fairly average, at least to the casual observer. But there is one trait that tends to separate serial killers from the norm: they are exceptionally skillful in presenting themselves so that they appear beyond suspicion. This is part of why they are so difficult to apprehend.

In the modern mythology of serial murder, the killer is characterized also as a nomad whose compulsion to kill carries him hundreds of thousands of miles a year as he drifts from state to state and region to region, leaving scores of victims in his wake. This may be true of some well-known and well-traveled killers like Ted Bundy and Henry Lee Lucas, but not for the majority. John Wayne Gacy, for example, killed all of his 33 young male victims at his Des Plaines, Illinois, home, conveniently burying most of them there as well. Gacy, like Milwaukee's Jeffrey Dahmer, Kansas City's Robert Berdella, and Long Island's Joel Rifkin, operated within driving distance of home. Moreover, most serial killers are not the recluses that movies often portray them to be. They typically have jobs and families, go to church on Sunday, and kill part-time—indeed, whenever they have some free time to kill.

The Profile of Serial Killers

A more specific profile of the typical serial killer is that of a white male in his late 20s or 30s who targets strangers at or near his place of residence or work. According to criminologist Eric Hickey, who has assembled the most extensive database on the demography of serial murder, 88% of the serial killers were male, 85% were Caucasian, and the average age when they claimed their first victim was 28.5. In terms of victim selection, 62% of the killers targeted strangers exclusively, and another 22% killed at least one stranger. Finally, 71% of the killers operated in a specific location or area, rather than traveling wide distances to commit their crimes.

In terms of motivation, most serial murderers kill not for love, money, or revenge, but for the fun of it. Like Andrei Chikatilo, they enjoy the thrill, the sexual satisfaction, or the dominance that they achieve over the lives of their victims. Not only do they savor the act of murder itself, but they rejoice as their victims scream and beg for mercy. Like Leonard Lake and Charles Ng, the buddies who killed dozens of people in Calaveras County, California, some serial killers record on video or audiotape their victims' worst moments of terror for the purpose of later entertainment.

The thrill-oriented killer hardly ever uses a firearm. A gun would only rob him of his greatest pleasure: exalting in his victim's suffering and misery. He enjoys the whole experience of murder—of squeezing from his victim's body the last breath of life. California serial killer Douglas Clark's greatest fantasy was to kill a woman as he was having intercourse with her; his wish was to feel her death spasms in the heat of passion.

For some thrill killers, the need for dominance is not expressed through sexual sadism. A growing number of murders have been committed by hospital caretakers who seek to "play God," exploiting their patients in order to feel the exhilaration of making life-and-death decisions. In 1987, registered nurse Richard Angelo was arrested and later convicted for poisoning a number of patients in a hospital in West Islip, Long Island. Because of a burning desire to be recognized as a hero, he purposely poisoned his patients and attempted to "save" their lives. Sometimes he succeeded, but not always.

Though not in an official caretaker role, a few serial killers find satisfaction by making healthy human beings into totally dependent pets or sex toys. Milwaukee's Jeffrey Dahmer, for example, expressed his need to control others by attempting literally to lobotomize his victims into submission. He was not interested in inflicting pain and suffering; he actually sedated his victims before performing surgery on them.

As another expression of their need for power and quest for attention, thrill-motivated serial killers often crave the publicity given to their crimes. It is not just the celebrity status that they enjoy; more importantly, they are able to control the lives of thousands of area residents, who are held in their grip of terror. These killers do not specifically turn to homicide as an attention-getting move, but the media hype is a powerful fringe benefit. Some might even exaggerate the scope of their crimes to attract the television cameras and front-page coverage.

Murder for profit, jealousy, or revenge, although unjustifiable, makes sense to most people at some level. By contrast, anyone who kills for fun, pleasure, or power would appear to be insane; after all, it would not seem to make logical sense that taking another person's life could be in any respect entertaining. Contrary to the popular view, however, most serial killers are not insane in either a legal or medical sense. They know right from wrong, know exactly what they are doing, and can control their desire to kill, but they choose not to do so. They are more cruel than crazy.

Psychologically the thrill-motivated serial killer tends to be a sociopath (or antisocial personality), someone with a disorder of character rather than of the mind. He lacks a conscience, feels no remorse, and cares exclusively for his own pleasures in life. Other people are seen merely as tools to fulfill his own needs and desires, no matter how perverse or reprehensible.

It has been estimated that 3% of all males in our society could be considered sociopathic. Most sociopaths are not violent: They may lie, cheat, or steal, but rape and murder are not necessarily appealing to them. The other critical ingredient to the profile of the serial killer is an overpowering need for control. Most thrill killers, for the sake of sexual gratification, tie up their victims in order to watch them squirm and torture their victims to hear them scream. Others find personal fulfillment and control by taking the life out of their victims—by "mercifully" killing a hospital patient or drugging a captive to make him or her an obedient zombie.

The overwhelming majority of serial killers pursue their victims for the thrill; they seek to satisfy their cravings for sexual or psychological dominance through murder. Some serial murderers, however, are motivated instead by a strong urge to further a social, political, or religious cause. This second kind of killer is on a mission to rid the world of filth and evil. This kind of moral crusade sometimes motivates killers to target marginal groups, such as prostitutes, gays, or homeless people, who are seen as destroying the moral fiber of the community or country. In a profoundly warped sense of good and evil, the criminals view their killing spree as "self-defense."

From 1981 to 1987, for example, at least a half-dozen members of a Miami-based cult known as the Temple of Love conspired to kill "white devils" in retaliation for the oppression of blacks. Their black-separatist leader, Yahweh Ben Yahweh (translated from Hebrew as "God, Son of God") preached that all whites were "demons and serpents." The temple's "entry fee" required that new members murder a white man and then produce his severed ear as proof. In the name of racial justice, temple members savagely murdered eight homeless vagrants, who probably had no idea that they were chosen for slaughter strictly because of the color of their skin.

As a result of severe mental illness, other mission killers actually see their victims as devils. In their delusions, they believe that they must extinguish the lives of their victims for the good of the world. Their inspiration to kill is not religious or political fanaticism, but psychosis. They hear the voice of the devil or God instructing them to kill. Driven by these delusions, they tend to be psychotic, confused, and disorganized.

In 1972 and 1973, for example, Herbert Mullin of Santa Cruz, California, killed 13 people over a span of 4 months in order to avert an earthquake—at least according to what his voices told him. Mullin was raised in an oppressively religious home, and his crimes had decidedly religious overtones. He believed that he was obeying God's "commandment" to make human sacrifices for the greater good of humanity.

Mullin's severe psychological problems began in late adolescence, a point in life when schizophrenia characteristically surfaces. He was institutionalized on several occasions, diagnosed as a paranoid schizophrenic. The same voices that told him to kill had previously commanded him to shave his head and to burn his penis with a cigarette—orders that he also dutifully obeyed. While hospitalized, Mullin wrote dozens of letters to strangers, signing them, "A human sacrifice, Herb Mullin."

There are very few serial killers whose motivation, like those of Mullin, arises out of a psychotic illness. Though many more mentally ill individuals may repeatedly have thoughts that compel them to commit murder, most lack the clearheaded state of mind needed to carry it out. For example, 26-year-old Cleo Green of Louisville, Kentucky, had the ambition, but not the wherewithal, to become a serial killer. During the summer of 1984, he assaulted four elderly women by inflicting multiple stab wounds to their necks and throats. Each attack gave him temporary relief from the "red demon" that he felt inhabited his body and unmercifully tortured his soul. In one case Green was able to succeed in taking a life, but only after stabbing his victim 200 times and decapitating her. On other occasions, he was simply too out of touch to complete the act of murder. . . .

The third kind of serial murderer kills for the sake of expediency or profit. In 1992, for example, a series of murder/robberies occurred in "Mom and Pop" convenience stores through the Midwest. After taking the money from the cash register, the robbers would attempt to cover up their identity by executing their victims. The important distinction between the thrill killer and the profit-motivated killer can be seen in the style of murder: Whereas the thrill killer eliminates his victim in the most brutal manner possible, the profit-oriented serial killer almost always uses a gun. The former enjoys the killing, whereas the latter just feels that it is necessary.

In 1989 and 1990, 35-year-old prostitute Aileen Wuornos perpetrated a 13-month serial-killing spree along Florida's highways. Her motive was greed. Typically she would be picked up by a stranger, have sex with him, ask for payment, shoot him several times, take his money, and then dump his body. After being found guilty of first-degree murder, Wuornos whispered in the direction of the jurors as they filed out of the courtroom, "I am innocent; I was raped." In her view, it was absolutely necessary to kill each and every one of her seven victims—men whom she felt had threatened her—in order for her to stay in business. Given the constant danger under which she operated as a highway hooker, Wuornos saw killing a few violent johns as self-defense. Of course, most people would get out of the business rather than shoot seven customers in "self-defense," and Wuornos's failure to do so is why the jury found her guilty.

Although her premise was reprehensible, Wuornos's way of thinking was not unlike that of a liquor store proprietor in a crime-ridden neighborhood who decides to keep a gun at his side. Rather than closing the store, he reasons that he might have to shoot some intruders. The key difference between the proprietor and Wuornos is, of course, that the liquor store business is legitimate, but highway prostitution is not.

Female Serial Killers

Aileen Wuornos was not the first female serial killer, as the press often made her out to be. For example, Beverly Allitt murdered four children and attempted to kill nine others under her care at the Grantham Hospital in Lincolnshire, England. The 24-year-old nurse suffocated some of her young victims and injected others with fatal doses of insulin or potassium. Over an 18-month period, teenager Christine Falling of Perry, Florida, killed six children for whom she baby-sat. The deaths were initially diagnosed to be the result of sudden infant death syndrome (SIDS), but when the death toll reached alarming proportions, authorities took a closer look at the 19-year-old high school dropout. Falling later described her method of killing as "smotheration." In 1985 Betty Lou Beets was sentenced to death for murdering her fifth husband, a Dallas firefighter, in order to collect his $100,000 insurance benefits. Suspected of foul play in the mysterious deaths of her former spouses, she was charged with murder when the body of her "missing" fourth husband was discovered buried in the back yard.

Although Wuornos is far from alone in the annals of female serial killers, she is unique nonetheless. Unlike other women who killed repeatedly, she targeted perfect strangers rather than family members or acquaintances. Also unusual was the fact that her victims were exclusively middle-aged males. While almost anyone is at some risk of victimization, serial killers tend to prey on the most vulnerable targets—prostitutes, drug users, skid-row alcoholics, homeless vagrants, hitchhikers, runaways, children, and elderly hospital patients. Part of the vulnerability concerns the ease with which these classes of victims can be abducted or overtaken. Because of physical stature or disability, many children and elders are not able to defend themselves against a sudden attack by a 200-pound killer. Hitchhikers and prostitutes become vulnerable as soon as they step into the killer's car or van; hospital and nursing home patients are vulnerable because of their total dependency on their caretakers.

Taking Advantage of the Vulnerable

The vulnerability of the elderly is shown dramatically in the case of 64-year-old Sacramento landlady Dorothea Montalvo Puente. Her victims, because of their advanced age and relative poverty, had nowhere else to go and no one else to take care of them. And take care of them she did: In 1988 Puente was arrested and charged with killing nine of her boarders and then stealing their government checks. . . .

Prostitutes (with the exception of Wuornos, of course) are also quite vulnerable because of the accessibility required by their trade, which explains their extremely high rate of victimization by serial killers. A sexual sadist can cruise a red-light district, shopping around for the woman who best conforms to his deadly sexual fantasies. When he finds her, she willingly complies with his wishes—until it is too late.

Because of these risk factors, prostitute slayings have occurred in Rochester, New York; Seattle, Washington; New Bedford, Massachusetts; San Diego, California; Detroit, Michigan; and dozens of other locales across the country. Even when it is widely known that a killer is prowling the streets, far too many prostitutes place profit over protection, hoping or assuming that they can avoid death. Some see no other life for themselves, particularly if they have expensive drug habits to support.

The vulnerability of one additional class of victims—young boys and girls—stems both from their naïveté and their small size. For decades, pedophiles (adults who desire sexual relations with children) have capitalized on the ease with which many children can be deceived by a contrived story or ruse. Even the most streetwise child will not necessarily think twice about going with someone impersonating a police officer. Still other children can be easily grabbed, so that their attempts to scream or flee are futile.

From Molesting to Murder

By the time he was 27, Westley Allan Dodd had logged years of experience in molesting and raping young boys. As a teenager, Dodd started out by exposing himself. But as he grew into adulthood, that simply wasn't enough to gratify him. His sexual desire for young boys continued to escalate. "[Exposing myself] wasn't fun anymore," recalled Dodd. "I needed more physical contact. I started tricking kids into touching me. Then that wasn't fun anymore, so I started molesting kids."

At first, Dodd's passion was purely sexual; he never felt compelled to murder any of his victims. Because many of his young victims reported him, Dodd had had numerous brushes with the law, and he served 4 months of a 10-year sentence in an Idaho prison. Upon his release from custody, he was determined to stay out of jail. He had no intention to "go straight," however—only to avoid apprehension.

"In Seattle, June 13, 1987, I tried to kidnap a boy," said Dodd. "My intentions, at this point, were to kidnap him, rape him, and kill him so that he couldn't report me." He realized at that point that murder would be a necessary evil to enable him to continue his career of rape and molestation. The boy he accosted in Seattle screamed his way to freedom, however, sending Dodd back to prison for another short stay. Dodd had to prepare himself mentally—to psych himself up—to cross the line into homicide. "I wasn't sure that I could kill, so in my mind I had to fantasize about it. To be able to kill, I had to make that thought exciting," Dodd explained. "And in a matter of just a couple of weeks . . . I was ready to kill."

After his release, Dodd was prepared to try again, and this time he was determined not to fail. His first murder occurred during Labor Day weekend of 1989. Dodd jumped 11-year-old Cole Neer and his 10-year-old brother Billy as they rode their bikes through a park in Vancouver, Washington. Dodd stabbed both children to death after molesting the older boy. One month later, he abducted 4-year-old Lee Iseli from a playground, molested him, and then hanged him by a rope in the bedroom closet. Dodd had clearly developed a taste for murder; he was totally hooked. In his own words, "I became obsessed with [killing]. That's all I thought about 24 hours a day. I was dreaming about it at night, constantly all day at work—all I thought about was killing kids."

Fortunately, Dodd had neither the skill nor the luck of more prolific serial killers. Two weeks after the Iseli murder, Dodd was again on the prowl. He attempted to abduct a boy from a movie theater bathroom, but his victim started screaming frantically. Dodd managed to wrestle the boy into his car. The vehicle was in poor mechanical shape, however, and not equipped for a quick getaway. Unable to accelerate, Dodd was captured only two blocks from the theater. On January 15, 1993, following months of intense publicity surrounding his unusual choice of mode of execution, Dodd was hanged at Walla Walla prison in eastern Washington state.

The vulnerability of certain groups of victims rests not so much in their naïveté, accessibility, or small stature, but in the sense that serial killers can feast upon them with relative impunity. Specifically, when extinguishing the lives of elderly nursing home residents, a caretaker can capitalize on the normalcy of death in such an environment. A thrill killer, when trolling for prostitutes along a red-light strip, can be reasonably assured that because of their typically transient lifestyle, the disappearances of his victims will not be immediately deemed foul play. Moreover, society devalues women and men who sell their bodies. The capture of their killer therefore often takes low priority, and the killer knows it. Some serial killers select other marginal groups—minorities, immigrants, or gays—to assure themselves that the public and police response will be muted. If nothing else, serial murderers are opportunists, and they seek out conditions that will allow them to kill repeatedly without detection or apprehension.

ORGANIZED AND DISORGANIZED SERIAL KILLERS

Robert K. Ressler and Tom Shachtman

Robert K. Ressler is a retired special agent of the Federal Bureau of Investigation (FBI) and reserve colonel in the U.S. Army's Criminal Investigation Division (CID). Ressler and writer Tom Shachtman are the coauthors of *Whoever Fights Monsters,* from which the following selection is taken. Ressler and his colleagues at the Behavioral Sciences Unit of the FBI developed a distinction between organized and disorganized serial killers, which he and Shachtman describe. Disorganized killers are generally psychotic, suffering from severe mental illness and delusions, they explain. Although organized killers are less likely to be obviously mentally ill, the authors maintain that they are often sociopaths who see themselves as victims of a society that does not recognize their greatness. While disorganized killers do not choose victims logically and often take no steps to avoid discovery of the body, Ressler and Shachtman write, organized killers plan every aspect of their crime, from targeting specific strangers to disposal of the body at great distances from the site of abduction.

To most people, when confronted by evidence of violent criminality, the behavior may seem an enigma, even a unique occurrence. Very few of us are used to grisly murders, mutilations, bodies thrown into ravines—and the majority who are ignorant of such matters includes most local police, who seldom encounter crimes of this sort. Even outrageous, unspeakable criminal behavior is not unique and not incomprehensible, however. These sort of murders have occurred before, and, when properly analyzed, can be understood well enough so that we can even break them down into somewhat predictable patterns. By the late 1970s, the Behavioral Sciences Unit [of the Federal Bureau of Investigation] had accumulated a large amount of experience in assessing these sort of crimes. The usual police officer might never have seen an act of disembowelment or cannibalism during his career, but because so many police departments sent us their unusual cases for analysis, we were used to looking at such crime scenes and could get past the average person's disgust at them and discern what the evidence revealed about the probable perpetrator.

Characterizing Offenders

Amassing this knowledge was one thing. Communicating it to our audience—those police officers who sought our help in tracking down violent criminals—was another. To characterize the types of offenders for police and other local law-enforcement people, we needed to have a terminology that was not based in psychiatric jargon. It wouldn't do much good to say to a police officer that he was looking for a psychotic personality if that police officer had no training in psychology; we needed to speak to the police in terms that they could understand and that would assist them in their searches for killers, rapists, and other violent criminals. Instead of saying that a crime scene showed evidence of a psychopathic personality, we began to tell the police officer that such a particular crime scene was "organized," and so was the likely offender, while another and its perpetrator might be "disorganized," when mental disorder was present.

The organized versus disorganized distinction became the great divide, a fundamental way of separating two quite different types of personalities who commit multiple murders. As with most distinctions, this one is almost too simple and too perfect a dichotomy to describe every single case. Some crime scenes, and some murderers, display organized as well as disorganized characteristics, and we call those "mixed." For instance, Ed Kemper was a highly organized killer, but his mutilation of bodies after death was more typical of a disorganized one. In the following pages, I'll paint the principal characteristics of both classic organized and classic disorganized offenders. Please remember that if I say that a particular attribute is characteristic of an organized offender, it is not so 100 percent of the time, but is something that is *generally* applicable. For instance, I say that the organized offender hides the bodies of his victims; in our research interviews, and in analysis of crime scenes, we found this to be true more than three-quarters of the time. That's enough to make the generalization hold up pretty well, but not enough to make it an absolute condition for our characterization. All of the "rules" of profiling are like that. Though the distinction between organized and disorganized itself is very apparent once recognized, the list of attributes that go along with each of the categories has grown, over the years, as we have learned more details about these murderers, and it continues to be enlarged.

Analyzing the Crime

When trying to figure out whether the crime has been perpetrated by an organized or disorganized offender, we look at crime-scene photographs, and, if possible, we examine information from or about the victim. For instance, we try to assess whether or not this particular victim meant a low risk for the criminal. It would be a low risk if the victim was frail or weak. Where did the victim become a victim? When Monte Rissell abducted a prostitute from a deserted parking lot in the early-morning hours, he chose a victim who might not be missed for some time. Knowledge that the perpetrator would deliberately choose such a victim can be important in trying to apprehend him.

We ordinarily divide the crime into four phases. The first is the pre-crime stage, which takes into account the "antecedent behavior" of the offender. Often, this is the last stage about which we finally obtain knowledge, though it is the first in temporal sequence. The second phase is the actual commission of the crime; in this stage, we place victim selection as well as the criminal acts themselves, which may include far more than murder—abduction, torture, rape, as well as the killing. The third phase is the disposal of the body; whereas some murderers do not display any concern about having the victim found, others go to great lengths to avoid its discovery. The fourth and final phase is postcrime behavior, which in some cases can be quite important, as some offenders attempt to inject themselves into the investigation of the murder, or otherwise keep in touch with the crime in order to continue the fantasy that started it.

The major attribute of the organized offender is his planning of the crime. Organized crimes are premeditated, not spur of the moment. The planning derives from the offender's fantasies, which have usually been growing in strength for years before he erupts into overt anti-social behavior. John Joubert had his crimes in mind for years before the opportunity for a slashing murder presented itself and he crossed the line into action. Rissell, too, had had violent fantasies for years before a likely victim showed up in that parking lot after the night when, in his mind, he had been spurned by his former girlfriend.

Choosing a Victim

Most victims of organized offenders are targeted strangers; that is, the offender stakes out or patrols an area, hunting someone who fits a certain type of victim that he has in mind. Age, appearance, occupation, hairstyle, and lifestyle may be elements in the choice; David Berkowitz looked for women who were alone or sitting with men in parked cars.

The organized offender often uses a ruse or con to gain control over his victim. This is a man who has good verbal skills and a high degree of intelligence, enough to lure the victim into a vulnerable area. Control is of the essence for the organized offender, and law-enforcement personnel learn to look for control as an element in every facet of the crime. An organized offender might offer a prostitute a fifty-dollar bill, give a hitchhiker a ride, assist a disabled motorist, tell a child that he's taking him to his mother. Since the crime has been planned, the offender has devoted time to figuring out how to obtain victims, and may have perfected the ruse. John Gacy promised money to young men in a homosexual transient district in Chicago if they would come home and perform sex acts with him. Ted Bundy used his charm, but also the aura of authority that some police paraphernalia gave him, to lure young women into his car. With the organized killer, the victims are personalized; the offender has enough verbal and other interchange with the victims to recognize them as individuals prior to killing them.

The disorganized killer doesn't choose victims logically, and so often takes a victim at high risk to himself, one not selected because he or she can be easily controlled; sometimes this lack of choice produces a victim who will fight back hard enough so that later their body reveals defensive wounds. Moreover the disorganized killer has no idea of, or interest in, the personalities of his victims. He does not want to know who they are, and many times takes steps to obliterate their personalities by quickly knocking them unconscious or covering their faces or otherwise disfiguring them.

Therefore, the major attribute of the organized killer is planning, which in this sense of the word means that the killer's logic is displayed in every aspect of the crime that is capable of being planned. The disorganized offender's actions are usually devoid of normal logic; until he is caught and tells us his version of the crimes, chances are that no one can follow the twisted reasoning he uses to pick his victims or to commit his crimes.

Organized Killers Are Adaptable

During the criminal act, the organized offender adapts his behavior to the exigencies of the situation. After Ed Kemper shot two young women on a college campus, he had the presence of mind to drive past security officers at the gate with the two dying women in his car, without alarming the officers. Though admittedly in a state of anxiety, Kemper was not on a hysterical shooting spree. He was able to adapt his behavior to the danger of getting past the checkpoint. Other murderers, less organized, might have panicked and attempted to drive through the gates at high speed, thereby attracting attention, but Kemper behaved as if he had nothing to hide, and was "successful" in getting away with his crime that night. Adaptability and mobility are signs of the organized killer. Moreover, organized killers learn as they go on from crime to crime; they get better at what they do, and this shows in their degree of organization. If the police have a series of five homicides that demonstrate the same method of operation (MO), we advise looking most closely at the earliest one, for it will most likely have "gone down" closest to the place where the killer lived or worked or hung out. As he becomes more experienced, the killer will move the bodies farther and farther away from the

places where he abducts his victims. Often that first crime is not thoroughly planned, but succeeding ones will display greater forethought.
When we see more planning in a later crime than in an early one, we
know we're after an organized killer.

This leap forward in criminal expertise is an important clue to the
nature of the offender. An offender who improved his crimes, and
steadily escalated them in violence, was Monte Rissell. Only after he
was caught and convicted for a series of rape-murders did he confess
that he had committed a half-dozen rapes earlier in his teenage years,
rapes for which he was never caught. He began by attacking victims in
the apartment complex in which he and his mother lived; later on,
while at a youth facility, he forced a woman whom he abducted in a
parking lot to drive to her residence, where the rape took place. Still later, he drove a car out of state to find a victim. Each time, he made it less
and less likely that he would be identified as the rapist. It was only
when he reversed this pattern that he was actually caught: Rissell's last
six crimes, of which five were murders, again occurred in or near the
apartment complex where he lived. Even in that last series of murders,
there was some escalation: With his first three murder victims, he made
the decision to kill them during the rapes; with the last two, he had
consciously decided to kill them even before the actual abductions.

Evidence Identifying Offender Types

Further evidence of planning that sometimes becomes available to
police investigators lies in the organized offender's use of restraints—
handcuffs, ropes, and the like. Many murderers take what we call
"rape kits" along when they hunt victims, so that they will not have
any difficulty restraining those whom they wish to assault. The presence of a rape kit also allows the offender to have a submissive victim,
something essential to his fantasies. We once assisted in the investigation of a bizarre sexual murder on a Bronx rooftop: We noticed that
the murderer had not brought anything with him to immobilize the
victim; he had taken his tools for that task from her own clothing and
handbag. The absence of a rape kit helped us profile a killer who was
not organized.

Was there a vehicle used? To whom did it belong? Someone as disorganized as Richard Trenton Chase, I had told the police when his
murders were still unsolved, would most likely have walked to the
scene; I was certain of this, because I had decided that the killer displayed all the signs of a disorganized offender, one too mentally ill to
drive a vehicle while at the same time controlling his victims. The
part of the profile that really helped the police a good deal was my
insistence that the killer would reside within a locus of a half mile
from the site of his latest victims. Like Chase, the disorganized killer
walks to the scene or takes public transportation, whereas the organized offender drives his own car or sometimes takes the victim's car.

If the disorganized offender owns a car, it will often appear unkempt and in poor condition, as will his dwelling. The organized offender's car will be in proper condition.

Taking one's own car, or a victim's car, is part of a conscious attempt to obliterate evidence of the crime. Similarly, too, the organized offender brings his own weapon to the crime and takes it away once he is finished. He knows that there are fingerprints on the weapon, or that ballistic evidence may connect him to the murder, and so he takes it away from the scene. He may wipe away fingerprints from the entire scene of the crime, wash away blood, and do many other things to prevent identification either of the victim or of himself. The longer a victim remains unidentified, of course, the greater the likelihood that the crime will not be traced back to its perpetrator. Usually the police find the victims of an organized killer to be nude; without clothing, they are less easily identified. It may seem a very large step from wiping away fingerprints on a knife to decapitating a body and burying the head in a different place from the torso, but all these actions are in the service of preventing identification of the victim and of the killer.

The disorganized killer may pick up a steak knife in the victim's home, plunge it into her chest, and leave it sticking there. Such a disorganized mind does not care about fingerprints or other evidence. If police find a body rather readily, that is a clue that the crime has been done by a disorganized offender. Organized ones transport the bodies from the place that the victims were killed, and then hide the bodies, sometimes quite well. Many of Ted Bundy's victims were never found. Bob Berdella, a Kansas City, Missouri, killer who, like John Gacy, abducted, tortured, and killed young boys, cut up their bodies into small pieces and fed them to the dogs in his yard; many that were so treated could never be identified

A different dynamic seems to have been at work in the instance of the Hillside Strangler, who was later identified as two men. The victims were found, and the killers later turned out to have been quite organized offenders. Their desire seems to have been an egotistical one—to flaunt the bodies in front of the police rather than to conceal them in an effort to prevent tracing the killers through identification of the victim

Staging a Crime Scene

An organized offender may sometimes stage a crime scene or death scene in order to confuse the authorities. Such staging takes a fair amount of planning, and bespeaks a mind that is working along logical and rational lines. No disorganized offender is capable of staging a crime scene, although the very chaos of some crime scenes later attributed to disorganized offenders may at first give rise to various contradictory theories of what has happened at the site.

When law-enforcement personnel look at a crime scene, they should be able to discern from the evidence, or lack of it, whether the crime was committed by an organized or disorganized perpetrator. A disorganized crime scene displays the confusion of the killer's mind, and has spontaneous and symbolic qualities that are commensurate with his delusions. If the victim is found, as is often the case, he or she will likely have horrendous wounds. Sometimes the depersonalization of the victim by the attacker manifests itself in an attempt to obliterate the victim's face, or in mutilation after death. Often the death scene and the crime scene are the same for the disorganized offender, he does not possess the mental clarity of mind to move the body or conceal it.

Taking Trophies from Victims

The organized offender often takes personal items belonging to his victims as trophies, or to deny the police the possibility of identifying the victim. Wallets, jewelry, class rings, articles of clothing, photograph albums—all of these, once belonging to victims, have been found in the dwelling places of organized killers after their arrests. Usually, these are not items of intrinsic value, such as expensive jewelry, but, rather, items that are used to recall the victim. These trophies are taken for incorporation in the offender's postcrime fantasies and as acknowledgment of his accomplishments. Just as the hunter looks at the head of the bear mounted on the wall and takes satisfaction in having killed it, so the organized murderer looks at a necklace hanging in his closet and keeps alive the excitement of his crime. Many take photographs of their crimes for the same purpose. Sometimes trophies of the crime, such as jewelry, are given to the killer's wife or girlfriend or mother, so that when she wears it, only the killer knows its significance. John Crutchley was convicted only of kidnapping and rape, but I believed his actions to be extremely similar to those of an organized serial killer: He had dozens of necklaces hanging on a nail in his closet. Though Monte Rissell stole money from the purses of his rape and murder victims, he also took jewelry from them and kept it in his apartment. He further extended his fantasy involvement with the victims by driving their cars for hours after he had killed them.

The disorganized murderer doesn't take trophies; rather, in his confused mental state, he may remove a body part, a lock of hair, an article of clothing, and take it with him as a souvenir whose value can not be discerned.

All these crimes are sexual in nature, even when there is no completed sexual act with the victim. The truly organized killer generally completes a sexual act with a living victim, taking full advantage of the situation to rape and torture before murdering someone. Even if they are impotent in ordinary circumstances, while they are punching, slashing, strangling, and whatever, they are able to have sex, and do. The disorganized killer often does not complete the sex act, or, if he does, completes it only with a dead or entirely inanimate victim. The disorganized killer kills quickly, with a blitz style of attack. The organized offender seeks to increase his erotic interest through keeping the victim alive and performing perverted and destructive acts on the victim. Power over the victim's life is what this type of offender seeks. John Gacy brought his victims near death several times before the actual murders, so that he could enjoy their suffering while he raped them. During rapes, the organized offender demands that the victim display submissive behavior and act fearful and/or passive. If a victim fights back, the organized offender's aggressive behavior usually becomes heightened, sometimes so much that a man who had originally planned only on raping a victim escalates his violence into murder when the victim resists.

In stages three and four, the organized offender takes steps to hide the bodies of his victims, or otherwise attempts to conceal their identity, and then keeps track of the investigation. He does so in order to elongate the time period in which his fantasy seems to be in control of events. In one particularly egregious case of postcrime fantasy, the killer was a hospital ambulance driver. He would kidnap his victims from the parking lot of a restaurant and transport them elsewhere for rape and murder. Unlike many organized offenders, he would leave the bodies in locations that were only partially concealed, and then would call the police and report seeing a body. As the police rushed to the location of that body, the offender rushed back to the hospital, so that when the call from the police came to the hospital for an ambulance to be dispatched, he would be in a position to answer that call. He derived especial satisfaction from driving the ambulance to the dump site, retrieving the body that he himself had killed, and transporting it back to the hospital.

Personalities of Killers Differ

Organized and disorganized killers have very different personalities. The ways in which those personalities develop, and the behavioral consequences of those developmental patterns, are often important to unraveling a crime.

The disorganized offender grows up in a household where the father's work is often unstable, where childhood discipline is harsh, and where the family is subject to serious strain brought on by alcohol, mental illness, and the like. By contrast, our interviewing of murderers found that the organized killer's childhood was characterized by a father who had steady and stable work but where the discipline was inconsistent, often leaving the offender with a feeling that he was entitled to everything.

The disorganized offender grows up to internalize hurt, anger, and fear. While normal people also internalize these emotions to some degree—that's necessary in order to live together in a society—the disorganized offender goes far beyond the norm in his internalization. He is unable to let off steam, and lacks the verbal and physical skills for expressing these emotions in the proper arenas. He can't be easily counseled because he can't tell the counselor very much about the emotional turmoil inside him.

Part of the reason for unexpressed anger within the disorganized offenders is that they are not normally handsome people. They don't appear attractive, as measured by others, and they have a very poor self-image. They may have physical ailments or disabilities that make them different, and they are not comfortable being different. Rather than accepting their disabilities, they believe themselves to be inadequate, and they act in an inadequate manner, thus reinforcing their hurt, anger, and isolation. Disorganized offenders tend to withdraw from society almost completely, to become loners. Whereas many organized killers tend to be reasonably attractive, outgoing, and gregarious, the disorganized ones are incapable of relating to other people at all. Therefore, the disorganized offender will most likely not be living with a member of the opposite sex, and probably not even with a roommate. If they live with anyone else, chances are it will be a parent, and probably a single parent at that. No one else will be able to stomach their strange ways, so the disorganized offender is alone, possibly a recluse. Such offenders actively reject the society that has rejected them.

Commensurate with these disorganized offenders' poor self-image is that they are underachievers. In general, they are less intelligent than the organized offenders, but most are not seriously deficient. However, they never live up to their potential, either in school or in the workplace. If they work at all, it will be at a menial job, and they are habitually disruptive because of their inability to get along with other people. They also accept that they underachieve. When the killer of the young woman on that Bronx rooftop was questioned by the police, he said he was an unemployed actor. That was wishful thinking. Actually, he was an unemployed stagehand—certainly by his own lights an underachiever in the theatrical profession.

Differences in Behavior

By contrast, the organized offender, rather than internalizing hurt, anger, and fear, externalizes them. This is the boy who "acts out" in school, who does aggressive and sometimes senseless acts. In years past, the public has believed that all murderers have been disruptive and outwardly violent in their childhoods, but that stereotype is applicable only to the organized offender. The disorganized boy is quiet in school, maybe too quiet; often, when he is caught for a heinous crime, teachers and fellow students from his childhood hardly remember him. And when his neighbors are interviewed, they characterize him as a nice boy, never any trouble, who kept to himself and was docile and polite. On the other side of the coin, the organized offender is recalled by everyone from his childhood as the bully, the class clown, the kid who made people notice him. As opposed to being loners, organized offenders are gregarious and they like crowds. These are the guys who pick fights in bars, who drive cars irresponsibly, and who are described throughout life as troublemakers. They may land jobs that are above menial labor and commensurate with their intelligence, and then act out in such a way as to provoke a confrontation that will result in their being fired. Such stresses often lead to their first murders. A former Ohio police officer in the midst of job troubles, difficulties with the law, and woman troubles abducted a young woman and, almost by accident, murdered her. With disorganized killers, this important factor, the precrime situational stress, is often absent; their crimes are triggered by their mental illness, not by events in the outside world that impact on them.

Instead of feeling inferior to people, organized killers feel superior to nearly everyone. Gacy, Bundy, and Kemper all belittled the police who were too stupid to catch them and the psychiatrists who were too inept to understand them. They overcompensate, often believing themselves to be the smartest, most successful people to have come down the pike, even when they are only moderately so, and not particularly distinguished except by the monstrousness of their crimes. After the crime, they often follow the progress (or nonprogress) of the investigation in the news media; the disorganized offender takes little or no interest in the crime after it has been committed.

There is another area in which the organized offenders seem to be successful: in the sack. Often, they have had multiple sex partners. As good con artists, with excellent verbal skills, they are often able to convince women (or men, in some cases) to have sex with them. They may be superficially attractive, and good amateur psychologists. However, they are unable to sustain normal, long-term relationships. Their lives are characterized by having many partners, none of whom stick with them for very long. A disembowelment killer in Oregon had many affairs with women, none very deep or of long duration. Ted Bundy's main squeeze before his incarceration said that he was an unexciting sex partner. Most if not all of the organized killers have tremendous anger toward women, often expressed in the belief that a certain female is not "woman enough" to "turn him on." The ranks of organized offenders contain many rapists who beat up women, they reported, because the women did not stimulate them to orgasm.

Organized offenders are angry at their girlfriends, at themselves, at their families, and at society in general. They feel that they've been mistreated during their entire lives and that everything is stacked against them. If they're so smart and clever, why haven't they made a million dollars or—as Charlie Manson wanted—had a career as a rock star? They all believe that society has conspired to keep them down. Manson felt that had he not been in jail during his early life, his songs would have been very popular. Manson's rhetoric led his followers to believe they were stimulating class warfare by their murders. Ed Kemper believed he was taking victims from the rich and the middle class, and in so doing striking a blow for the working stiffs. John Gacy thought he was ridding the world of no-account punks and "little queers." In their murders, these men strike back not only at the individual victims but at society as a whole. . . .

Serial Killers and Society

Organized and disorganized: two types of killers. Which are the more prevalent and dangerous? That's hard to answer, but perhaps we can approach an answer by means of our research and some educated guesses about modern society. Our research into murderers is acknowledged to be the most broad-based yet completed. In it, we judged two-thirds of the murderers to be in the organized category, as opposed to one-third in the disorganized; perhaps those ratios carry through in the overall population of killers, only some of whom are behind bars, as our interviewees were.

My guess is that there has always been a certain unchanging fraction of disorganized killers in society, from the earliest days until the present—men who are quite deranged and who now and again go on killing sprees that stop only when they are caught or killed. We can't do much about the disorganized murderers; there'll probably always be one or two among us. It is my sincere belief, however, that the number and percentage of organized killers are growing. As our society grows more mobile, and as the availability of weapons of mass destruction increases, the ability of the antisocial personality to realize his rapacious and murderous fantasies grows apace.

THE SIGNATURE OF SERIAL KILLERS

Robert D. Keppel with William J. Birnes

Robert D. Keppel writes that signature killers, who comprise the largest subcategory of serial killers, are compelled to leave their own personal stamp—their unique signature—at the crime scene. The signature is often an unconscious pattern that includes the type of victim selected, the method used to control the victim, the type of wounds inflicted, any postmortem activity with the victim's body, and the method of disposing of the body. The author asserts that although some details may change from crime to crime, the basic signature of the serial killer will always remain the same. Keppel claims that years of experience with serial murder cases, as well as gut instinct, help law enforcement officials to identify a killer's signature. Keppel is the chief criminal investigator for the Washington State Attorney General's Office and author of *Signature Killers: Interpreting the Calling Cards of the Serial Murderer,* from which the following selection is taken. William J. Birnes is a freelance writer and journalist and the publisher of *UFO Magazine.*

The killer's signature is his psychological "calling card" that he leaves at each crime scene across a spectrum of several murders. I have come to recognize individual calling cards from the thousands of crime scenes I've investigated of the hundreds of serial killers whose paths I've crossed. So my life and work as a homicide detective have taught me to look for the unusual—what is rare—that makes one murder so very different from another. By that method, when one sees something rare in one murder and recognizes the same thing a week later, those unusual acts in two murders are often the signature of a lone killer. For example, when the killer in one murder intentionally leaves the victim in a position so the victim will be found open and displayed, posed physically spread-eagled and vulnerable; when he savagely beats that victim to a point of overkill and violently rapes her with an iron rod, you have to consider that fundamentally unusual. After a second murder in which the killer does the same things, even

though he may slightly modify one or two of the features, there is little doubt in my mind that the two murders are related. The killer has
left his signature. . . .

There are many, many killers not just satisfied with committing the
murder and going on their way. They have a compulsion to leave
their own personal stamp. The killer's personal expression takes the
form of his unique signature, an imprint left by him at the scene, an
imprint the killer is psychologically compelled to leave to satisfy himself sexually. In Ted Bundy's lingo, it's whatever the killer "gets his
rocks off on." The core of a killer's imprint will never change. Unlike
the characteristics of an offender's modus operandi (MO), the core
remains constant. However, a signature may evolve over time, such as
in cases where a necrophilic killer performs more and more postmortem mutilation from one murder to the next. The FBI's behavioral
scientists say that the signature elements of the original personal
expression don't change, they just become more fully developed

John Douglas once described the nature of the signature as the person's violent fantasies which are progressive in nature and contribute
to thoughts of exhibiting extremely violent behavior. As a person
dreams and thinks of his fantasies over time, he develops a need to
express those violent fantasies. Most serial killers have been living
with their fantasies for years before they finally bubble to the surface
and are translated into deeds. When the killer finally acts out, some
aspect of the murder will demonstrate his unique personal expression
that has been replayed in his fantasies over and over again. On the
same subject, retired New York Police Department homicide detective
Vernon Geberth wrote that it's not enough for these types of murderers just to kill, the murderer must act out his fantasies in some manner over and beyond inflicting death-producing injuries. From my
experience, I've seen lust killers who have a need to bludgeon to the
point of overkill, others who carve on the body, or signature killers
who leave messages written in blood. Some rearrange the position of
the victim, performing postmortem activities which suit their own
personal desires. In each of these ways, they leave their psychopatho-
logical calling card at the crime scene.

I begin to look at murder scenes as a series when I see the same type
of extraordinary violence similarities. This physical evidence is usually
accompanied by my gut instinct which tells me there's more that's
alike than different. But another homicide investigator might look at
the evidence and say the killer used a pipe wrench as a blunt instrument here, a ballpeen hammer there, and in this third crime we can't
even figure out what weapon he used. Maybe the killer draped a pair
of underpants on the victim's left leg. In the next crime scene, the
underpants were on her right leg or maybe still on the bed. These are
differences, I'll agree. Yet, in each case, I will argue that the victim was
obviously beaten well beyond the point of death by an assailant

whose violence seemed to increase in frenzy while he was attacking her. Also, the killer seemed preoccupied with the victim's clothing and took some time to arrange the crime scene, even though there might have been people living just upstairs. When I compare evidence like this, I see overwhelming similarities. These are the psychological calling cards the killer actually *needs* to leave at each scene. These constitute his signature and remain relatively constant from crime to crime, even when the killer deliberately changes his MO because of situational circumstances or as an attempt to throw us off his trail.

Through the years since Ted Bundy, I became increasingly aware of the nature of serial murder cases in which the killer seemed to be acting in an unconscious pattern when it came to victim profile, exercising control over the victim, inflicting wounds of specific types, postmortem activity with the victim's body, and disposing of the body. Even though the killer varied his MO, things about the crimes were eerily the same. What was this pattern? The more serial cases I examined or consulted on, the more aware I became of the pattern. I was intrigued as well as disturbed. Instinctive homicide investigators were able to home in on the patterns also, but didn't take conscious notice of it. I knew there had to be something there beyond the MO of the serial killer, something that told us more about the murderer than he wanted us to know, something that would allow us to make predictions not only about where the killer had come from and where he had been, but where he would go and what he might do next. The more research I did, the more it became clear that the killer was not just committing one crime in a series, but that each crime was a different act in a drama that had been going on throughout his entire life. The individual act contained the same plot, same characters, and same dialogue, and came to the same conclusion. But the psychodrama itself was an evolving story. If you knew the story, you might know how to stop the killer. . . .

Signature Killers Seek Control

Signature killers, the single largest subcategory of serial killers, are driven by such a primal psychological motivation to act out the same crime over and over again that their patterns become obsessive. All signature murderers seek some form of sexual gratification, and their crimes are expressions of the ways they satisfy that need. For example, inasmuch as most of the killers exert little or no control over their own existences or perceive themselves deep down inside as being life's losers and the victims of society, they gratify their sexual urges by demonstrating control over their murder victims. Whether that control manifests itself as necrophilia, bondage, humiliation, the torture of living victims, or the posing of dead victims, it is the control itself that supplies the killer with his gratification. The events leading up to the ultimate moment of control supply him with the excitement of anticipation.

In many ways, the behavior of signature killers so mirrors the behaviors of other types of addicts that it is important to see how the crime plays itself out as a progression of escalating, but linked, violent events. Like all addicts, signature killers work from a script, engaging in repetitive behavior to the point of obsessiveness. Their calling cards at the crime scenes—how they choose their victims, control their victims, mutilate or manipulate the bodies, and dispose of bodies—all display similar types of pathological deviance and repeat themselves no matter how their method of operation changes. Signature killers change their MOs, often experimenting with different ways of dealing with their victims and satisfying their sexual cravings. They often take mementos or souvenirs with them from their victims. The killers impart to these items a special kind of power to reinvigorate their excitement over taking the victim. When the excitement subsides over time, the killers go out hunting again, taking new mementos to sustain their fantasy life after the murder by reenergizing their sexual thrill so as to allow them to continue to experience the excitement of the crime they committed.

You can very often determine what type of psychological signature the killer has left by examining the crime scene, understanding the profile of the victims, and recreating the process of the crime. For example, prostitute killers fall into specific categories, child predators fall into another, and so do killers of gay young adults such as John Gacy and Jeffrey Dahmer. . . .

Different killers have different signatures. Killers who pulverize their victims leave one type of calling card while killers who torture living victims or who play with corpses leave another. Some killers go through different signature phases during the same crime, smashing or crushing the life out of their victims with many fatal wounds and then posing their bodies as if to play with them after the violence of overkill has been expended. Some killers are less intimate with their victims than others, or display their hatred of an aspect of themselves in their victims instead of their need to be sexually satisfied.

Whatever the specific signature or signatures we determine from the crime scene, they all fall into one or more of the basic traits of sexual sadism—control, humiliation, progression, posing, torture, overkill, necrophilia, and cannibalism. It is the combination of these that often gives us enough of a handle on whom we're looking for that we know where he might strike next, or when . . . he's probably passed us by. Each of these types of signatures is a clue not only to what the murderer does, but what he wants, what he seeks, and what drives him from victim to victim. Hidden among the evidence, often gleaned from the marks and wounds on the victim's body, or clues left at a body dumpsite, these signatures are the only ways the killer truly expresses himself. But if you're smart, you can figure out what the killer is really after.

CHAPTER 2

FEMALE SERIAL KILLERS

Gender Differences in Serial Murderers

Belea T. Keeney and Kathleen M. Heide

In the following selection, Belea T. Keeney and Kathleen M. Heide report the results of their study of fourteen female serial murderers. Although male and female serial murderers share similar backgrounds, the authors found more differences than similarities between female and male serial murderers: For example, female serial murderers do not generally stalk or torture their victims and usually use poison to kill. Keeney and Heide also write that their study revealed that most female serial murderers kill close to their home or workplace rather than displaying the mobility found in many male serial killers. The authors believe that further examination of this difference might help law enforcement officials to identify serial murders that had previously gone undetected, particularly in hospitals and within families. Keeney is a criminologist who has consulted with several Florida law enforcement agencies. Heide is a licensed psychotherapist and a professor of criminology at the University of South Florida in Tampa.

During the past two decades, serial murder has received increased attention from both law enforcement and the popular media. Recent research has suggested that female involvement in serial homicide was approximately the same as their representation in other types of murder in the United States. This finding contradicted theorists who stated that serial murder was an almost exclusively male behavior.

Research on this topic has been limited due to the rare occurrence of this phenomenon and the difficulty in obtaining access to these offenders. To date, no traditional, academic, empirical research has been attempted. This article reviews the participation of women in serial murder. After discussion of definitions of serial murder and female involvement in other types of murder, current knowledge of the phenomenon is examined. Analysis then focuses on female serial murderers, and the variables that appear to affect their behavior are discussed.

Excerpted from Belea T. Keeney and Kathleen M. Heide, "Gender Differences in Serial Murderers: A Preliminary Analysis," *Journal of Interpersonal Violence*, vol. 9, no. 3 (September 1994), pp. 383–98. Copyright ©1994 by Sage Publications, Inc. Reprinted by permission of Sage Publications, Inc. (Notes and references in the original have been omitted in this reprint.)

Definitions of serial murder reported in the literature have lacked uniformity. In this study, serial murder is defined as "the premeditated murder of three or more victims committed over time, in separate incidents, in a civilian context, with the murder activity being chosen by the offender," as Belea T. Keeney wrote in 1992. This definition excludes killing performed by military personnel as part of their job duties and assassinations by political terrorist groups. It does include health care workers who murder their patients, parents who murder their children, professional assassins who operate under the confines of organized crime syndicates, and persons who kill multiple spouses/lovers. The number of murder victims used in this definition coincided with the Federal Bureau of Investigation (FBI) designation.

Summarizing the Research

The United States has seen a fairly consistent rise in the reported murder rate, from 5.1% in 1965 to 9.8% in 1991. However, perusal of FBI statistics showed that the proportion of total homicide arrests involving females has actually decreased from 17.6% in 1965 to 10.3% in 1991. Notwithstanding the proportionate decrease in female involvement in homicide, the actual number of women arrested for homicide showed a generally increasing trend, particularly for 1965 through 1983. Since 1983, the numbers of women arrested for homicide have tended to decrease. Interestingly, however, the number of women arrested for homicide in 1991 was still 36% greater than the number arrested in 1965.

Two of the early historical studies on murder focused almost exclusively on male offenders. Subsequent studies of women who had been charged with and/or convicted of murders began to emerge during the late 1960s. Female murderers have shown more of a tendency to kill family members than have males, to be somewhat older than men who murder, and to have killed their victims in the home. They also have used guns and knives as their most common weapons of choice. Female homicide offenders have tended to be from the lower socioeconomic classes, with an attendant lack of education and employment skills.

In contrast to the pattern of female murderers, the profile of males who murder has been studied more extensively. Early research concluded that they were typically young black males who killed in response to an argument or physical provocation. Males have tended to murder outside the home—in bars or streets—and to use guns and knives most commonly as weapons. Like the victims of women who kill, the victims of male murderers have usually been family members, friends, or acquaintances. . . .

Male serial murderers have tended to inflict a great deal of victim damage in addition to causing death and to engage in the torture of their victims prior to death. Male serial murderers have also shown a tendency to use a "hands-on" approach in killing by using knives, blunt objects, and hands to kill their victims. The process of murdering and the power/domination effect have been cited as part of their motivation.

Male serial murderers have shown a tendency toward "stalking" behaviors such as actively patroling for victims, aggressively pursuing victims, and/or using physical force to procure victims. They also have tended to commit either organized or disorganized types of murders when crime scenes have been compared.

Male serial murderers have often attended their victims' funerals as a method of reliving the murder and as material for future fantasy experiences. They typically returned to their victims' graves, whether official or unofficial. Male serial murderers have generally had affective goals; that is, murders committed for emotional or psychological reasons versus instrumental goals for practical reasons.

The Backgrounds of Male Serial Murderers

Several studies showed similar findings in the backgrounds of serial murderers. Male serial murderers have tended to be "first-born" children in their families of origin or the oldest children in their family units. They have also tended to be raised in broken homes such as those of divorced parents, widows/widowers, single parents, or adopted families.

Male serial murderers have often been victims of childhood abuse and/or neglect in their families of origin. Their parents have frequently been alcohol dependent or drug dependent.

There has been no clear pattern in whether male serial murderers have had substance abuse problems themselves. Available data have indicated that some serial murderers had symptoms of the "MacDonald Triad" (bed-wetting, fire-setting, and cruelty to animals) during childhood and some sustained head injuries.

No clear pattern is discernible regarding male serial murderers' encounters with law enforcement agencies as juveniles. Some research has reported that they have been institutionalized at some point in their lives (juvenile incarceration, foster homes, adult incarceration, etc.) prior to their arrests for murder. Male serial murderers have tended to be psychiatrically diagnosed as antisocial personalities more often than schizophrenic or psychotic.

Male serial murderers have tended to be White and to have had low to average levels of education, with a mean of a 10th-grade level. Their household composition (single, married, living alone, or other) at the time of the murders has been varied. If working, male serial murderers have shown a tendency to be employed in low-level/blue-collar types of occupations.

Examining Female Serial Murderers

The present study was designed to determine to what extent female serial murderers fit the current profile of male serial murderers. A series of both general and specific findings about the behavior, background, and demographic characteristics of male serial murderers based on the literature reviewed were generated and investigated with respect to female serial murderers. Previous research had not focused systematically on most of these variables and had been largely limited to profiles of male serial murderers.

A total of 14 female serial murderers who acted alone were identified and selected through the use of several sources. First, newspaper indexes were examined to find women who were charged with multiple murders committed over time or charged with a single murder and strongly suspected by law enforcement of other murders. These indexes included the *New York Times* (1972–1992), *Los Angeles Times* (1972–1992), *Chicago Sun-Times* (1980–1992), *Atlanta Journal and Constitution* (1983–1989), and *St. Petersburg Times* (1975–1986). After perusal of the various indexes for identification purposes, the actual articles on microfilm were analyzed and used to gather information. Second, female serial murderers were identified by books, biographies, periodicals, and abstracts on murder. Cases that occurred between 1972 and 1992 were selected for examination because more recent cases tended to have more accurate information. . . .

The mean age at arrest for this sample was 37.9 years, with a range of 40 years (19–59). The average age that the women began their murders was 32.9 years with a range of 35 years (18–53). The 14 women were convicted of killing 27 victims; law enforcement agencies estimated that the women killed more than 88 people. None was charged with all of the murders for which she was allegedly responsible.

Of the 14 women, 13 were place-specific killers; that is, they operated in one small area such as a city, often in a hospital or their own homes. The remaining woman was a regional killer who operated in one state. Geographically, the state represented most often was Florida with four offenders; North Carolina and California each had two; Wisconsin, New York, Michigan, Texas, Georgia, and Alabama each had one offender in this sample. Nine offenders in the sample were from Southern states—the only pattern of regionality that was evident in this study.

The victim sample was taken only from confirmed victims, not those who were alleged or speculated. With regard to relationship to their victims, victims who were in the custodial care of their murderers (patients, children with babysitters) were the largest category, comprising 43% of the sample. Family members (children, husbands, in-laws, fathers) were the second largest category with 37%. The remaining 20% consisted of strangers, acquaintances, and nonspousal lovers.

Murder and Postmurder Behaviors

Victim Damage. Victim damage was measured by mutilation, dismemberment, and other evidence of "overkill" over and above what was required to cause death. Among the 62 victims, no sexual assault, mutilation, or dismemberment was evident.

Victim torture. Victim torture was measured by victim burns, evidence of multiple revivals and loss of consciousness, multiple stab wounds, and dismemberment while the victim was alive. Female serial murderers in this sample did not engage in torture of their victims prior to death. (It could be argued that a slow death by poison, spread over weeks and months, could be considered a form of torture.) There was no indication that females used their victims' suffering as a form of sexual release in the manner that some male serial murderers have done.

Weapon choice/method. The majority of female serial murderers used some form of poison to kill their victims. Overdoses of potassium, insulin, and prescribed medications, as well as arsenic and poison derivatives, were considered poisons for the purpose of this study. In the victim sample, 57% were killed with poison, 29% were smothered, 11% were killed by firearm, and 3% were killed by other methods (e.g., one instance of a victim deliberately being places on his back under a medical condition that made this fatal, and one instance of drowning). There was little variation in these murderers' methods; only two of the women used more than one weapon choice/method to kill their multiple victims.

Stalking versus luring behaviors. None of the female serial murderers engaged in traditional stalking behaviors such as following the victim for a period of time, watching the victim from a distance, or engaging in Peeping Tom type of activities. Five murderers in this sample were aggressive in procuring victims in that they actively sought out boarding home tenants, insured and killed multiple lover/husbands, or solicited prostitution clients apparently for the primary purpose of robbery.

Crime scene organization. The 14 female serial murderers left crime scenes that showed characteristics of both organized and disorganized offenders. According to FBI profilers, a planned offense, the personalization of the victim, the use of restraints, and the weapon/evidence absent from the scene are associated with organized offenders. Conversely, a spontaneous offense, a known victim and location, sudden violence, and the bodies left in view and at the death scene are associated with disorganized offenders. There was no definite demarcation in the female serial murderers in this study. Each offender's crime scene showed characteristics of both types of offenders. The typical crime scene involved a known victim who was helpless or powerless, and the weapon/cause of death was not immediately obvious. In addition, the typical crime scene involved a victim who was intimately known by the killer, with the body left in view and at the scene of death. Only one offender actually moved her victims from the death site and buried them.

Reasons for the murders. The sample was evenly divided between offenders who appeared to have had instrumental goals and those who appeared to have had affective goals. Seven apparently had instrumental goals, such as insurance benefits or other monetary gain upon the death of their victims. The other seven appeared to have had affective goals; that is, there was no apparent benefit except an emotional one upon the deaths of their victims. One woman was reported to have experienced some tension release as a result of her murders.

Social and Psychological History

Broken homes. Of the 10 women for whom data were available, 4 were adopted by nonrelatives, 4 were raised in nontraditional homes composed of various relatives and nonrelatives, and 2 were raised in traditional homes with both biological parents until age 18. Nearly half were raised with siblings, ranging in number from one to six brothers and sisters.

Childhood abuse. Of the eight women for whom data were available, five reported overt sexual abuse such as being fondled, molested, or raped. Five reported physical abuse such as being beaten, slapped, or hit with objects. Four reported sexual assault/rape before age 18. Three reported physical neglect. Two reported exposure to violence/cruelty such as spouse abuse. Emotional neglect was reported by two women, and one was a victim of medical neglect. (Totals do not equal 14 due to the nonexclusiveness of categories.)

Chemical abuse history. Of the eight women for whom data were available, four showed social illegal drug use such as marijuana or cocaine. Three were social drinkers and three were alcoholics. The one subject who was chemically addicted or dependent on prescription drugs allegedly committed her murders under the influence. Two of the eight had sought treatment for alcohol or drug dependency. One was a teetotaler. (Totals do not equal 14 due to the nonexclusiveness of categories.)

Psychiatric diagnosis. Of the nine women for whom data were available, six were diagnosed with an "other pathology" after their arrests. The other pathologies category included histrionic, manic-depressive, borderline, and dissociative disorders. Three were diagnosed as antisocial personalities, and one was diagnosed as schizophrenic. One woman unsuccessfully used the insanity plea. One was adjudicated guilty but mentally ill.

Demographic Information

Race. Of the 11 women for whom data were available, all were White.

Educational level. Of the 10 women for whom data were available, 5 graduated from high school, 4 dropped out of high school with a mean educational level of 9.5 years, and 1 had received a GED. Four women had education beyond high school, typically a 1-or 2-year nursing degree. One woman had a high performance level in school with awards and scholarship, whereas two women had a poor performance level with a history of learning difficulties and truancy. (Totals do not equal 14 due to the nonexclusiveness of categories.)

Household composition. Of the 14 women in the sample for whom data were available, 13 were living with others at the time of the murders.

Occupation. Among the sample subjects, 11 were employed in one capacity or another at the time of the murders. Five were employed in traditional "pink-collar"-type jobs, including licensed practical nurses, housekeepers, or store clerks. Three were self-employed as a babysitter, prostitute, or shopkeeper. Four showed a history of menial employment, and four reported an unstable work history with periods of significant unemployment. Three had a stable work history with nearly continual employment throughout most of their adult lives (two of these were nurses and one was a secretary). One was a former blue-collar worker who had previously worked at a factory.

Analyzing the Data

The findings suggested that there may be more differences than similarities between female serial murderers and their male counterparts. Of the 14 variables for which data were available and could be analyzed, 9 differences were found between female and male serial murderers with respect to behavior patterns, psychosocial history, and demographics. Differences between male and female serial murderers were evident in victim damage, victim torture, weapon/method, stalking versus luring behaviors, crime scene organization, reasons for the murders, substance abuse history, psychiatric diagnosis, and household composition. Similarities between the two groups were found with respect to broken homes, childhood abuse, race, education level, and occupation.

One major strength of this study was the focus on variables previously reported on male serial murderers. Eric W. Hickey completed a thorough analysis of basic demographic information and victim findings for female serial murderers but without comparison to the variables found important by the FBI. In relation to previous research, the differences found between males and females in the present study regarding victim torture, victim damage, crime scene organization, weapon/method, and victim procurement were particularly significant. The similarities found, especially those of childhood abuse and broken homes, implied some background commonalities among serial murderers. In addition, the findings suggested new areas of exploration with regard to female serial murderers.

Of the variables that were eliminated due to lack of information, funeral attendance and gravesite visits are among those that warrant further attention. Because a large proportion of female serial murderers' victims were family members, it could be postulated that these two postmurder behaviors were actually quite high. (However, the meaning of this behavior in females is likely to be different from what it has been in males.) Additionally, the extent of juvenile encounters with law enforcement and institutionalization prior to the arrest for murder should also be reexamined. It was disappointing that the MacDonald Triad and head injuries were two variables that had to be omitted. Interviews of offenders and examination of medical and social service agency records would be a useful tool in uncovering the prevalence of these two variables among female serial murderers. The use of primary data, especially Department of Corrections files, would also be helpful.

The findings of this study were for the most part consistent with previous research regarding female serial murderers. Differences between the two groups in crime scene organization, psychiatric diagnosis, geographic distribution, body disposal, and mobility were substantive and merit further discussion.

Findings Raise Further Questions

The crime scenes of the women in this sample showed characteristics of both organized and disorganized murderers. Although the FBI does concede that some male serial murderers appear to be "mixed"-type offenders, the use of such a category would not necessarily be useful to law enforcement investigations. A new set of criteria for female and custodial serial murderers seems to be in order.

One unusual finding of this study was the geographic distribution of these murderers. More than half of the women in this sample committed their crimes and were arrested in Southern states. In examining male serial murderers, Hickey found that the Pacific Northwest was the area in which most incarcerated male serial murderers had killed their victims. FBI statistics have shown that the murder rate has consistently been higher in the South than it has in other areas of the United States.

Another fascinating finding was the almost complete lack of mobility of these offenders. Only Aileen Wuornos, a Florida prostitute, traveled at all during the commission of her murders; the rest of the sample remained in one place. Accordingly, "linkage blindness" [the inability to link crimes to the same offender] may not be a problem in tracking these offenders. Rather, the problem appears to result from the failure of law enforcement and other professionals to recognize that a homicide has been committed and to respond appropriately. For female serial murderers who have killed their patients, for example, health care facilities appear to have been extremely reluctant to bring charges against an employee with the resultant possibility of a trial and media attention. One case in this sample was indicative of this type of administrative bungle. Genene Jones, a Texas nurse, was continually employed in a hospital long after numerous complaints and charges that she was injuring the children in her ward. In addition, family and friends may be unwilling to confront female killers with their suspicions regarding their behavior. The husband of Mary-beth Tinning, the New York woman who murdered eight of her children, apparently did nothing to stop her behavior, suggest that she get therapy, or take steps to prevent further births.

The prevalence of childhood abuse has been well documented in many types of criminal offenders but specifically with murderers. Various forms of abuse were reported by this sample. Abuse has different effects on different people. Experts agree that it often promotes future violence, breaks the human bond needed to empathize with others, and fosters angry, inadequate human beings. Research should focus on which types of abuse may have been experienced by these offenders. . . .

Further Research Is Needed

Three areas warrant further investigation: the parenting received by these murderers, health care workers who murder their patients, and the fantasy life of female serial murderers. Two women in this sample were born to teenage mothers. Christine Falling, a Florida babysitter who killed several of her charges, was born to a 17-year-old girl. Wuornos's mother was 16 years old when she was born. The inherent disadvantage to children born of teenage mothers (lack of attachment, low birth weight, cycle of poverty) puts them at risk for future behavioral and criminal problems. The patterns of parenting associated with serial murders may provide us with some answers for their behavior.

An additional question arises about health care workers who murder their patients. Several male nurses and nurses' aides have been convicted of killing their patients. An analysis of their backgrounds, crimes, and history might lend itself to a profile of male caregivers who murder. Further research into nurses who murder might uncover gender differences in that population group. For example, coworkers of nurse Brian Rosenfeld of St. Petersburg, Florida, implied he may have experienced some sadistic satisfaction from torturing the patients he killed. By contrast, none of the female nurses in this sample was implicated in sadism.

Robert K. Ressler emphasized the importance of a violent, sadistic fantasy life in his sample of male serial murderers. Perhaps females also have an active fantasy life, although it may be oriented in other directions. Genene Jones was said to have had grand ambitions about being a "super nurse." She administered select drugs to children that induced seizures and then attempted to save them by using the antidotal drugs that she knew would have a counteracting effect on the patients. These dynamics appear to be similar to those of the Munchausen syndrome by proxy [in which offenders injure or induce illness in children in order to gain sympathy and attention for themselves].

A Need for Understanding

Although serial murder is a statistically rare phenomenon, these findings and previous research indicate that it affects all age and demographic groups. Some female offenders have preyed solely on children whereas others have victimized middle-aged persons, the infirm, and the elderly in health care facilities. As our population ages and our family structure continues to change, families are experiencing more stressors that may cause them to harm their children, whether intentionally or not. Careful parenting may prove to be the most important factor in the prevention of future violent behavior.

Preliminary findings from this study suggest that important differences may exist between male and female serial murderers. Further research is needed to develop a reliable profile of female serial murderers. Perhaps factors could be found that might indicate to parents, educators, and others that some girls are at a higher risk than others of acting destructively.

In addition, research needs to proceed with respect to discovering the motivational dynamics that undergird serial murder. Although there may be genuine differences between male and female serial murderers, there may be motivations to destroy other human beings that transcend gender. Erich Fromm's theory of character holds promise in this regard. In *The Anatomy of Human Destructiveness,* Fromm distinguished between benign aggression and malignant aggression. Benign aggression is defensive in nature and is designed to promote life and preserve vital interests. Malignant aggression, by contrast, is destructive and unique to human beings. Men and women have existential needs such as needs for a frame of orientation and an object of devotion, for rootedness, for unity, and for a sense of effectiveness. Those who lack a sense of belonging and peace and who cannot achieve fulfillment in constructive ways (education, work, family, money) can affect society through acts of destructiveness. The serial murderers examined in this and previous research appear to be unhappy, unsuccessful individuals who choose to make their mark on society through violent means. Uncovering the neurophysiological, social, and psychological conditions that lead certain individuals to chart a destructive course appears essential if efforts at prevention are to be entertained seriously.

AN EVOLVING CRIMINALITY

Candice Skrapec

According to Candice Skrapec, although female serial killers often use different methods than men, when their motives are examined, male and female serial killers have much in common. Skrapec claims that both male and female serial killers may have a variety of motives not necessarily linked to gender: For example, not all male serial murderers are sexually sadistic and some female serial murderers exhibit sexual sadism. Moreover, the author explains that like male serial killers, female serial killers come from diverse backgrounds. Because the typical methods used by female serial killers are influenced by their role in society, she writes, as the role of women expands, the methods used by female serial murderers may become more like those typically employed by male killers. Skrapec is a Canadian psychologist who has studied serial murder since 1984 and has worked on specific cases with police departments in Canada and the United States. She lectures at John Jay College of Criminal Justice in New York.

Editor's note: The author wishes to assure the reader that in its original publication, the following material is properly documented with endnotes and references according to scholarly convention. Such documentation has been omitted from this reprint for ease of reading.

Violent criminality has been marked out as an essentially male province by the criminal justice system, criminological researchers, and the media. Homicide, in particular, is viewed as a predominantly male crime, female offenders tending to be relegated to an 'exceptional case' status that rests upon some exceptional or untoward, compelling circumstance: the battered wife who kills her abusive husband; the postpartum psychotic mother who kills her newborn infant. The motif of a threatened Medea killing those in her charge surfaces repeatedly. Murders are the solution to real or imagined tensions.

Excerpted and adapted from Candice Skrapec, "The Female Serial Killer: An Evolving Criminality," ©1993 by Candice Skrapec, in *Moving Targets: Women, Murder, and Representation*, edited by Helen Birch (Berkeley & Los Angeles: University of California Press, 1993). Reprinted with permission from the author.

Women as Murderers

Despite recent sensational portrayals of women murderers in Holly-wood cinema, they still do not figure regularly as killers in fact or fic-tion. Women hold even smaller claim to our perception of multiple murderers (the image of a woman killing a number of people, over a period of time or upon a single occasion, is not familiar). As one who has delivered many presentations on the subject of serial and mass murder to a wide range of audiences, I frequently encounter amaze-ment at the revelation that women have long been, and continue to be, multiple murderers. The notion so violates the idea of femaleness, tied to her traditional nurturing role, that a woman is denied her identity as a multiple murderer. Indeed, an FBI spokesperson distin-guished Aileen Wuornos [who was convicted and sentenced to death in 1992 for the killing of four men whose bodies were found along Florida highways] as 'the first female textbook case of a serial killer', contributing to this prevailing misconception.

Serial murder is typically presented as a male phenomenon, but the reality does not support this. Women do kill. Moreover, American soci-ety's experience with female serial killers is consistent with its experi-ence with female murderers in general. If we look at rates of homicides committed by each gender in the United States over time, females account for roughly 12 to 15 per cent of all murderers. Intriguingly, women represent the same proportion of serial murderers. In criminol-ogist Eric Hickey's research on serial murderers and their victims, 17 per cent of the 203 offenders he studied were females.

Looking for Similarities and Differences

Typically presented as case studies and summarily typecast as 'black widows' (women who kill a series of husbands, their children and other relatives), 'angels of death' or 'mercy killers' (women who kill patients in their care), and the like, female multiple murderers have not been examined as a group, apart from the 'celebrity' and inherent sensationalism of individual cases. This case-by-case, largely biograph-ical approach certainly owes part of its currency to the relatively small number of cases, but case studies, while they are valuable in and of themselves, so dominate the literature on female multiple murder that the larger picture is obscured. Scant attempt has been made to see how the women who kill repeatedly are like one another, or to see how they compare, as a group, with their male counterparts. Do these women come from similar places, psychologically and socially? What are the methods and motives of their crimes? Is there a discrete social phenom-enon of female serial murder? The answers require a systematic look at the women and their crimes. I wish, however, to caution against view-ing male and female serial killers as different 'breeds'. Indeed, it is a main point of this chapter that while it is tempting to focus on the readily apparent differences between the two, it is misguided to do so. I believe that these differences serve to mask more substantive, underlying similarities between male and female serial murderers.

The key distinction between male and female serial murderers is at the level of *modus operandi,* not of underlying motive: the how, not the why. The motive in each instance is a need for a sense of self as actor; a need for power that has generally arisen out of a formative history in which the individual as a child experienced him- or herself as powerless. This experience—as Alice Miller and others point out—can lead to a simmering yet pervasive rage which, if it is not resolved in a healthy manner, will result in violence. A critical element in determining how such children develop, and in particular how they express their rage, is their sense of entitlement. It has been more socially acceptable for men, who are more likely to feel entitled by virtue of their gender, to express this rage outwardly. Women have, until recently, been accorded less entitlement and have been more likely to turn their anger inward and to become self-destructive.

Serial and Sexual and Male?

Disagreement prevails among academics, law enforcement agents and journalists on what constitutes serial murder. While most definitions specify a minimum number of victims killed over time as the principal distinction, some are quite vague. Attorney Donald Sears, for example, speaks of 'many' killings. The relationship between murderer and victim has also been held to be a defining characteristic. Criminologist Steven Egger includes only strangers in his definition of serial murder. My own research suggests that serial murderers, both male and female, share varying degrees of closeness in their relationships with their victims. While most serial murderers do not know their victims, an impressive number do. Some even know them intimately; some are relatives.

Early press accounts of serial murders typified them as random and motiveless. It is my sense that, by and large, they are neither random nor lacking in discernible motive. The killings tend to be selectively targeted and appear to be committed in the service of some inextinguishable personal need. Rather than using factors such as relationship to victims or motive to *define* serial murder, they are more meaningfully viewed as ways in which serial murderers can *differ* from one another. After studying the literature and interviewing male serial and mass murderers, I am comfortable with the basic definition of a serial killer as one who kills a number of people, at least three, over a period of time.

The inclusion of a sexual component as part of the definition of serial murder is particularly problematic—so much so that when some people think of serial killers they can conceive only of the 'lust' killer, such as Ted Bundy. Bundy was convicted of the serial murders of two women and a girl and, within forty-eight hours of his execution in 1989, admitted to killing twenty-five other women across six US states in the 1970s. He often used a ruse to lure victims into a vulnerable position, and then bludgeoned, raped and strangled them. While it does not appear that he was a sexual sadist who drew erotic pleasure from the actual suffering of his victims, Bundy sexually violated them when they were unconscious and dying, or dead. This is the image of serial murder that a number of people hold: a series of victims are stalked by a predator who kills them as part of a scene of perverse sexual frenzy. While this is not an uncommon scenario, neither is it the only one.

Serial murder includes—but is in no way limited to—sexual murders that are perpetrated by both men and women. There are serial killers who do not violate their victims sexually. And while many offenders do not engage in any kind of overt sexual behaviour during the commission of their crimes, the killing scenarios may none the less be highly sexually charged for them. Memories and 'souvenirs' of the murders in the form of personal items or body parts from the victims become stimuli for later masturbatory fantasies, enabling the offender to relive the crimes.

Female Sexual Serial Killers

Most of the serial murderers familiar to the public did violate their victims sexually. Sexual or lust murder, in which the act of killing is itself eroticized, as feminist writers Deborah Cameron and Elizabeth Frazer view it, is held by them to be an exclusively male phenomenon. They consider Myra Hindley, convicted in 1966 with her lover Ian Brady of murdering two children and being an accessory to the murder of a third, a lone exception in the 'tradition of sadistic sexual murder . . . [in which] . . . women are virtually non-existent', but their dismissal does not appear to be adequately informed by empirical study of other cases. Tom Kuncl and Paul Einstein, for example, cite the Georgia case of Janice Buttram, who, with her husband, killed a teenage acquaintance in 1980. The victim was stabbed ninety-seven times in her face, neck, breasts, abdomen, legs and vaginal areas. There were also wounds on her hands which showed that she had tried to defend herself. The dying victim had apparently been raped and sodomized by Danny Buttram, and afterwards by Janice, who penetrated her rectally and then vaginally with the base of an electric toothbrush. Her husband told prosecutors that when he finished and went to wash blood from his hands, he saw Janice continue to stab the victim's breasts while performing oral sex on her. Psychologist Henry Adams described Janice Buttram as 'a genuine sexual sadist . . . obtaining sexual gratification [through] acts of perversion committed on an unwilling female victim'. Although not all the experts called into the case agreed with this depiction, they all believed that 'had

[she] not been apprehended so swiftly, there was an almost certain chance she would have killed again in a sexually sadistic assault'. . . .

Charlene Williams and her 'husband', Gerald Gallego, were responsible for the sexual murders of ten people in Oregon, California and Nevada from 1978 to 1980. She pleaded guilty to second-degree murder in Nevada as the basis of a plea-bargain arrangement. Her primary role was to lure victims to Gerald, who wanted them as sex slaves. Eric Van Hoffmann presents information that clearly implicates Charlene in the crimes. For example, bite wounds around the anus and nipples of different victims were from different sets of teeth, presumably Gerald's and Charlene's. It appears that Charlene actively participated both in abduction and sexual violation of victims. While there was no evidence that she killed any of their victims, Charlene testified that she did nothing to stop Gerald from doing so. There are also numerous reports of male and female workers in child daycare centres who sexually violate the children in their care. In 1987, for example, a twenty-three-year-old New Jersey woman, Margaret Michaels, was sentenced to forty-seven years in prison on 115 counts of sexual abuse against pre-school children in the day nursery in which she worked. Clearly, women are not immune from sexual perversions. A number of documented cases, then, involve women operating alone or as accomplices to sexual murders with their male partners. The extent of their involvement varies from awareness of the crimes to active participation.

Looking for the Motive

The sexual nature of crimes such as those committed by the Gallegos tends to render them more reprehensible in the eyes of the media and the public than they would be had there been no sexual assault. Perpetrators like these are often given monikers such as 'monster' or 'sex fiend' to reflect their heightened depravity. Even so, to focus on the sexual component of lust killings, as do Cameron and Frazer, is at the expense of a deeper understanding of the murders themselves. If one considers by analogy a sexual fetish, and focuses on the sexual behaviours involved, the underlying anxiety that is believed to drive the fetish will probably be neglected. Why does the fetishist need the red patent leather high-heeled shoe to reach sexual orgasm? Why do so many (male) serial murderers appear to need a suffering, dying, and/or dead victim to be sexually gratified? This is not to say that the link between sexual gratification and aggression among serial murderers is without meaning, but it may not represent the primary underlying motivation. While the gratification that accompanies sexual violation in a series of murders may be one reason why a killer repeats his or her crimes, it is, none the less, only part of the picture that is serial murder.

The ostensible motive for serial murder is sometimes monetary. While there are cases of 'black widowers', they appear to represent a much smaller proportion of male serial killers than 'black widows' do of female serial killers. Nevertheless, serial poisoners killing for money have long been a part of the criminal profile of women. Louis Charles Douthwaite cites many examples of serial killing by arsenic poisoning in sixteenth- to eighteenth-century Europe, particularly by women seeking to gain fortune and/or status. Among the most prodigious black widows in American history was Belle Gunness of Indiana, who may have begun her criminal career by killing husbands for insurance, and then changed her mode of operating to advertising in newspapers for suitors with dowries and killing them once she got access to their money. In 1908, the charred remains of her three children were found alongside the headless, burnt corpse of a woman thought at the time to be Gunness. In a search for the missing head, the authorities unearthed the bones of one to two dozen bodies on her property. The handyman, who was found guilty of arson, confessed to disposing of the bodies of some forty men who had been drugged, bludgeoned, and then dismembered by Gunness over five years. She was also linked to the death of her adopted daughter and, possibly, her two husbands. If, indeed, Gunness escaped, as the handyman contended, she may have got away with as much as $100,000 from her victims. . . .

There have also been instances in which women team up with men in a scheme of serial murder as a means to profit. During the 1940s in the states of New York and Michigan, Martha Beck and Raymond Fernandez, the 'Lonely Hearts Killers', murdered a number of women (and the baby of one of the victims) in a scam whereby Fernandez would promise marriage, secure the fiancée's funds, and then kill her. Beck and Fernandez were convicted of three such cases but were strong suspects in seventeen others.

Establishing Trust

The history of female serial killers, recent and remote, is littered with examples of women who have killed relatives and/or non-relatives whom they get to know and with whom they secure a position of trust for personal gain. While some appear to have had some measure of conscience about their deeds, others were decidedly more calculating. In 1989, for example, fifty-two-year-old Geraldine Parrish of Baltimore was indicted and jailed for killing four people for insurance money and making three attempts at killing a fifth person. This prompted an investigation into the death of her husband, who had died fifteen days after they were married in 1988, leaving her his social security benefits, his house, and a small inheritance. When police searched Parrish's house they found forty-five policies locked in closets and safes insuring the lives of various people. Fifty-nine-year-old Dorothea Montalvo Puente murdered tenants in California and collected their pension and disability benefits. The nine known victims, residents of her boarding-house, were between fifty-two and eighty years old. Before the series of murders, Puente had spent a decade in jails and prisons for drugging victims, stealing from them, and forging cheques in their names. While she was on parole for drugging and robbing ill and elderly people, she approached a local social worker offering to provide lodging for people on fixed incomes. In 1988, she was convicted of poisoning nine of them. . . .

Care-Takers as Killers

The means in cases like these are extreme, but the ostensible motive is comprehensible: personal gain. How, then, are we to understand women who kill those entrusted to their care, for no apparent financial gain? So-called 'angels of death' have claimed to kill terminally ill or suffering patients in their charge as a humane gesture. But many cases suggest perversity of purpose, where people in little immediate health risk or discomfort are killed by their care-takers. A remarkable example comes from Austria and involves four nurse's aides (aged twenty-eight to fifty-one) who were convicted of killing twenty patients since 1983 with lethal injections in a Vienna hospital. The women alleged that they were 'mercy killings to end suffering of terminal patients'. Further police investigation revealed that while all the deceased patients were feeble (they were between seventy-five and eighty years of age), not all were terminal. It is alleged that some were deemed 'bothersome' or too demanding. The nurse's aides used overdoses of—for example—insulin or a tranquillizer, or forced infusions of water into lungs. Remarkably, each nurse knew the others were killing patients: in some cases, two acted together to administer lethal injections.

Of all serial murderers, none are held to be so reprehensible as the baby-killers. Nurse Genene Jones was found guilty of the murder of a fifteen-month-old child following lethal injections of the muscle relaxant succinylcholine, which is extremely difficult to trace. Indeed, in earlier criminal cases, forensic medicine identified succinylcholine as the perfect murder weapon. Jones was also convicted of injecting heparin, an anticoagulant, into a four-week-old infant who survived. How many babies Jones actually killed will probably never be known. It has been estimated by experts from the Center for Disease Control in Georgia, who investigated a series of questionable deaths, that one paediatric intensive care unit alone where Jones had worked may have been the site of as many as fifteen murders by lethal doses of digoxin. Investigators also determined that forty-seven babies died 'suspicious' deaths during Jones's four-year nursing tenure at another facility. At her murder trial the prosecution alleged that the divorced mother of two had sought to become a heroine by causing a life-threatening condition from which she would then try to save the child. This kind of motivation is also seen in the arsonist who sets fires and then proceeds to be the hero who saves everyone. If this was true for Genene Jones, however, it would seem that she construed such self-importance differently. The indications are that rather than attempting to save the babies, her role was to ensure that they died. Possibly she was responding to what she believed were goals of a higher-order, albeit a deluded mission. Serial murderers in care-taking roles have been known to claim that they killed to prevent further or anticipated suffering by the people in their charge.

Among cases apparently devoid of any possible monetary or 'humanitarian' motive are those in which mothers kill their own children. Much infanticide goes unrecognized. In part this is because suffocation, the method used most frequently, is very difficult to distinguish from natural death and perhaps even more difficult to imagine. In the United States, cases often tend to be prosecuted only when they are sufficiently unusual or repeated often enough that they signal foul play. Mary Beth Tinning was convicted in 1987 of smothering her three-month-old daughter. Astoundingly, no one, not even her husband, disputed the explanations that her seven other babies (plus an eighth child she was caring for and planned to adopt) died of natural causes—possibly a genetic condition, or sudden infant death syndrome. Not until the death of the ninth child was it acknowledged that all the deaths but the first, which had definitely resulted from meningitis, were consistent with suffocation. A similar hindsight suggested that Tinning may have suffered from postpartum psychosis, or some other form of serious mental disorder. Certainly, rational motive for a series of killings like this is elusive. . . .

Examples like these illustrate how different female serial murderers can be. Not unlike their male counterparts, female serial murderers are diverse in their backgrounds. Some have been impoverished individuals without status in their community; others come from the privileged classes or the nobility. They are single, married, living in common-law relationships, or divorced. Many are mothers. About a third of the female serial killers in Hickey's study were housewives and a fifth were employed in health-care positions. Fifteen per cent were 'career criminals', deriving their primary source of income from criminal activities. Another 15 per cent were housekeepers, waitresses, and the like. Twenty per cent of the sample were transient or living with relatives, and declared no occupation. There is, therefore, no one profile of the kind of woman who commits serial murder. . . .

The Means to an End

Modus operandi, the method or means employed in accomplishing a task, is different from motive. It is the way in which a person goes about committing a crime: what he/she does and—just as significantly—does not do. In the case of homicide, *modus operandi is* the means by which one person kills another; literally, the means to an end. Beyond its importance to nuts-and-bolts police investigations, *modus operandi* helps to inform us about underlying motive. Elements of rage, disdain, greed, sadism, and the like can be inferred from what the perpetrator does. Are the victims subjected to 'overkill', a degree of violence that exceeds that necessary to kill the victim? Are corpses treated with any degree of respect, or are they humiliated in some way? For example, are the bodies found off the beaten track, fully clothed and perhaps even cleansed, or are they left nude along a well-travelled roadside, with the legs spread apart? Does a period of sadistic torture, psychological or physical, precede death? The emotional underpinnings of the acts of murder are often evidenced through *modus operandi* and, as such, provide clues about motive.

Generally, the victims of women are conned or overtaken while naturally in—or rendered into—a vulnerable state. They are killed by various means, including poisoning, smothering, stabbing and shooting. We should not be surprised that women tend not to kill by means that require overpowering physical force unless the physical strength of their victims—as children, or frail and elderly—makes this possible. A killer chooses his or her method according to what it takes to do the job and how familiar (and confident) he or she is with those means. It is unusual for a murderer to choose means that are outside her realm of life experience. Most female serial killers we know about, as the 'black widow' and 'angel of death' motifs indicate, killed people by poisoning or asphyxiating them: both means which are likely to be closer to their life experience than, say, shooting. They do not usually use a weapon like a gun or knife in confrontation.

Similar Motive; Different Method

Paradoxically, the fact that male *modi operandi* are more likely to involve sexual activity is an illustration of the *similarity* of basic motive for male and female serial killers, all of whom, regardless of their gender, seek a very specific end. Both will seek this through what we can call empowerment.

Men are traditionally expected to seek domination, particularly in sexual relations. Psychological and cultural evidence suggests that men experience feelings of power through sex, and since serial murder is essentially about power, we would expect those murders committed by men to be sexually charged. Men are expected to direct their anger at its source. In cases of sexual murder, perhaps the clearest example of this, the source of anger is the object that has power over him, the object he needs. He may fear the power of the need he has for the sexual object, feeling that it threatens his sense of control. Taken to its extreme, this fear, coupled with an underlying feeling of entitlement, may result in a need to exert absolute life-and-death control over the object of his desires. Women do not generally experience sex in the same way. They are not socialized to experience power directly through the sex act, and may even feel diminished by the way some men view them as sex objects. It is not surprising, then, that female serial killers do not tend to sexualize their killings.

Serial murderers first present themselves to us via their *modus operandi*. So struck are we by the terrifying image of the intensive-care nurse overdosing her infant patients, or the greed of the landlady who subjects her ageing tenants to the agonizing effects of poison in a scheme to collect their social security money, that typologies have been created based upon *modus operandi*. In terms of gender, differences manifest themselves through such aspects as physical strength, the male serial murderer being generally more able and more inclined to use physical force in the commission of his murders and his means more visceral (e.g. strangulation rather than suffocation).

Murderous Comfort Zones

We have yet to see a significant increase in the proportion of women who kill, but we are witnessing changes in the methods women use in killing. Perhaps the most useful concept to understand these changes is that of 'comfort zones', a term used by the law enforcement community. Generally speaking, people choose to behave in ways that do not arouse discomfort. While comfort zones are often physical places, they also include psychological environments that do not evoke undue anxiety. From our real and imagined experience we develop a repertoire of behaviour. We learn that there are a number of ways to deal with a situation to get what we want and to act in ways that generate the least unease. Criminals tend to behave in ways that at once maximize their sense of mastery and minimize any anxiety. They experience confidence and a sense of security when they operate in particular ways, under known conditions. This familiar arena or comfort zone may in large part account for the differences in *modus operandi* between men and women. Like men, women choose means that are accessible to them in terms of their familiarity and availability. It is more likely, for example, that a man will be exposed to and (in the USA at least) socialized in the use of weaponry during his life than it is for a woman; therefore a man will use a gun when he commits a crime, while a woman, who experiences guns as more foreign, is less likely to do so. None the less, in the United States, we are beginning to see cases of women who, like Aileen Wuornos, take up arms and commit serial or mass murder. . . .

Another point of departure between male and female serial murderers is that women are more apt to kill in or close to their home or workplace, presumably where they feel most secure. Male serial killers often travel hundreds, or even thousands of miles during the course of their crimes. The greater geographic mobility of male serial murderers is consistent with the idea of broader zones of comfort for men in general. The Wuornos case is evidence of a broadening of women's comfort zones, paralleling women's increasing integration into society. We may find that, increasingly, female serial murderers will kill in ways that have historically been the province of the male.

From Prey to Predator

It is important to distinguish killings that are essentially crimes of opportunity from those in which the murderer deliberates on and carefully executes his or her plan. Opportunists take advantage of situations in which they happen to find themselves. Their crimes lack premeditation. Predatory criminals operate according to a preconceived cognitive map that will guide them to their prey; they purposely seek out those they can violate in the service of some rational or irrational need. Perhaps the key distinction, though, is that the opportunist is reactive, responding to a particular situation with a criminal act. By contrast, while the predator may capitalize on any opportunity that presents itself, he or she will also, with single-minded determination, create opportunities.

Predation has been more characteristic of male criminals—although, as a long history of 'black widows' attests, it is by no means unheard of among women. As she moves further out into the world, through work or travel or social mobility, today's woman will acquire a broader base of competence and confidence. Her comfort zones of psychological tolerance and physical location expand. She moves from reactive object to proactive agent. Increasingly, over time, the prey becomes predator.

The vulnerability of victims of female serial killers tends to be inherent in their condition (as children, elderly or ill) or circumstance (the offender is in a position of trust, or manipulates this). Moreover, the female killer has the advantage of not being considered capable of or inclined to murder. For the multiple killer, the chosen victims will be those who can serve as a vehicle for the experience the killer is seeking. At the same time, she must be able to overtake the victim by virtue of her greater size, strength, or cunning. In most cases, the female serial murderer kills by her wits.

Changing Roles May Change Methods

Sociologist Gwynn Nettler argues that 'culture and opportunity expand or contract the exercise of biological differentials. This is particularly apparent with changes in the social roles of women'. Changing social factors affect women in ways that result in changes in their behaviour. One of these—and one where we may see further developments—is in the *modus operandi* of the female serial killer. Largely owing to the feminist movement, increased social awareness of women's growing sense of entitlement has begun to legitimize the outward expression of tensions that arise out of unmet needs. For the female killer, this can mean that the opportunist may become a predator. For Aileen Wuornos, early experience of herself as powerless, particularly at the hands of men, may have produced an underlying vulnerability, coupled with anger,

on which a growing sense of entitlement fed. Then as an adult prostitute, possibly feeling subjugated by her male clients, she may have felt
disdain for those who (ab)used her. The targets of this hatred may be
specific men who press to go beyond a line she found unacceptable
(e.g. demanding a sexual service she does not wish to provide), or the
rage may become generalized to all men who, in her mind, want to
(ab)use her and therefore deserve to be punished. Some media accounts
suggest that because of her lesbian relationship with Tyria Moore and
her choice of male victims, Wuomos was a man-hater. While man-
hating, or 'misandropy' as I call it, *might* describe Wuornos, more needs
to be learned about her, particularly how she experienced herself with
others both male and female, before her killings could simply be attributed to man-hating. . . .

Gender differences in *modus operandi* turn on differences in the
social construction of masculinity and femininity, on individual psychological make-up, as well as on physical constraints. Women, for
example, are more prone to turning their rage inward, becoming
depressed or self-destructive—victims rather than victimizers. Men are
generally encouraged and rewarded for expressing their anger outwardly, and will do so to the extent to which they feel entitled.

If certain preconditions are in place, the individual feels powerless
and either lacks a sense of self or may develop a distorted self. If that
fragile self is threatened, the individual may become fearful. To protect
himself, a man will tend to try to control the threat. Paradoxically, in
order to defeat his powerlessness he must control the source of power
that threatens his own. When rage is coupled with powerlessness, and
the individual feels entitled to express this state as intolerable and
unacceptable, then he or she must have access to the means of disposing of the source of these feelings. For each individual, there are tem-
peramental differences—to some degree biologically based—as well as
differences that result from social conditioning, that help to determine
how this release will occur. In the past, gender has exerted its main
effect as an additional level of restraint on women's behaviour.

Emerging Female Predators

Serial and mass murder is but one colour in a disturbing portrait of
society. We respond by filtering out the blinding spectrum of violence
before us. Our collective sense of security is particularly threatened by
the notion of female serial murderers. In the matter of women who
kill, we have been fatally complacent. We seem to need to look at the
women who are agents of multiple murder as aberrations rather than
as symptoms of a phenomenon. I believe that many homicide cases
remain unsolved, without viable suspects, because the offender was
falsely assumed to be male. Current statistics indicate that the prevalence of female serial murder—as a phenomenon in its own right and
as a phenomenon relative to male serial murder—is exceedingly

small. But the Wuornos case should give us pause to reflect on our state of knowledge: it may be that women are becoming increasingly comfortable in those realms of human experience that have been traditional male preserves. It is probable that the number of female serial killers will increase as more law enforcement agents consider women as viable suspects.

As women become more a part of the workings of society, we will, I expect, increasingly observe predatory kinds of serial murders perpetrated by women. By virtue of her femaleness, a woman lacks exposure to many of the means that are more readily accessible to males. But feminism has arguably given women a greater sense of entitlement, facilitating the outward expression of emotion, and in practical terms, women's comfort zones have expanded. They are now more likely than ever to come into contact with a wider array of means to gratify their needs in general (and express their fears and rage in particular). In this way, feminism is serving a catalytic role in the evolution of the female serial killer, although the basis for the behaviour remains the same—a need for a sense of being and vitality that is experienced through empowerment. In certain cases her anger and need for empowerment will be directed at the power-brokers, those she has experienced as victimizing her. More specific than misanthropy, this emerging female is 'misandropic', decidedly hateful of men. She will seek to punish them for being men, the symbol of her oppressed sense of self. The victim becomes the victimizer. Murder is, in its most elemental aspect, an act of self-preservation. I believe that how it is committed is largely a function of gender; why it is committed is a function of the human condition.

AILEEN WUORNOS: SEXUAL PREDATOR

Michael D. Kelleher and C.L. Kelleher

Michael D. Kelleher and C.L. Kelleher coauthored the book *Murder Most Rare: The Female Serial Killer,* from which the following selection is taken. The authors explore the life and crimes of Aileen Wuornos, the woman they believe to be the only female sexual serial killer in history. Beginning with details of Wuornos's birth to teenage parents, the authors provide an account of her abusive and troubled childhood, her life as a petty criminal and prostitute, her arrest and trial, as well as an account of the murders she committed. The authors also question Wuornos's claim that all of the murders were necessary to defend herself, arguing that the evidence points to a conscious and brutal attack on her victims.

The female sexual serial killer who acts alone in carrying out her egregious crimes is so unusual that America has only experienced a single female sexual serial killer in its history—Aileen Wuornos. Although it is not unusual for a woman to partner with a male sexual predator as a member of a serial-killing team, the female sexual predator who acts alone unquestionably represents the most extraordinary of perpetrators in the history of this crime. Indeed, her crimes are murder most rare.

Troubling Questions

Despite the fact that we have a growing knowledge of the male sexual predator and his crimes, it is uncertain if any of this knowledge is applicable to the female sexual serial murderer. To draw conclusions about this type of perpetrator from what is known about her male counterpart may or may not prove to be valid; it is, at best, risky guesswork. In the final analysis, male and female serial murderers differ in fundamental ways that make workable comparisons difficult and uncertain. Likewise, female sexual predators who are members of a serial-killing team do not provide a sure point of comparison for the obvious reason that their motives are shared and intermingled with their murderous partners.

The questions raised by the crimes of Aileen Wuornos are complex and troubling. Since her case is unique in the history of criminology, very little of what has been learned from her background and criminal activities can be generalized. It is certainly impossible to even begin to profile such a murderer. The only other female sexual predator whose crimes approximate those of a male sexual serial killer was Marti Enrequeta, who was active in Spain shortly after the turn of the twentieth century. Unfortunately, far less is known of Enrequeta and her crimes than of Wuornos, who claimed her victims between 1989 1990 in America.

An obvious question that arises in the context of the rarity of the female sexual serial killer is one of significance. Were the crimes of Wuornos an anomaly, as many criminologists believe, or was she the first of a new category of lethal criminal with which future law enforcement personnel must grapple? Today, the answer to this question is unknown. However, a longer view of the crime of serial murder leads to a different answer. The crime of serial murder is evolving in lockstep with its perpetrator and the complexities of our society. The serial killer of today is more pernicious, diverse, and active than in the past. The crimes committed by this perpetrator are more complex today than in previous decades; and they are also more numerous. There is no reason to exclude the possibility of other female sexual serial killers in the coming decades. However, the history of serial murders committed by women indicates that sexual motivations for this crime are rare. Therefore, it is reasonable to assume that there will be other female sexual serial killers in the future, but it is also reasonable to assume that they will be few in number. Since any definitive answer obviously lies in the future, the best one can know of this most rare of murderers can be learned from the crimes of Aileen Wuornos.

Serial Murder or Self-Defense?

Aileen "Lee" Carol Wuornos clearly stands apart from other American female serial killers. She has been persistently, and mistakenly, portrayed in the media and on television as the first American female serial killer. In reality, she was neither the first such murderer nor the most prolific. However, Wuornos could be the first female sexual serial killer who acted alone in committing her crimes, if one discounts the possibility that she acted in self-defense when she murdered seven men in Florida in 1989 and 1990.

Wuornos has remained steadfast in her position that each of the murders that she committed was necessary in order to protect her own life. Because Wuornos worked as a prostitute for over twenty years, she had any number of violent and abusive encounters with men. Each man Wuornos murdered had become involved with her for sexual reasons, and in at least one instance, the victim was known to be an extremely violent individual with a history of rape. However, most of her victims did not have such a background, and there would have been little or no reason for Wuornos to suspect a violent out-come to the encounter. All of Wuornos's victims were shot with a .22-caliber handgun that she kept constantly in her possession, and each of her victims was robbed of personal effects, their automobile, or both. Each crime scene indicated that Wuornos was able to gain con-trol over her victim and shoot him to death. In each instance, she had the presence of mind to rob her victim and make some attempt to secret the body. Given the method and pattern of her crimes, it is dif-ficult to accept an argument of self-defense in each crime. However, Wuornos's background and long history of abusive encounters with men must have played a major role in her later crimes.

The evidence and testimony surrounding the crimes of Aileen Wuornos overwhelmingly points to a series of conscious and brutal attacks against her victims—attacks predicated on some form of sexu-al encounter for money. However, it seems clear that the murders were not motivated by a drive for bizarre sexual satisfaction, as is often the case with male serial killers. Rather, Wuornos lashed out against her victims in a rage that originated in decades of abusive and debilitating encounters with men that began in her early childhood.

A Childhood of Horrors

It is difficult to image a more horrendous childhood than the one experienced by Aileen Pittman Wuornos. Fathered by a psychopathic child molester and rejected by her mother as a toddler. Wuornos was raised by her grandparents and older sister. She was physically abused by her grandfather and subjected to even more physical and sexual abuse by older boys and young men throughout her childhood years. It was not until the age of thirteen that Wuornos learned the truth about her parents. (She had long been told that her grandparents were, in fact, her birth parents). By the age of fifteen, Wuornos had been rejected by her grandfather, her grandmother was dead, and she was a ward of the court. In 1971, at that young age, she began a life of petty crime, prostitution, and drifting that eventually led to a year of serial killing in Florida. Nothing came easy for Wuornos, who strug-gled throughout her childhood with the kind of physical and sexual abuse that would be inconceivable to most individuals.

February 29, 1956. Aileen Pittman (Wuornos) is born to teenage par-ents, Diane Pratt and Leo Pittman, in Rochester, Michigan. Pratt and Pittman had separated several months prior to Wuornos's birth. Leo Pittman was a habitual sex offender who suffered from significant psy-chological problems. He would later be jailed for molesting a seven-year-old girl and eventually institutionalized in mental hospitals in Kansas and Michigan. Pittman played no role in Wuornos's childhood and later committed suicide while institutionalized for his crimes.

January 1960. Diane Pratt, Wuornos's birth mother, claims that she can no longer tolerate the demands and incessant crying of her two young children, Aileen and her older brother, Keith. Pratt leaves her children in the care of her parents and Wuornos's older sister, Lauri.

March 18, 1960. Wuornos's maternal grandparents legally adopt Aileen and Keith. Wuornos would later describe her grandfather as an abusive alcoholic who beat his wife and the children regularly. According to Wuornos, she was thirteen years old before she was told the truth about her birth parents and her true relationship with Mr. and Mrs. Wuornos.

1962. At the age of six, Wuornos is severely burned while she and Keith set fires with lighter fluid. Although she recovers, she is permanently scarred on her face.

A Series of Losses

June 1970. Wuornos, who later claims to have been sexually active for over a year by 1970, becomes pregnant after being raped. According to Wuornos, her grandparents refuse to believe that she was raped and begin to incessantly refer to her as a "whore." She is only fourteen years old.

March 23, 1971. Wuornos gives birth to a son at a Detroit maternity home for unwed mothers. She immediately gives the infant up for adoption.

July 7, 1971. Grandmother Britta Wuornos dies, allegedly of liver cancer. However, Diane Pratt (Wuornos's birth mother) believes that her father actually murdered her mother. By the time of Britta Wuornos's death, Grandfather Wuornos had incessantly threatened to kill both Aileen and Keith if they were not removed from his home. Shortly after her grandmother's death, Wuornos and her brother become wards of the court.

1971. Wuornos begins a life of drifting and prostitution that will span nearly twenty years. She is completely alone, destitute, unskilled, virtually uneducated, and only fifteen years old. Her only close personal relationship is with her brother, Keith.

1974. Wuornos celebrates her eighteenth birthday. She would later state that she was raped at least five times before she turned eighteen.

May 1974. Using the alias Sandra Kretsch, Wuornos is jailed in Jefferson County, Colorado, for disorderly conduct, drunk driving, and firing a .22-caliber pistol from a moving vehicle. She skips town before her trial date.

July 13, 1976. Wuornos is arrested in Antrim County, Colorado, for assault and disturbing the peace after she throws a cue ball at the head of a bartender with whom she has been arguing. She is also served with outstanding arrest warrants from Troy, Michigan, for driving without a license and consuming alcohol in a motor vehicle. Her brother, Keith, helps her pay a $105 fine to clear the cases.

July 17, 1976. Keith Wuornos dies of throat cancer, devastating Aileen Wuornos. To her surprise, Wuornos receives $10,000 from the proceeds of his life insurance. Within two months, she has spent all the money and is again destitute and drifting.

A Life of Crime in Florida

When Aileen Wuornos arrived in Florida at the age of twenty, she was destitute, angry, and had a lengthy history of minor criminal activities. Although she had long demonstrated a propensity for violence against men, Wuornos was certainly not yet a killer. However, the bitter experiences of her childhood and adolescence continued into her adulthood in Florida. Wuornos was unable to sustain a meaningful relationship with any man. Although she did briefly marry while in Florida, the relationship was with a man who was some fifty years her senior, and it was brought to a sudden end when each accused the other of physical abuse. For well over a decade, Wuornos continued to earn a meager living as a prostitute. Eventually, she met another woman in a bar, with whom she began a relationship that would last throughout her year of serial killing.

September 1976. Wuornos hitches rides to Florida and sporadically, continues to earn money through prostitution. Sometime during the next few years, she marries a seventy-year-old man; however, the marriage quickly fails when the two partners accuse each other of physical abuse. Wuornos then drifts through a series of short-lived heterosexual relationships. Two years after her divorce, she attempts to commit suicide by shooting herself in the stomach.

May 20, 1981. Wuornos is arrested in Edgewater, Florida, for the armed robbery of a convenience store. On May 4, 1982, she is sentenced to prison for the robbery; she is released thirteen months later, on June 30, 1983.

May 1, 1984. Wuornos is arrested for trying to pass forged checks at a bank in Key West, Florida.

November 30, 1985. Wuornos is named as a suspect in the theft of a pistol and ammunition in Pasco County, Florida.

December 11, 1985. Using the alias Lori Grody (the name of her aunt in Michigan), Wuornos is cited for driving a motor vehicle without a valid license.

January 4, 1986. Wuornos is arrested in Miami, Florida, under her own name and charged with automobile theft, resisting arrest, and obstruction of justice by giving false information to a law enforcement officer. A .38-caliber handgun and ammunition are impounded from her car at the time of her arrest.

June 2, 1986. Wuornos is detained as Lori Grody after a male companion accuses her of threatening him with a gun and demanding $200. At the time she is detained, law enforcement personnel discover a .22-caliber handgun and ammunition in Wuornos's automobile. Wuornos later denies that the incident ever took place.

June 9, 1986. While using the alias Susan Blahovec, Wuornos is ticketed for speeding in Jefferson County, Florida.

June 1986. Wuornos meets Tyria Moore in a South Daytona, Florida, bar. The women soon become homosexual lovers and begin a relationship that will last for the next four years. The couple is supported by Wuornos's prostitution.

July 4, 1987. Using the alias Susan Blahovec, Wuornos and Moore are detained for assaulting a man with a beer bottle.

December 18, 1987. Using the alias Susan Blahovec, Wuornos is cited for walking on the interstate and possessing a suspended driver's license.

January 11, 1987. Using the alias Susan Blahovec, Wuornos writes a threatening letter to a circuit court clerk regarding her citation of December 18, 1987.

February 9, 1988. Using the same alias, Wuornos writes a second threatening letter to the circuit court clerk.

March 12, 1988. Using the alias Cammie March Green, Wuornos accuses a Daytona Beach bus driver of assault, claiming that he pushed her off his bus after an intense verbal argument. Tyria Moore is listed as a witness to the incident.

July 23, 1988. A Daytona Beach landlord accuses Tyria Moore and Susan Blahovec (Wuornos) of vandalizing their apartment.

November 1988. Using the alias Susan Blahovec, Wuornos attempts to buy lottery tickets at a Zephyr Hills, Florida, supermarket and becomes embroiled in a heated argument with the store manager. For the next six days she makes incessant threatening telephone calls to supermarket employees.

A Year of Murder

Aileen Wuornos began her lethal career at the age of thirty-three. By this age, she was clearly a hardened and angry, woman who had experienced two decades of debilitating abuse and horror, which in retrospect seemed to inevitably impel her to murder. However, her first victim was a man who proved to be a brutal rapist—a fact that lends credence to Wuornos's later claims of self-defense. Unfortunately, the background of this victim was never disclosed by law enforcement personnel, and in fact, was never brought to light until well after Wuornos had been convicted of murder and given the death penalty.

Wuornos has relentlessly claimed that she acted in self-defense in attacking each of her male victims. Although this argument was considered completely specious until 1992—the year in which the violent background of her first victim was made known—it now seems likely, that Wuornos may have acted to protect her own life in at least one instance. Is it possible that Wuornos's first murder was all act of self-defense that led to a compulsion to attack future victims? Although it seems unreasonable to believe that each of her murders was an act of self-defense, one cannot discount the possibility that Wuornos's first victim may have threatened her life and prompted an ultimate act of retaliation. Given her long history of abusive relationships with men, could this incident have triggered Aileen Wuornos's short, but spectacular, career as a serial murderer?

November 30, 1989. Richard Mallory, a fifty-one-year-old electrician from Clearwater, Florida, is last seen alive by his coworkers. Those who know Mallory consider him a volatile and difficult character. He has been divorced five times, has a reputation as an unusually heavy drinker, is considered extremely paranoid, and exhibits an insatiable obsession with pornographic material. Despite his unsavory reputation with coworkers, Mallory had no criminal record, according to local police.

December 1, 1989. Mallory's 1977 Cadillac Coupe de Ville is found abandoned at Ormond Beach, in Volusia County, Florida. Nearby, law enforcement personnel discover his wallet (without any cash) and personal papers, along with several condoms and a half-empty bottle of vodka.

December 13, 1989. Mallory's partially decomposed body is found in the woods northwest of Daytona Beach by two men who are searching the area for junkyard scrap to sell. The body is naked from the waist up. Investigators on the scene determine that Mallory was shot three times in the chest with a .22-caliber pistol, thus becoming Wuornos's first known victim.

According to later testimony, Wuornos claimed that the encounter started as a routine proposition for sex. However, Mallory, soon became physically abusive and began to attack the woman. As they struggled, Wuornos pulled the .22-caliber pistol from her handbag and shot him a single time in the chest. Seeing that he was injured, she considered what to do next. Fearing that if the incident was discovered, she would be arrested for attempted murder, Wuornos fired two more shots, killing Mallory. She then wrapped the victim's body in a piece of carpet and drove off in his car, after relieving Mallory of the valuables in his possession.

Murder in a Series

May 19, 1990. Forty-three-year-old David Spears, a construction worker from Sarasota, Florida, leaves his workplace to visit his ex-wife in Orlando. However, he neither arrives in Orlando nor reports back to work.

May 25, 1990. David Spears's supervisor happens on his pickup truck on interstate I-95, south of Gainesville, Florida. However, law enforcement officials are unable to discover Spears's whereabouts.

May 31, 1990. Charles Carskaddon, a forty-year-old part-time rodeo worker from Missouri, is reported missing after he leaves Booneville, Missouri, to drive interstate I-95 to meet his fiancée in Tampa, Florida.

June 1, 1990. The nude body of a male is discovered in a wooded area forty miles north of Tampa, in Citrus County, Florida. The victim has been shot six times with a .22-caliber pistol. Law enforcement personnel recover a used condom near the body. Less than a week later, on June 7, 1990, the body of David Spears is identified from dental records; he is Wuornos's second known victim.

June 6, 1990. The naked body of Charles Carskaddon is discovered thirty miles south of the location of David Spears's corpse. He has been shot nine times with a .22-caliber weapon. The next day, Carskaddon's abandoned automobile is located. Missing from the vehicle is the victim's .45-caliber automatic pistol and his personal effects. Carskaddon is Wuornos's third victim.

June 7, 1990. Peter Siems, a sixty-five-year-old missionary and former merchant mariner, is last seen leaving his home in Jupiter, Florida, to visit relatives in Arkansas. On June 22, 1990, a missing person report is filed with Florida law enforcement personnel. Siems would later be identified as Wuornos's fourth victim, although his body was not located.

July 4, 1990. Siems's automobile is involved in an accident in Orange Springs, Florida. Although the vehicle is quickly abandoned, witnesses describe the occupants as two women—one blonde (Wuornos) and one brunette (Moore)—and provide sufficient information to produce police-artist sketches. The occupants of the automobile were injured in the crash but fled. However, the driver left a bloody palm print behind, on the trunk of Siems's car.

July 30, 1990. Eugene Burress, a fifty-year-old sausage deliveryman, leaves his workplace in Ocala, Florida, to start his normal rounds of commercial deliveries. He never returns to work, and a missing person report is filed early the next morning after his abandoned delivery van is located.

August 4, 1990. Burress's body is discovered by picnickers in the Ocala National Forest. He has been shot twice with a .22-caliber pistol. Near the body, law enforcement personnel find some of his personal effects, credit cards, and an empty cash bag in which he carried the cash receipts from his deliveries. Burress is later identified as Wuornos's fifth victim.

September 11, 1990. Richard Humphreys, a fifty-six-year-old retired police chief from Alabama, fails to return home from his job as a child abuse claims investigator in Ocala, Florida. The next day, his body is found in an empty lot, shot seven times with a .22-caliber pistol. All Humphreys's pockets are empty and his personal effects are missing. A week later, on September 19, Humphreys's car is found abandoned and missing the license plates. A month later, on October 13, 1990, his badge and some personal effects are discovered in Lake County, Florida, seventy miles south of where his body had been found. Humphreys is Wuornos's sixth victim.

November 19, 1990. The body of Walter Antonio is discovered in the woods northwest of Cross City, Florida. Antonio was a sixty-year-old truck driver from Merrit Island, Florida, who also worked as a reserve police officer for Brevard County, Florida. The victim had been shot three times in the back and once in the head with a .22-caliber pistol. His body was found nude except for his socks. Antonio had been robbed of his police reserve badge, handcuffs, cash, and a gold ring. His car is located five days later in Brevard County. Antonio is Wuornos's seventh victim.

Arrest and Trial

By any standards, Aileen Wuornos was not a precise, methodical serial murderer, unlike the vast majority of female serial killers. Whatever their causes, these murders were opportunistic in nature and brutal in their commission. Although it is true that Wuornos made some efforts to hide the corpses of her victims, she repeatedly used their automobiles, flaunted their personal effects, and attempted to publicly pawn their assets. Wuornos made only feeble attempts to avoid apprehension and gave little or no thought to planning her crimes. Because these murders were spontaneous and her activities after each killing continued to be flagrant, it was only a matter of time before law enforcement personnel caught up with their prey. By the end of November 1990, the police were well aware that they had a pernicious serial killer operating in their area, and they were beginning to close in on Aileen Wuornos.

November 30, 1990. Law enforcement personnel release sketches of the suspect they believe has been involved in some or all of the seven related homicides that occurred over the past twelve months. Over the next month, police receive several tips regarding two women identified as Tyria Moore and "Lee" Blahovec. Investigators soon discover the aliases used by Aileen Wuornos (Grody, Green, and Blahovec) and are able to link Moore and Wuornos to the accident involving Peter Siems's automobile.

December 6, 1990. Wuornos, using the alias Cammie Green, pawns items belonging to Richard Mallory in Daytona, Florida; she later pawns articles belonging to Richard Spears in Ormond Beach.

January 9, 1991. Aileen Wuornos is apprehended at a bar known as the Last Resort in Ormond Beach, Florida. The next day, Tyria Moore is located at a relative's home in Pennsylvania and agrees to cooperate with law enforcement personnel. Subsequently, police arrange for Wuornos and Moore to talk on the telephone; during these conversations, Moore pleads with Wuornos to confess to the murders.

January 16, 1991. Wuornos confesses to six murders, claiming that each was an act of self-defense. She denies murdering Peter Siems, whose body was never located, as well as another male victim who had been discovered in 1990 but never identified. Explaining her crimes to police, Wuornos made this statement:

I shot them because, to me, it was like a self-defending thing. Because I felt if I didn't shoot them and didn't kill them, first of all . . . if they had survived, my ass would be getting in trouble for attempted murder, so I'm up shits creek on that one anyway; and if I didn't kill them, you know, of course, I mean I had to kill them . . . or it's like retaliation, too. It's like, you bastards, you were going to hurt me.

January 13, 1992. Wuornos's trial for the murder of Richard Mallory begins. During her testimony, Wuornos explains that her actions were necessary to defend herself after Mallory threatened her life. However, Wuornos's former lover, Tyria Moore (who was not a participant in any of the murders), testifies against her and discloses conversations that took place after the murder of Richard Mallory that prove harmful to the defense. These conversations indicate that Wuornos was probably not acting in self-defense when she shot Mallory.

On January 27, 1992, the case is handed over to the jury, which deliberates for less than two hours before finding Wuornos guilty of first-degree murder. After hearing the verdict, Wuornos shouts at the jurors: "I'm innocent! I was raped! I hope you get raped! Scumbags of America!" On January 29, 1992, the same jury recommends the death penalty for Aileen Wuornos.

April 1992. Wuornos pleads guilty to the murders of Burress, Humphreys, and Spears.

May 7, 1992. Wuornos receives a second death penalty for the murders to which she confessed the preceding month.

November 10, 1992. A nationally televised program (Dateline NBC) airs information about the Wuornos murders and various law enforcement investigations surrounding the case. During the program it is disclosed that Richard Mallory had served ten years in prison for rape—a fact that had not been discovered by law enforcement personnel and that would have lent credence to Wuornos's statements at her trial, in which she claimed to have been acting in self-defense. However, no information about any of Wuornos's other victims has ever been brought forward to substantiate her long-standing claim that she acted only in self-defense in attacking her other victims.

Throughout 1992, Aileen Wuornos underwent a series of legal proceedings and was involved in one of the most sensational media events ever to surround such a case. However, to law enforcement officials, officers of the court, and the majority of the public, her guilt was clear and her motives obvious. Since that time, while awaiting her fate on death row, Wuornos has become a born-again Christian. Facing multiple death sentences and now (as of this writing) involved in the last of her mandatory appeals, Aileen Wuornos remains unshakable in her assertion that she acted in self-defense, despite the near-universal belief that she was America's first female sexual serial murderer.

CHAPTER 3

WHY DO SERIAL MURDERERS KILL?

WHY SERIAL MURDERERS KILL: AN OVERVIEW

Steven A. Egger

In the following selection, Steven A. Egger summarizes various theories that attempt to explain the behavior of serial killers. Egger includes theories that provide biological, psychological, or cultural explanations as well as theories that examine multiple characteristics, known as a profile approach. The theories that he describes range from the hypothesis that head injuries may lead to a biological compulsion to serial murder to the theory that childhood neglect and abuse may predispose some children to grow up to be serial killers. However, Egger writes that more research is necessary in order to gain an accurate understanding of serial killers. Egger is a professor of criminal justice at the University of Illinois at Springfield and was formerly the project director of New York State's Homicide Assessment and Lead Tracking System (HALT), the first statewide computerized system designed to track and identify serial murderers.

The killing of a stranger is not seen as motivated principally by previous interpersonal friction in the killer-victim relationship, but rather, must be seen as the outcome of some other interpersonal motive. While the ability to identify and capture serial killers is the critical short-term objective of law enforcement, it is becoming more and more important to understand why these killers behave as they do. As they are identified, apprehended, and studied, some description of these murderers has developed. Older references in the literature tend to reflect a Freudian orientation to this phenomenon.

Explaining the Behavior of Serial Killers

Some researchers tend to classify theories that explain behavior into very broad categories. Those examining serial murder might classify theories of the behavior and motivation of the killers as falling within three general areas: sociological, psychological, and cultural. Others would add the biological category. The problem with placing serial mur-

Excerpted from *The Killers Among Us: An Examination of Serial Murder and Its Investigation*, by Steven A. Egger, ©1998. Reprinted by permission of Prentice-Hall, Inc., Upper Saddle River, N.J.

der behavior into specific categories is that the behaviors found in serial killers that have been identified and studied do not necessarily fall within neat and tidy theories—or groups of theories, for that matter.

Some researchers will study the serial killer from their own specific frame of reference. In other words, a sociologist will examine and concentrate on those behaviors or characteristics which in total tell us something about the serial killer in the aggregate. Sociologists attempt to use data and empirical evidence from a large group of subjects (serial killers) to explain what these subjects are "like."

Psychologists and psychiatrists are in the business of studying individuals, and much of their research is reported in the form of clinical case studies. Data from clinical studies of larger populations of subjects are frequently reported in journals and research reports. Psychiatrists differ from psychologists by holding a medical degree, and their research frequently combines the biological and social science information on the subjects of their study. Cultural explanations of serial murder behavior are provided by anthropologists, sociologists, social psychologists, and a number of other social science disciplines who look to the broader issues of historical development, media influence, trends, marginal members of society, and so on. Biological explanations of serial murder generally deal with genetics (XYY chromosomes), neurology (brain abnormality or dysfunction), and biochemistry (chemical imbalance in the brain).

All of these disciplines have contributed to our understanding of serial murder. However, many theories and explanations of serial murder behavior combine one or more of these disciplines, and these theories do not fit tightly within a discipline or theoretical framework. . . .

Inadequate Socialization

Theories regarding inadequate socialization or childhood trauma are frequently cited in the homicide literature and often referred to regarding serial murderers. A. Storr states that human cruelty (which describes the acts committed by serial murderers, i.e., torture, mutilation, dismemberment, etc.) is "a phenomenon which can only be understood if we take into account the fact that many people suffer from persistent feelings of powerlessness and helplessness which date from a very early period in childhood."

The intense rage of the serial killer may be a mirror of the horror suffered in childhood. This rage reflects an intense hatred bred in childhood and which can now be targeted on victims. J.M. Reinhardt's case studies of multicides (mass and serial murders) found a prevalence of neglect and early years spent in wretched states of social and psychological deprivation. According to Reinhardt, "They gave preponderant evidence of never having experienced normal communication with a dependable, understanding part of the social world about them. They had no workable system of social or personal frames of reference."

W.S. Willie, who concurs with Reinhardt, found the most common feature of the family backgrounds of the murderer to be the violent punishing practices inflicted on the child, and that there "appears to be no other factor which is as specific in the family backgrounds of homicidal offenders."

FBI agents R.R. Hazelwood and J.E. Douglas state that, "Seldom does the lust murderer come from an environment of love and understanding. It is more likely that he was an abused and neglected child who experienced a great deal of conflict in his early life and was unable to develop and use adequate coping devices (i.e. defense mechanisms)."

In their extensive reading of the case histories of murderers, A. Ellis and J. Gullo found that "whenever sufficient material is given on the murderer's background, it is consistently found that (1) his upbringing particularly in relation to being treated kindly by his parents and his being emotionally close to them and to his other family members, left much to be desired; and (2) from an early age, he acted peculiarly, especially in his interpersonal relations with others, and began to get into some kind of school, social or vocational difficulties."

Serial murderers are frequently found to have unusual or unnatural relationships with their mothers. D.T. Lunde notes: "Normally there is an intense relationship with the mother. Her death is often one of those fantasized during adolescence. Later on, she may become one of the victims." "Many serial murderers have had intense, smothering relationships with their mothers—relationships filled with both abuse and sexual attraction."

In his classic 1927 study of murder, A. Bjere states:

> Time after time during my studies among murderers I was struck by the fact that just the most brutal criminals—men who, however different their psychological natures may have been in the beginning, and who had a stereotyped incapacity to conceive their fellow creatures as anything but dead matter or as the means to the satisfaction of their animal lusts; in other words men who for a long time had been cut off from any sort of association with humanity—were nevertheless frequently attached to their mothers by bonds which seemed even stronger than those which one ordinarily finds between mother and son.

Sex as a Motive

The killer's sexual preference or orientation is not a consistent correlate when known serial murderers are examined. As D.J. West notes, "there is no reason to suppose that the likelihood of becoming homicidal is associated with a particular sexual orientation." For example, Albert DeSalvo, Ted Bundy, and Ed Kemper preferred females as sexual partners and as prey, whereas John Wayne Gacy, Dennis Nilsen, and Dean Corll preferred males in these roles.

The author has argued that sex is only an instrument used by the killer to obtain power and domination over his victim. Although the sexual component is frequently present in a serial murder, it is not the central motivating factor for the killer but an instrument used to dominate, control, and destroy the victim.

Helen Morrison, who has reportedly interviewed a number of serial murderers, argues against the sexual theme of serial murder. She states: "The incidence of sadomasochistic sex is very high. The incidence of mass murders is not, at least in the sheer number of perpetrators." Storr also discounts the sexual nature of sadomasochism or cruelty. He argues that "sado-masochism is less 'sexual' than is generally supposed, and is really a 'pseudo-sexual' activity or preoccupation, much more concerned with power relations than with pleasure." The emphasis on power relations or control was, for J. Levin and J.A. Fox, an important characteristic of serial murderers. They state: "Domination unmitigated by guilt is a crucial element in serial crimes with a sexual theme. Not only does sadistic sex—consensual or forcible—express the power of one person over another, but in serial homicides, murder enhances the killer's sense of control over his victims."

Variations on Power and Control

Levin and Fox contend that the serial murderer is trying to achieve a feeling of superiority over the victim and to triumph or conquer by destruction; further, that "as the serial killer becomes more and more secure with his crime, however, he may also become increasingly more sadistic and inhumane," and that "the pleasure and exhilaration that the serial killer derives from repeated murder stem from absolute control over other human beings." The psychological need to control and the wish to command the fate of those around them is, for Fox and Levin, often evident in serial murderers. However, in their study of 36 sexually oriented murderers, R.K. Ressler, A.W. Burgess, C.R. Hartman, J.E. Douglas, and A. McCormack found every indication that their motivation was a complex developmental process based on needs for sexual dominance based on violent sadistic fantasies.

J.D. Sewell analyzed the case of Ted Bundy from the literature dealing with Bundy and Sewell's own involvement as an investigator of the Chi Omega sorority house murders committed by Bundy at Florida State University. The purpose of Sewell's analysis was to apply E.I. Megargee's "algebra of aggression" to Bundy's behavior. Megargee's multidisciplinary approach to criminal behavior contends that "an individual automatically weighs alternatives and chooses a response to a situation which maximizes his/her benefit and minimizes potential pain distress."

Sewell argues that the behavioral characteristics of Ted Bundy provide a clear application of Megargee's algebra of aggression:

> Bundy's overall violent response exemplified an instigation to aggression which was grounded in his rage against women and magnified by his need for excitement, attention, and ego gratification. His habit strength drew on his repeated successful acts of violence . . . to obtain control of the victims and the unsuccessful attempts by a number of states to charge him with these crimes. A number of situational factors added to his predisposition towards violence as an acceptable response.

Sewell concludes that "it would appear that Bundy chose a violent response as an acceptable reaction to many situations."

Similarities to Rape

As the author has noted elsewhere, the motivational dynamics of serial murder seem to be consistent with research on the nature of rape. Power would appear to be a vital component in either crime. Although this is conjecture without an empirical foundation, the similarity of these acts becomes evident when one realizes that, as D.J. West put it, "it may take only a small increase in the desperation of the assailant or the resisting victim to convert a violent rape into a murder."

D. Canter has also recently noted this similarity in his research. Canter states that "men I have spoken to who have admitted a series of rapes have often also admitted that they would have killed subsequent victims if they had not been caught. Rape has the same roots as murder. The difference between rape and murder lies in the form and degree of control the offender exerts over his victims." The implication from Canter's statement is that the motivations of these two violent acts may be similar. However, the motivational dynamics of either violent act are certainly complex and their similarities may only explain a certain level of action, in this case the form and degree of control, not necessarily the inner thoughts and drives of the violent actor.

In discussions with FBI agent Roy Hazelwood (who has since retired), he readily agreed that there was a similarity between rape and serial murder. He acknowledged that they were repetitive and there seemed to be a number of similarities between the two crimes. He agreed with the author that there was a power component to each and that further study was needed to determine if motivational factors were similar in these crimes.

It is certainly true that the crime of rape can be found in the criminal histories of numerous serial murderers. In some cases the rapes are found to have been committed months and sometimes years before the act of murder is committed. In other cases, the killer may vary his crimes, raping some of his victims and killing others. . . .

Biological Predisposition

There is a developing body of literature which suggests that certain biological characteristics may cause a person to commit violent acts or may contribute to violent actions. These characteristics may be certain abnormalities in the brain caused from trauma, brain damage, or genetic traits from birth. For example, Adrian Raine, professor of psychology at the University of Southern California, Los Angeles, recently completed a series of psychological studies of Danish men, schoolboys in York, England, and murderers on California's Death Row which all point specifically to mild brain dysfunction in early life as playing a crucial role in determining whether a young boy turns into a violent man. Raine's research results strongly imply that birth complications can lead to mild brain damage that may go unnoticed throughout childhood, yet predispose a boy to violent behavior in adulthood. Raine suggests that these studies in the three cities show that birth complications could have produced the prefrontal dysfunction, which then goes on to lead to low levels of arousal, which result in a tendency to commit violent crime. Raine states: "We suspect that under-aroused people seek out arousal to increase their levels back to normal. One way to do this as a kid is to join a gang, burgle a house or beat somebody up."

Jonathon Pincus, a noted neurologist, believes that it is a combination of factors, including brain damage and psychiatric impairment, that produces illogical thinking and paranoia in the serial killer. The other factor which he believes is always present in these killers is physical and/or sexual abuse. Brain damage alone will not cause violence in a person but when brain damage, abuse, and psychiatric impairment are all present, "those factors interact, and produce a very violent person."

The serial murderers that Pincus has seen have been a bit less obviously neurologically impaired than those who aren't serial murderers and less psychiatrically impaired than those who aren't able to function in society at all. All had been abused sexually and physically. Pincus suggests that "a number of them [serial murderers] have had episodic disorders of mood that have made them unable to control their impulses at a particular time." The fact that serial murderers have a mood disorder may explain, according to Pincus, why these murderers don't kill all the time and kill only when their mood swings dictate such behavior.

A Dissenting Opinion

Richard Restak, neurologist and neuropsychiatrist, disagrees with Pincus. He argues that serial murderers have not been found to have episodic dyscontrol—that these killers are often stalkers who follow their victims. Restak argues that society has difficulty understanding and putting a person like a serial killer into a framework. Restak says,

"Circular arguments start from the idea anybody will have to be crazy in order to do this, and this person did it, and therefore they must be disturbed. . . . It's easy to say they must be insane or they must be suffering from some mental disorder. But it's also a way of eliminating, or I should say refusing to look at the outer limits of human freedom, and even human, evil if you will."

Restak thinks that to a lesser extent, psychiatry and neurology are being drawn in again and asked to explain behavior in a court of law that the public have difficulty understanding. Rather than explaining behavior from a Freudian perspective, which juries, judges, and the public spurned and rejected, the idea of brain damage is being proposed and discussed. Restak argues that "behavior doesn't necessarily imply brain damage at all."

Restak sums up the current state of psychiatric and neurological knowledge of the serial killer by stating:

> I think we're at the beginning, we're going to study different brain functions with pet scans, and new computer-assisted electro-cephalograms, and things like that, but I don't think we're going to turn up some type of magic bullet, or magic key that's going to explain this. . . . We've learned more about the brain in the last ten years than we did in the previous two hundred. So you could say that about any particular behavior that you want to look at, serial killers as well as anything else . . . but I don't think we are going to predict or prevent, because not every person that fits a certain profile goes on to become a serial killer. The current state about knowledge of the brain of serial killers is at a very elemental level.

Richard Kraus, a rural psychiatrist from New York, has taken a somewhat different approach to studying the biology of the serial killer. Kraus studied Arthur Shawcross, a serial killer who was convicted of killing 11 women in the Rochester, New York, area between 1988 and 1989. Kraus's examination of Shawcross revealed some unusual results. Kraus states:

> In this case, there was no predisposing family history of alcoholism, violence, criminality, or psychiatric disorder and no evidence of parental abuse, neglect, abandonment, or cruelty. However, at age seven years, this "bright, well-dressed, neat" child (as he was then described) was beginning to exhibit solitary aggressive conduct disordered behaviors which set him apart from his family, alienated him from his peers, and probably contributed to his becoming a loner. In the years that followed, his life style became that of repeated aggressive and antisocial behaviors, with convictions for burglary, arson, manslaughter, and finally, the serial homicides of 11 women.

A Series of Head Injuries

In examining Shawcross's medical history, Kraus found a number of serious accidents. When he was 9, Shawcross suffered leg paralysis and was hospitalized for one week. At age 16 he suffered a skull fracture and cerebral concussion. When he was 20 he was accidentally struck in the head with a sledgehammer and was involved in an auto accident the same year. In each of these instances he suffered a cerebral concussion. The following year he fell from a ladder. While in prison his record shows numerous complaints of passing out, headaches, and similar problems. Shawcross received a 10% medical disability for numbness in his left hand related to a military injury when he was in Vietnam.

Shawcross stated that his homicides were due to an "uncontrollable rage . . . it wasn't everyone, just certain ones [who] were more aggressive . . . the first one, she bit me . . . some tried to rob me . . . some belittled me . . . some didn't care . . . one threatened to tell my wife" (about his infidelities).

Kraus found that Shawcross was not too impaired to understand the nature and consequences of his acts and to know that what he did was wrong. But Shawcross did have a "hair-trigger" temper and would lose control when provoked or under stress.

A battery of psychological tests on Shawcross revealed a primary diagnosis of antisocial personality disorder. Laboratory examinations revealed that Shawcross had a 47, XYY karyotype chromosome. Kraus found a great deal of controversy in the research literature on this XYY chromosome condition and whether or not it was suggestive of abnormality in some men. Further lab tests also revealed that he had 10 times the normal level of krytopyrroles, which according to Kraus's research "correlated with marked irritability, rages, terrible problems with stress control, diminished ability to control stress, inability to control anger once provoked, mood swings, poor memory, a preference for night time, violence and antisocial behavior."

In summary, Kraus found that

> these clinical findings revealed a matrix . . . of genetic, biochemical, neurological, and psychiatric impairments, which at least partially explain the "actual inner workings" of this serial killer. . . . Such matrix of findings in one individual can reasonably be expected to result in behavioral disturbance. While biological influences do not control behavior or predetermine outcomes, this case demonstrates that criminal tendencies do have biological origins.

The Anthropological Viewpoint

C. Wilson and P. Putnam state: "If man is deprived of meanings beyond his everyday routine, he becomes disgusted and bitter, and eventually violent. A society that provides no outlet for man's idealist passions is asking to be torn apart by violence." C. Wilson and D. Seaman carry this line of thinking one step farther by attempting to examine the thoughts of those who commit murder. While the argument for unmotivated resentment as a prerequisite for such violence is extended and developed further, the authors also attach an explanation for what they label as "motiveless viciousness." According to Wilson and Seaman, "Such violence, as frequently committed by the serial killer, is the result of [Jean Paul] Sartre's magical thinking, that is, thinking that cannot possibly accomplish its objective." However, such an etiological argument seems specious given the fact that such thinking is apparently nothing more than a lack of self control and an unwillingness to delay gratification. Explanations of this nature are indeed almost trite and frequently found in much of the more mainstream true-crime literature.

E. Leyton argues that multiple murders are a "kind of sub-political and conservative protest which nets the killer a substantial social profit of revenge, celebrity, identity and sexual relief" and "and is viewed by them as a mission or crusade." For Leyton, these killings are "a kind of rebellion against the social order"; "a protest against their [the killers] perceived exclusion from society."

Leyton concludes by rejecting arguments of sexual excitement or of conquest over the victim. He argues that motivation is, rather, a solution of those problems resulting from denied ambition. Multiple murderers act "to relieve a burning grudge engendered by their failed ambition."

Leyton expands on a frequently cited explanation for homicide. Leyton, an anthropologist, identifies relative deprivation, which he also extends to absolute deprivation, as the provocation for the multiple murderer's frustration. From a cultural perspective, the multiple murderer (Leyton includes both mass and serial murderers) is then "a profoundly conservative figure who comes to feel excluded from the class he so devoutly wishes to join. In an extended campaign of vengeance, he murders people unknown to him, but who represent to him (in their behavior, their appearance, or their location) the class that has rejected him."

The Problems with Explanations

There are indeed a number of different theories that claim to explain the behavior of the serial killer. In *Serial Killers,* J. Norris presents a list of behavior patterns which he offers as the epistemology of the "serial killer syndrome." These 22 patterns are symptoms of episodic aggressive behavior, which for Norris provides a profile of predisposition. Norris contends that these patterns or profiles are the "combined symptomatology of hundreds of serial killers." It would seem that the reader must accept such a statement as fact based on Norris's assertion of having interviewed "more that a dozen serial killers." and that the remaining data for such a synthesized symptomatology stem from interviews of secondary data sources. Such acceptance is indeed difficult, given the total lack of empirical documentation, footnote, or references in Norris's work.

Few, if any, of the theories of serial murder described above have been tested empirically against a large number of serial killers. Frequently, psychologists and other researchers who have interviewed serial killers have approached their interviews with a structured format or protocol intended to verify an already developed theory of the behavior. Frequently, when those interviewed have produced information inconsistent with already established theories, the information obtained is not considered important or relevant.

We are locked into a single-factor approach or the belief that there is a common profile for the serial killer and that each serial killer has certain common characteristics. The mass media tend to drive this approach by constantly asking for a "profile" of the serial killer. It is quite possible that by failing to consider those characteristics of the serial killers that do not distinguish these killers from other non-killers, we are missing an important and critical ingredient in the behavior of serial murder. If these nondistinguishing characteristics of serial killers are present in concert or combination with other factors, this combination may be what drives the desire of these killers to kill and kill again. More research is undoubtedly necessary.

PATTERNS OF CHILDHOOD NEGLECT

Robert K. Ressler and Tom Shachtman

The following selection is taken from the book *Whoever Fights Monsters*, by retired FBI agent Robert K. Ressler and writer Tom Shachtman. The authors describe the results of a study performed by Ressler and his FBI colleagues in which they interviewed thirty-six murderers, most of whom were serial killers, and found similar patterns of severe childhood neglect. Ressler and Shachtman trace the development of these patterns from birth through adolescence, citing examples from the interviews. They explain that most of the killers had poor relationships with their mothers and consequently never learned appropriate ways to relate to other human beings. For instance, the authors write that the mother of "vampire killer" Richard Chase was schizophrenic, while serial murderer Ed Kemper was banished to the basement by his mother when he was only ten years old. Although Ressler and Shachtman acknowledge that many individuals who suffer from neglect in childhood do not become killers, they maintain that without intervention at crucial points in childhood development, abused and neglected children are at high risk for growing up to become violent murderers.

"Where do we come from? Who are we? Where are we going?" These three great questions were the real subject of the prison interviews of murderers I had started on my own in the late 1970s. I wanted to know what made these people tick, to understand better the mind of the murderer. Shortly, my curiosity became systematized and the interviews brought under the umbrella of the FBI; they became the core of the Criminal Personality Research Project, partially funded by the Justice Department, and involving Dr. Ann Burgess of Boston University, and other academics, with myself as principal investigator. Using a research protocol of some fifty-seven pages, we interviewed thirty-six individual incarcerated murderers, concentrating on their histories, their motives and fantasies, their specific actions. Eventually, we were able to discern important patterns in their lives and learn something about their developing motivation to murder. . . .

Before going into the details of who these murderers are and how they became murderers, let me state unequivocally that there is no such thing as the person who at age thirty-five suddenly changes from being perfectly normal and erupts into totally evil, disruptive, murderous behavior. The behaviors that are precursors to murder have been present and developing in that person's life for a long, long time—since childhood.

A Family History

A common myth is that murderers come from broken, impoverished homes. Our sample showed that this wasn't really true. Many of the murderers started life in a family that was not desperately poor, where family income was stable. More than half lived initially in a family that appeared to be intact, where the mother and father lived together with their son. These were, on the whole, intelligent children. Though seven of the thirty-six had IQ scores below 90, most were in the normal range, and eleven had scores in the superior range, above 120.

Nonetheless, though the homes seemed to outward appearances to be normal, they were in fact dysfunctional. Half of our subjects had mental illness in their immediate family. Half had parents who had been involved in criminal activities. Nearly 70 percent had a familial history of alcohol or drug abuse. All the murderers—every single one—were subjected to serious *emotional* abuse during their childhoods. And all of them developed into what psychiatrists label as sexually dysfunctional adults, unable to sustain a mature, consensual relationship with another adult.

From birth to age six or seven, studies have shown, the most important adult figure in a child's life is the mother, and it is in this time period that the child learns what love is. Relationships between our subjects and their mothers were uniformly cool, distant, unloving, neglectful. There was very little touching, emotional warmth, or training in the ways in which normal human beings cherish one another and demonstrate their affection and interdependence. These children were deprived of something more important than money—love. They ended up paying for that deprivation during the remainder of their lives, and society suffered, too, because their crimes removed many people from the world and their assaultive behavior left alive equally as many victims who remain permanently scarred.

The abuse that the children endured was both physical and mental. Society has understood somewhat that physical abuse is a precursor to violence, but the emotional component may be as important. One woman propped her infant son in a cardboard box in front of the television set, and left for work; later, she'd put him in a playpen, toss in some food, and let the TV set be the baby-sitter until she came home again. A second man reported to us that he had been confined to his room during his childhood evenings; when he wandered into the living room at such times, he was shooed away and told that evening was the time when his mother and father wanted to be alone together; he grew up believing he was an unwanted boarder in his own home.

Inadequate Parenting

These children grew up in an environment in which their own actions were ignored, and in which there were no limits set on their behavior. It is part of the task of parenting to teach children what is right and wrong; these were the children who managed to grow up without being taught that poking something into a puppy's eye is harmful and should not be done, or that destroying property is against the rules. The task of the first half-dozen years of life is socialization, of teaching children to understand that they live in a world that encompasses other people as well as themselves, and that proper interaction with other people is essential. The children who grow up to murder never truly comprehend the world in other than egocentric terms, because their teachers—principally their mothers—do not train them properly in this important matter.

Richard Chase, the "vampire killer," killed a half-dozen people before he was apprehended in 1978. According to psychiatric interviews conducted in conjunction with Chase's sentencing, Chase's mother was a schizophrenic, emotionally unable to concentrate on the task of socializing her son or to care for him in a loving way. The mothers of nine more subjects of the study also had major psychiatric problems. Even those mothers whose problems did not reach the level where they came to the attention of a mental-health professional could be considered dysfunctional in other ways; for instance, many were alcoholic. Neglect has many faces. Ted Bundy summed it up when he reminded an interviewer that he had not come from a "Leave It to Beaver" home. He had been brought up by a woman who he thought was his sister but was actually his mother, and although there was no neglect or abuse pinpointed in that relationship, there were strong indications that Bundy was physically and sexually abused by other members of his family.

Sometimes the mother, even when nurturing, cannot balance out or offset the destructive behavior of the father. One murderer came from a family in which the father was in the Navy, was often away on assignments, and was present only occasionally; the children went into a panic when he did come home, because he would then beat up his wife and the children, and sexually abuse the son, who later became a murderer. Over 40 percent of the murderers reported being physically beaten and abused in their childhoods. More than 70 percent said they had witnessed or been part of sexually stressful events when young—a percentage many times greater than that usually found in the general population. "I slept with my mother as a young child," said one; "I was abused by my father from age fourteen," said another; "My stepmother tried to rape me," reported a third; "I got picked up downtown one night by some guy when I was around seven or eight," said a fourth man.

The quality of a child's attachments to others in the family is considered the most important factor in how he or she eventually relates to and values nonfamily members of society. Relationships with siblings and other family members, which might make up for a parent's coolness in these situations, were similarly deficient in the murderers' families. These children, nurtured on inadequate relationships in their earliest years, had no one to whom they could easily turn, were unable to form attachments to those closest to them, and grew up increasingly lonely and isolated.

Missing Fathers

It is true that most children who come from dysfunctional early childhoods don't go on to murder or to commit other violent antisocial acts. As far as we could see, the reason for this is that the majority are rescued by strong hands in the next phase of childhood, that of preadolescence—but our subjects were definitely not saved from drowning; they were pushed further under in this phase of their lives. From the ages of eight to twelve, all the negative tendencies present in their early childhoods were exacerbated and reinforced. In this period, a male child really needs a father, and it was in just this time period that the fathers of half the subjects disappeared in one way or another. Some fathers died, some were incarcerated, most just left through divorce or abandonment; other fathers, while physically present, drifted away emotionally. John Gacy killed thirty-three young men and buried them beneath his home before he was caught in 1978. In Gacy's youth, his father used to come home, go down into the basement, sit in a stuffed chair, and drink; when anyone approached, the father would chase them away; later, drunk, he'd come up for dinner and pick fights and beat his wife and children.

John Joubert killed three boys before he was caught in 1985. John's mother and father divorced when he was a preadolescent, and when John wanted to see his father, his natural mother refused to take him to the father's residence or provide money for his trip. That's abuse, too, in a manner psychologists call passive-aggressive. Now, divorce in the United States is a very common occurrence, and hundreds of thousands of children grow up in single-parent homes. Only a handful of them go on to commit murder. I'm not impugning single-parent homes; rather, I am recognizing the fact that the preponderance of murderers in our study came from dysfunctional settings, many of which were rendered dysfunctional by divorce. . . .

Potential murderers became solidified in their loneliness first during the age period of eight to twelve; such isolation is considered the
single most important aspect of their psychological makeup. Many
factors go into fashioning this isolation. Among the most important
is the absence of a father. When there's no father or father figure present for an eight- or ten- or twelve-year-old boy, this is embarrassing
for the child in front of his peers. He begins to avoid friends, to avoid
situations in which father-and-son teams are usually present, such as
Little League or the Boy Scouts. His preadolescent sexual activity,
rather than being connected to other human beings, starts as autoerotic. More than three-quarters of the murderers we investigated
began autoerotic sexual practices as preadolescents; half reported rape
fantasies occurring between the ages of twelve and fourteen; more
than 80 percent admitted to using pornography, and to tendencies
toward fetishism and voyeurism. Again, we must realize that many
boys grow up in homes without a father and do not turn into
sociopaths; but for the ones who do become sociopaths, the eight-to-
twelve period is critical. Investigation often leads back to just this
time, and the set of circumstances in which the father figure is absent,
as the period when bizarre behavior began.

When Ed Kemper [who confessed in 1973 to killing his mother and
six other women] was ten, after his parents' divorce, he returned
home one day to find that his mother and older sisters had taken his
belongings from his second-floor room and moved them into the
basement. His mother, Clarnell Strandberg, was greatly respected at
the university, where she worked as an administrator, for her concern
for the students; at home, she was a terror, continually belittling Kemper, telling him he was responsible for all the shortcomings in her life.
She told him that she had banished him to the basement because he
was so large that he was making his adolescent sisters uncomfortable.
Shortly afterward, Kemper, a big hulk brooding alone in a windowless
room, began to have murderous fantasies.

Dysfunctional Sexual Development

As the psychologically damaged boys get closer to adolescence, they
find that they are unable to develop the social skills that are precursors to sexual skills and that are the coin of positive emotional relationships. Loneliness and isolation do not always mean that the
potential killers are introverted and shy; some are but others are gregarious with other men, and good talkers. The outward orientation of
the latter masks their inner isolation. By the time a normal youngster
is dancing, going to parties, participating in kissing games, the loner
is turning in on himself and developing fantasies that are deviant.
The fantasies are substitutes for more positive human encounters, and
as the adolescent becomes more dependent on them, he loses touch
with acceptable social values.

Jerome Brudos, at twelve and thirteen, began to abduct girls his own age or younger at knife point and take them into the barn on the family farm. There, he would tell them to disrobe, and then he would photograph them but do nothing else, since he was not sexually aware enough to go further. Then he'd lock them in a corncrib and go away. Minutes later, he would reappear in the barn with his clothes changed and his hair combed differently, unlock the corncrib, and announce to the girl that he was Ed, Jerry's twin brother. He would profess horror that Jerry had locked her in there, and say, "He didn't hurt you, did he?" The girl would explain that Jerry had taken pictures, and "Ed" would locate the camera and destroy the film in it, then say, "Jerry's been in therapy; we have him in psychological counseling. This is going to set him back a lot. Please don't tell my parents or anyone about this." The girl would acquiesce. Later in life, between 1968 and 1969, Brudos put advertisements in campus newspapers asking for women to come and model shoes and hose for him. When they arrived for appointments in his motel room, he would abduct and murder some of them, then hang them in his garage and photograph them, either nude or in various outfits (and especially shoes) that he had put on the dead bodies.

The key to these murderers, if there is one, lies in the unremittingly sexual nature of their deeds. To a man, they were dysfunctional sexually; that is, they were unable to have and maintain mature, consensual sexual experiences with other adults, and they translated that inability into sexual murders. Not everyone who is unable to participate in kissing games becomes a sexually dysfunctional adult. It's also important to recognize that having a good adult sexual relationship does not imply only heterosexual activity. There is such a thing as a successful homosexual relationship that is normal when looked at from the standpoint of encompassing two people who care for each other. Those killers in our sample who were homosexual were also dysfunctional in this regard, unable to maintain long-term relationships, showing a decided preference for bondage, torture, and sadomasochism in their short-term partnerships. Nearly half the murderers reported to us that they had never had a consenting sexual experience with another adult. As important, all the murderers knew they had not had normal relationships, and they resented not having them; it was this resentment that fueled their aggressive, murderous behavior. Richard Lawrence Marquette picked up a woman in a bar; they had known one another slightly during their childhoods. At his residence, according to his later confession, he was unable to perform sexually; the woman ridiculed this inability, so he killed her and chopped her up in small pieces. Incarcerated for thirteen years for this murder, and then released, Marquette picked up two more women in similar circumstances, tried and failed to have sex with them, and killed them, too, before being apprehended and returned to prison.

Pursuing Negative Outlets

Adolescence in these troubled youngsters was dominated by increasing isolation and "acting out" behavior, with lots of daydreaming, compulsive masturbation, lying, bed-wetting, and nightmares as concomitants of the isolation. There was more opportunity at this stage for antisocial behavior. Instead of being in the house or yard all the time, the youngster was now in school, on the streets, away from the home. Cruelty to animals and to other children, running away, truancy, assaults on teachers, setting fires, destroying the property of others and their own property—these overt acts began in adolescence, though the mind-set that generated them was present earlier but had been below the surface because the child had been controlled in his home environment.

Many of the murderers were intelligent, but they did not do well in school. "I failed the second grade because I was uneducable," one murderer told us. His parents wanted to take him out of school to work on their farm, "but then I skipped the third grade because I passed the second grade and went on and excelled in many areas and dropped out in others. I excelled in math but couldn't spell." Their spotty record in school was a pattern that carried over later in life. Most were incapable of holding jobs or living up to their intellectual potential. They were not successful employees, and were fired often, involved in disputes at the workplace, and had continual problems with authority. They had the intellect necessary for skilled jobs, but most of them were employed in menial capacities. When they went into the military, as about 40 percent did, most of them received less than honorable discharges.

Just as there had been very little love in the family environment, there was also a lack of stimulation or encouragement to achieve within the family (and the school). Their energy became directed to negative outlets. In school, they were either chronically disruptive or subdued and withdrawn to the extent that no one paid them any attention.

"I felt guilty of having those thoughts [toward family]," Monte Rissell [who killed five women before he was nineteen] told me—after years of listening to psychologists and picking up their jargon—"and submerged them and built up lots of hostility, and then it gets off into fantasy. . . . They should have noticed it at school, so excessive was my daydreaming that it was always in my report cards. . . . I was dreaming about wiping out the whole school."

Schools Add to Neglect

School systems as well as families fail these children. Too often, confronted with a problem child, a school system does not get him to counseling, or, if counseling is done, it does not address the significant issues in his life, especially including those pertaining to the dysfunctional home. If a teacher says, "You ought to look at Joe, he has problems," the school system is unable to properly examine Joe's life, unable to get at the root of those problems in the home, unable to move other bureaucracies, such as the social services system, to the point where these could interrupt the downward spiral to salvage the child. Moreover, since the damage to the child is emotional, it is not easy to reach. These above-average-intelligence children find ways to disguise and conceal their mental wounds until they are covered over with thick scar tissue.

Many people survive enormous difficulties in childhood and don't grow up to murder. However, when the problems of childhood are reinforced by added neglect in the school, the social services system, and the neighborhood, they steadily worsen. In a situation where you find a distant mother, an absent or abusive father and siblings, a non-intervening school system, an ineffective social services system, and an inability of the person to relate sexually in a normal way to others, you have almost a formula for producing a deviant personality.

THE DARK SIDE OF THE SERIAL-KILLER PERSONALITY

Al C. Carlisle

Al C. Carlisle is a retired psychologist who worked with inmates at Utah State Prison, including serial killers Ted Bundy and Arthur Bishop. In the following article, Carlisle explores the theory that serial killers have a divided personality: a good side that often maintains the public appearance of an upstanding citizen, and a dark side that is ultimately compelled to act out the killer's murderous fantasies. In order to escape from painful memories and experiences, he explains, these people often resort to fantasy, and their personalities become divided between their fantasy self and the face they show to the real world. Not only do their dark fantasies become sexually violent, but they turn to their fantasies with increasing frequency, Carlisle writes. When a situation similar to the fantasy arises in real life, he argues, the person may automatically act out his fantasy without consciously deciding to kill. Carlisle suggests that although the killer may experience some remorse, the excitement and satisfaction experienced by his dark side compel him to murder again and again.

"I knew myself, at the first breath of this new life, to be more wicked, sold a slave to my original evil; and the thought, in that moment, braced and delighted me like wine."

—Robert Louis Stevenson,
The Strange Case of Dr. Jekyll and Mr. Hyde

The Jekyll and Hyde story is a fictional account of a person who, through chemical experiment, becomes transformed into two separate entities, each with his own set of realities, and each having diametrically opposite intentions. Even though it is fiction, this story is often used as a simile to describe opposing personality states of an offender whose violent acts appear incongruent with the image others have of them. Ted Bundy, Christopher Wilder, and John Wayne Gacy,

Excerpted from Al C. Carlisle, "The Divided Self: Toward an Understanding of the Dark Side of the Serial Killer," *American Journal of Criminal Justice*, vol. 17, no. 2 (1993). Reprinted by permission of the *American Journal of Criminal Justice*. (References in the original have been omitted in this reprint.)

for example, were each perceived as upstanding citizens, yet each was a vicious killer. Each was intelligent, energetic, and actively involved in the community. Bundy graduated from college and later went to law school. He worked on a crisis line in an attempt to help others, and was a field worker in political campaigns. He obtained adequate grades in his law classes even though he was simultaneously killing victims. He is believed to have killed over 30 victims.

Wilder was a wealthy co-owner of a construction business, owned Florida real estate worth about a half million dollars, always had plenty of girlfriends and was liked by those who lived around him. He killed eight victims, torturing many of them. Gacy had a successful business, would dress up like a clown to cheer up sick kids in hospitals, and was Jaycee "Man of the Year." When the snow became deep he would hook up a snowplow and clean out the driveways of the homes on his block. Each year he sponsored a celebration for about 400 people in Chicago at his own expense. He killed more than 30 victims. Each of these was admired by many, yet each was a serial killer whose dark side was demonstrated by the vicious manner in which a victim's life was taken.

Were they originally good people who went astray or were they born evil and had the ability to hide their sadistic homicidal tendencies from those around them? The evidence accumulated on each would suggest the first postulation to be the accurate one. The pathological process that leads to the development of an obsessive appetite (and possibly an addiction) to kill is still one of the most perplexing psychological mysteries yet to be solved.

Is the Serial Killer Mentally Ill?

While it is tempting to explain the behavior of these killers by labeling them psychotic, or insane, psychiatric data usually contradicts such a conclusion. Each of these three, for example, was able to carry out a fairly high level of daily functioning while committing crime. each made logical, and often creative, decisions in his work. Those closest to each of them generally did not see indications of mental illness, nor of violent tendencies, and were surprised when the person was arrested for murder. While most serial killers are not insane in the legal sense (that is, they knew the difference between right and wrong at the time of the crime), it is commonly accepted that there is some deviant or pathological process occurring within them which is directly related to the commission of multiple homicides.

A second frequently used explanation in the attempt to understand the serial killer is to label him a psychopath, a term which refers to a person who has a clear perception of reality, but one who seems to lack feelings of guilt, and commits criminal acts for his own immediate gratification, having little regard for the pain and suffering caused by his acts. In other words, a person who has no conscience. While this term may describe the killer's behavior, it still doesn't explain the psychological processes that go on within the person that cause him to "kill for pleasure." No more does it answer the question of whether this lack of conscience resulted in the killing, or if psychological pain caused violent tendencies which in turn resulted in suppressing moral prompting. There are many indications that some serial killers experience strong remorse when they kill, at least in the beginning, which shows some capacity to experience guilt. Yet, in spite of the regret for their act, they go on to kill again. Clearly, there have to be some ingredients in the process of the development of the serial killer which have excepted our focus. It is not acceptable any longer to use the terms "monster" or "psychopathic killer" as explanatory mechanisms. An increased understanding of the psychological processes that take place within the offender prior to, during, and following the criminal act may help in recognizing and alleviating the problem earlier in the person's life.

While there are many explanatory possibilities, one area which has been minimally explored utilizes the concepts of fantasy, dissociation and compartmentalization which result in what many offenders refer to as a dark, sinister, twisted self that hungers for sordid and depraved experiences which would have created deep feelings of revulsion earlier in the killer's life. The purpose of this article is to suggest how this sinister dark side of the person is sparked into existence and develops through common psychological processes. The utility of understanding the process for the mental health profession is in recognizing and redirecting this process in youth. For law enforcement, the utility is towards the development of investigation and interviewing techniques which can enhance the detection and conviction process.

Dissociation and the Separate Self

The concept of an altered self, or altered identity, has its scientific root in the findings of such persons as Sigmund Freud, Carl Jung, Pierre Janet and Josep Breuer. Freud postulated the subconscious mind, a "hidden" level of consciousness generally not accessible to the conscious processes. He demonstrated fairly conclusively that traumatic memories and emotions from a person's past could be housed in the subconscious which could later have a strong effect on the emotional life and behaviors of that person. Breuer and Freud found a connection between behavioral symptoms and subconscious memories which they referred to as a "splitting of consciousness" or dual consciousness processes. . . .

The process of dissociation is a normal psychological process which provides the opportunity for a person to avoid, to one degree or another, the presence of memories and feelings which are too painful to tolerate. Dissociation is a continuum of experiences ranging from the process of blocking out events going on around us (such as when watching a movie) to Multiple Personality Disorder (MPD) where personalities are separate compartmentalized entities. . . . The concepts of the entity, dark side and shadow referred to by various homicide offenders are somewhere between the two extremes. These are sub-MPD level states of consciousness which have been created by the person in an attempt to better adapt to his world.

The Role of Fantasy

While in the usual case of dissociation traumatic memories are buried, allowing the person to avoid experiencing the pain, on the opposite side of the coin is the process of creating fantasy imagery, or illusions, for the purpose of avoiding pain and generating excitement. Walter Young found that a traumatized child who became MPD would incorporate fantasy imagery into a personality identity. In the same manner, a child who experiences excessive emptiness and engages in extensive daydreaming may reach the point where the identity or entity generated through the fantasy becomes a compartmentalized and controlling factor in the person's life.

A fantasy is an imagery process in which a person attempts to obtain vicarious gratification by engaging in acts in his mind which he currently isn't able to do (or doesn't dare to do) in reality. Fantasy is a mechanism by which a temperament, such as anger, begins to take a form with a specified purpose and direction. Ongoing and intense fantasy is also a mechanism by which hate and bitterness can begin to become dissociated and compartmentalized from the more ethically focused aspects of the mind. Intensely painful memories and deep emptiness can lead to intensely experienced fantasies, which over time take on a greater and greater degree of reality. When a person is totally absorbed in a fantasy, he dissociates everything around him. Anger and emptiness become the energy and motivating forces behind the fantasy. While in the fantasy the person experiences a sense of excitement and relief. However, when it is over there is still a feeling of emptiness because the fantasy has whetted an appetite for the real thing, which he anticipates will be even more enjoyable than the fantasy. Thus, through fantasy, the person creates a make-believe world wherein he can accomplish what he can't do in reality. Over time, the person may turn to this pseudo-existence with increasing rapidity when he feels stress, depression or emptiness. This leads to a dual identity, one being that associated with reality and the people he associates with every day and the other the secret identity which is able to manifest the power and control he would like over others. If the person is angry and bitter, this alter identity is usually an animal of destruction. The major problem is that heavy fantasy is inexorably linked to the process of dissociation and compartmentalized. As the person shifts back and forth between the two identities in his attempt to meet his various needs, they both become an equal part of him, the opposing force being suppressed when he is attempting to have his needs met through the one. Over time, the dark side (representing the identity or entity the person has created to satisfy his deepest hunger) becomes stronger than the "good" side, and the person begins to experience being possessed, or controlled by this dark side of him. This is partly because the dark side is the part anticipated to meet the person's strongest needs, and partly because the good side is the part which experiences the guilt over the "evil" thoughts, and therefore out of necessity is routinely suppressed. Thus, the monster is created. Bill (a pseudonym), a person who became a multiple homicide offender, describes the need he had for fantasy as a child:

> Without that (hero fantasies) I would have had to live with myself. What would have been the alternative? I go out into the garage and I'm in there reading a book or reading one *Reader's Digest* article after another. If I'm not doing that I'm back inside the house where I'm a nobody. If I'm not doing that, I'm out there on the school yard playing ball, maybe, but still a nobody (personal correspondence).

The Development of Opposing Forces
Bill would become absorbed in the fantasies to the point that he had a difficult time living his day-to-day life with them:

> I think that anybody who would look upon me, at least for the first hour after reading the book, would think I was preoccupied. . . . With most people when they put the book down they are back to the real world . . . whereas in my case, these would provide scenarios that I would yearn for, and wish could happen. I was in there (the story). I could almost smell the smells, see the sights. I was gone. I was in another world (Ibid).

Over the years, Bill relied on his fantasy life for his major satisfaction, always still yearning for the fulfilling social life which would replace the fantasies. However, when it didn't come bitterness and revenge fantasies replaced the hero fantasies. Still wanting to be a socially respected person, he attempted to suppress his violent urges while concomitantly relying on his increasingly more violent fantasies to gratify his urges for retribution. This created a serious motivational imbalance in his mental system which resulted in a compartmentalization of the opposing motivational forces (the desire to be a respectable citizen and the opposing desire to get revenge) so that he could have some sense of balance in his life. Ted Bundy described an attempt to keep the two opposing forces separate:

> As we've witnessed the development of this darker side of this person's life, we'd expect to see how very closely controlled

and separated this part of him became, and how he was able to keep it, ah, more or less, from those around him who thought he was normal. And because this separation was so distinct and well maintained, we would find it unlikely [that] the roles could get confused (Michaud and Aynesworth, 1989, p. 195).

However, the roles do begin to get confused which results in an even greater attempt to keep these identities or forces separate in order to maintain the appearance of normalcy. The process of suppression results in the development of the sinister or dark side of the personality.

The Creation of the Shadow

The vicarious enjoyment of fantasy is enhanced through a self-sustained hypnotic trance, and creates an appetite which gets out of control. Ted Bundy, in telling S. Michaud and H. Aynesworth (1989) how a psychopath killer is created, stated:

> there is some kind of weakness that gives rise to this individual's interest in the kind of sexual activity involving violence that would gradually begin to absorb some of his fantasy . . . eventually the interest would become so demanding toward new material that it would only be catered to by what he could find in the dirty book stores . . . (p. 68).

As this process continues, it begins to dominate his life. Bundy continues:

> By peeping in windows, as it were, and watching a woman undress, or watching whatever could be seen, you know, during the evening, and approaching it almost like a project, throwing himself into it, uh, literally for years. . . . He gained, you'd say, a terrific amount of . . . at times . . . a great amount of gratification from it and he became increasingly adept at it as anyone becomes adept at anything they do over and over again . . . and as the condition develops and its purposes or characteristics become more well defined, it begins to demand more of the attention and time of the individual . . . there is a certain amount of tension, uh, struggle between the normal personality and this, this, uh, psychopathological, uh, entity (Ibid. p. 70).

Bob (pseudonym), a homicide offender, described his experience of the development of this entity, dark side, or shadow within him prior to his homicide:

> The beast can take over to complete an identity if you leave a hole in yourself. In other words, it seeks a vacuum. In a healthy person the vacuum doesn't exist. There's a sense of identity that prevents a need for the dark awareness.

It was very much like a battlefield in my head, wrestling with what I as a human being felt to be reasonable alternatives. It was a battle between two very different parts of myself—goodness and evil. When you feel evil, there is a sense of power. It can consume you. There is not much intellect involved with making an evil decision. It is a more gripping thing, more animalistic. It's so much simpler and so much easier to give into it than to hang on to a moral structure that you don't understand, or an ethic or value or commitment, all the things that make us human beings (personal correspondence).

The offender may attempt to curtail the problem which is developing:

I just kept trying to shake it off and physically I would shake my head to rid myself of the thoughts. I wondered where it could come from, or without my pulse going, how I could consider such an ugly sequence of events (Ibid).

When this doesn't work, he attempts to indulge the fantasy rather than fight it to see if that would work. He continued:

Let's give in to the thoughts. Let's not try to resist it. Let's grovel in it for maybe 20 minutes. Maybe that will dissipate it. Maybe it will blow off some steam. Let's have a fantasy, OK? What happened was, I became preoccupied with the fantasy. It did not resolve itself (Ibid).

This process begins to get more and more out of the person's control, as evidenced by the Boston Strangler:

I could not stop what I was doing. This thing building up in me—all the time—I knew I was getting out of control (Frank, 1966, p. 326).

The Fantasy Becomes a Reality

Ultimately, when a person has visualized killing over and over again, a time may come when an actual event, similar to what he has been fantasizing about, presents itself. At such time, under the right circumstances, the offender finds himself automatically carrying out an act he has practiced so many, many times in his mind. Finally, inevitably, this force, this entity, makes a breakthrough. Bundy commented:

The urge to do something to that person (a woman he saw) seized him—in a way he'd never been affected before. And it seized him strongly. And to the point where, uh, without giving a great deal of thought, he searched for some instrumentality to, uh, uh, attack this woman . . . there was really no control at this point . . . (Ibid. pp. 72–73).

The offender may partially, or completely, dissociate the crime. Following the event, the offender's mind returns to the realm of the real world and he often experiences surprise, guilt, and dismay that such an act could have happened. Bundy adds:

> What he had done terrified him. Purely terrified him. And he was full of remorse . . . and, you know, he quickly sobered up, as it were. . . . The sobering effect of that was to . . . for some time, close up the cracks again. And not do anything. For the first time, he sat back and swore to himself that he wouldn't do something like that again . . . or even, anything that would lead to it . . . within a matter of months, slowly but surely, the impact of this event lost its, uh, deterrent value. And within months he was back, uh, uh, peeping in windows again, and slipping back into that old routine (Ibid, pp. 74–75).

By acting out the fantasy, the dark side or Shadow, now becomes a more permanent part of the person's personality structure. Bundy adds:

> Well, we, we . . . ah, described this individual and found that his behavior, which was becoming more and more frequent, was also concomitantly . . . occupying more and more of his mental and intellectual energies. So he's facing a greater, ah, more frequent challenge of this darker side of himself to his normal life (Ibid, p. 171).

Within the offender there is a revulsion of the act, but there is also a sense of excitement, satisfaction, and peace. If the feeling of peace is profound, as if a great load has been taken off the person's shoulders, he is especially likely to become a serial killer. The Shadow becomes stronger because the person has now transcended that final boundary and most inhibitions against killing are gone and overwhelmingly painful guilt is suppressed. Still, there are some feelings and beliefs against killing. The good side isn't dead. Just pushed away. Thus, there is generally a period of time before another homicide occurs.

The offender may begin tempting the fates a little by allowing himself to engage in some of his earlier pre-homicide activities, thinking this will help satisfy the need that is still growing within him, yet promising to himself he will never go as far as he did the last time. However, a time comes when the urge to again feel that power and control becomes so strong the offender gives into it. Bob describes his experience of the fantasy about the plan to commit homicide:

> My mouth would dry up, my peripheral vision would narrow, and I would be at peace. This was a plan that whatever cost would accomplish what I wanted and would create balance in my life. There is a sweetness in surrendering to any plan. To allow yourself to commit provides a platform in your life

where you're not at drift. . . . Here there is power. Here there is meaning, logic and order and stability. If I have to give in to an evil thing to do it, it is worth it (personal correspondence).

Another homicide is committed. He may again experience guilt and may again promise to himself that it will never happen further. However, his identity has now drastically changed.

The Obsession

He has become the very being he had so often visualized in his fantasies, even though the possibility of becoming such was so abhorrent to him. He has stepped over the line and cannot step back. The only way he can handle the guilt is to compartmentalize it and thus not consciously experience it. But the guilt doesn't go away. It remains hidden beneath the surface grinding on the offender, which often produces an eventual deterioration in the killer's personality.

The homicides are often not as satisfying as the first one was, and do not reach the level of satisfaction of his fantasies. The killer's search for the ultimate high becomes an obsession. Usually by this time the offender senses the entity within as being a dark side that is very evil and is controlling him, and it terrifies him. He detests it, is fearful of it, yet he basks in its power. He may continue his attempt to fight against its controlling influence, but soon he gives up his struggle against it and allows it to dominate him. His new life becomes a secret existence, often known only to him.

A drastic identity change has occurred, with the opposing identities being farther apart than ever before. Strong self-hate is engendered and in order to avoid it, the offender has to idealize the pathology. The Shadow has advanced to the level of having become the Controller and is now the dominant force in the offender's life. He can't undo what he has done nor can he face the guilt or accept the responsibility for his behavior. By doing so he would have to face what he has become.

Thus, his sickness becomes his idol and he places himself on a pedestal and worships his own image. For Bill, the two most common traits he experienced at the time of the killings were, "my 'SENSE OF BEING PERFECT' and my sense of feeling that I was 'ALMOST LIKE A GOD.'" To be divine is to be sinless. To be sinless abnegates blame, and the "evil" act become mentally transformed into a divine judgement. . . . The offender is hooked. An addiction begins to build, due partly to the attempt to chase the high, and partly in an attempt to find the gratification in reality which the person has found through fantasy.

The offender may begin to flaunt his prowess and feelings of superiority, such as did the Son of Sam. He may toy with the police. He savors the knowledge that he is skillful, he can kill people and no one can catch him. He plans, stalks, observes and executes his crimes with great skill, at times taking great chances because he feels invulnerable. Edmund Kemper, who killed his grandparents, six college-age girls, his mother, and finally his mother's friend, stated:

> It was getting easier to do. I was getting better at it. . . . I start-ed flaunting that invisibility, severing a human head, two of them, at night, in front of my mother's residence, with her at home, my neighbors at home upstairs, their picture window open, the curtain open, eleven o'clock at night, the lights are on. All they had to do was walk by, look out, and I've had it. Some people go crazy at that point. I felt it. It was one helluva tweek.

A Compulsion to Kill

The uncontrollable nature of the urge is expressed by Charles Hatch-er, a serial murderer who began his killing spree in the early 1960s, murdering 13 adults and three children. His spree finally ended when he committed himself to a mental hospital the day after he abducted and murdered an 11-year-old girl in St. Joseph, Missouri. He admitted to FBI agent Joe Holtslag:

> I kill on impulse. It's an uncontrollable urge that builds and builds over a period of weeks until I have to kill. It doesn't matter if the victims are men, women, or children. Whoever is around is in trouble (Ganey, 1989, pp. 216–217).

Bob described it this way:

> It was like obeying somebody else. I felt as though I was tak-ing orders and the Shadow was about to say, "No longer will you think of other alternatives" (personal correspondence).

Regarding the compulsion, Bill stated:

> Once the compulsion is there, it is not a matter of should I or shouldn't I. At this point it's too late. It's a psychological impossibility to stop that activity (personal correspondence).

The compulsion is a combination of the planning, the hunt, the capture, the power and control over the victim, the terror she shows and the possession of the person, often both before and after death.

The excitement combined with the need for companionship and possession is demonstrated in the Dennis Andrew Nilsen and Jeffrey Dahmer cases. Nilsen, a 37-year-old executive officer at the Jobcentre in Kentish Town, London, killed 16 young men at Cranley Gardens and 13 at his residence on Melrose Avenue. He would invite the vic-tim to his apartment for an evening of companionship and then would kill him. He stated:

It was intense and all consuming . . . I needed to do what I did at the time. I had no control over it then. It was a powder keg waiting for a match. I was the match. . . . The kill was only part of the whole. The whole experience which thrilled me intensely was the drink, the chase, the social seduction, the getting the "friend" back (meaning the essence of the "friend" would still be there), the decision to kill, the body and its disposal.

The pressure needed release. I took release through spirits and music. On that high, I had a loss of morality and danger feeling. . . . I wished I could stop but I could not. I had no other thrill or happiness (Masters, 1985, p. 241–243).

There may be dissociation during the act as indicated by Albert DeSalvo regarding looking in a mirror and seeing himself strangling a Scandinavian woman a week before he killed Anna Slesers:

I looked in a mirror in the bedroom and there was me strangling somebody! I fell on my knees and I crossed myself and I prayed, "Oh, God, what am I doing? I'm a married man. I'm the father of two children. . . . God, help me!". . . Oh, I got out there fast. It wasn't like it was me . . . it was like it was someone else I was watching (Frank, 1966, p 313).

Or, dissociation of the event may occur following the crime, as indicated in another of the Boston Strangler's crimes:

You (meaning himself) was there, these things were going on and the feeling after I got out of that apartment was as if it never happened. I got out and downstairs, and you could of said you saw me upstairs and as far as I was concerned, it wasn't me. I can't explain it to you any other way. It's just so unreal. . . . I was there, it was done, and yet if you talked to me an hour later, or half hour later, it didn't mean nothing, it just didn't mean nothing (Ibid, pp. 320–321).

Habituation, Decline, and Fall

Habituation occurs and the act does not produce the anticipated satisfaction. In an attempt to obtain the level of excitement and fulfillment so desperately sought for, the killer escalates his activities in the form of increased frequency of the crimes and/or increased sadistic acts. Parallel to this there is often a deterioration in the self-image of the offender. He becomes very repulsed by his acts and he begins to hate himself. He feels out of control and helpless in the presence of the Shadow he has created. He feels mastered by his Dark Side. The moralistic side of himself fights against the killer within which thirsts for blood. The killer may then reach out for help in some manner. After his eighth victim, the Zodiac Killer of the 1960s wrote a letter to attorney Melvin Belli:

> Dear Melvin, This is the Zodiak speaking.
>
> I wish you a happy Christmas. The one thing I ask of you is this, please help me. I cannot reach out for help because of the thing in me won't let me. I am finding it extremely difficult to hold it in check. I am afraid I will loose control again and take my ninth and possibly tenth victim. Please help me. I am drowning . . . (Graysmith, 1976, p. 207).

The Zodiac Killer went on to take at least 49 lives. In another case, Bill Heinrens wrote a plea for help in red lipstick on a wall of the apartment of his victim just before he killed her:

> For heavens
> Sake catch me
> Before I kill more
> I cannot control myself (Freeman, 1956, p. 15).

The overpowering urges to kill pitted against the hate he has developed for himself, results in a deterioration in the consistency of his emotions and behavior and it is more difficult for him to continue to kill as singularly in intent as he had done so in the past. He becomes more sloppy in his criminal activities, almost as though he were trying to get caught. The Chi Omega killings, for example, were very different from the approach Bundy had used in the past. Arthur Bishop, an offender who sexually molested and killed five boys, began to engage in criminal activities in an attempt to get caught by the police following the fourth homicide. When he got caught following the fifth victim he fully confessed all of the details of each crime to the police and later said that was a tremendous relief to get rid of the load he was carrying. Charles Hatcher voluntarily committed himself to a mental hospital the day following his final homicide and confessed to the other killings, partly because another person had been found guilty of his first three victims. Westley Dodd attempted to abduct another victim from a movie theater. The boy fought him and Dodd was able to narrowly escape. However, the following week he attempted the same thing in another theater and got caught. Two contract killers I have worked with each reached the point where they had so much self-hate because of their crimes that they ceased to care whether they got caught or not, and thus they were apprehended easily while committing an amateurish crime. Once the offender has been caught and placed in prison, he often seeks psychological counseling out of a need to understand how he developed into the person he became.

While every serial killer does not fit the model suggested here, many do. Finding that a killer has an inner part, or some internal entity that becomes an overwhelming force in his life and compels him to kill again and again doesn't excuse or justify the person's actions. There is no way to rationalize away a killer's responsibility for his crimes. There may have been some event or events which started the process, but the person himself fed it and allowed it to build and to get out of control. Thus, the person created his own monster which then controlled him, causing him to do the things he actually wanted to do in the first place. An understanding of the psychological processes regarding splitting and compartmentalization will aid in the detection process. If this process is not recognized and corrected, it continues unabated. The final product is best summarized by a statement Bundy made to the Florida police when they were interrogating him: "I'm the most cold blooded son of a bitch that you will ever meet" (Michaud and Aynesworth, 1983, p. 113).

References

Breuer, J. and S. Freud (1957). Studies on hysteria. New York: Basic Books.

Carlisle, A. (1991). Dissociation and violent criminal behavior. *Journal of Contemporary Criminal Justice*, 7, 273–285.

Damore, L. (1981). In his garden: The anatomy of a murder. New York: Dell Books.

Ellenberger, H. (1970). The discovery of the unconscious. New York: Basic Books.

Frank, G. (1966). The Boston strangler. New York: Signet.

Freeman, L. (1956). Before I kill more. New York: Kangaroo Books.

Ganey, T. (1989). Innocent blood. New York: St. Martins Press.

Graysmith, R. (1987). Zodiak. New York: Berkeley.

Hilgard, E. (1977). Divided consciousness: Multiple controls in human thought and action. New York: John Wiley and Sons.

Home Box Office. (1984). Murder: No apparent motive. American Undercover Series.

Jacobi, J. (1973). The psychology of C.G. Jung. New Haven: Yale Press.

Jung, C. (1983). Psychiatric studies: The collected works of C.G. Jung (Vol 1). New York: Bolingen Series XX/Princeton University Press.

Masters, B. (1985). Killing for company: The case of Dennis Nilsen. New York: Stein and Day.

Michaud, S. and Aynesworth, H. (1983). The only living witness. New York: Linden Press/Simon and Schuster.

Michaud, S. and Aynesworth, H. (1989). Ted Bundy: Conversations with a killer. New York: Signet Books.

Serial Killers. (1992). New York: Time-Life Books.

Stevenson, R. (1963). Dr. Jekyll and Mr. Hyde. New York: Scholastic Book Service.

Watkins, J. (1978). The therapeutic self. New York: Human Sciences.

Young, W. (1988). Observations of fantasy in the formation of multiple personality disorder. *Dissociation*, I.P. 13–20.

CHAPTER 4

THE STRUGGLES OF SURVIVING VICTIMS AND FAMILY

REACTIONS OF SURVIVING FAMILY MEMBERS

M. Regina Asaro

In the following selection, psychiatric nurse M. Regina Asaro describes the typical reactions experienced by people who have lost a loved one through murder, explaining how their grief and loss differ from those who lose a family member in a less violent manner. Surviving family members, Asaro claims, are at high risk for developing Posttraumatic Stress Disorder, which causes survivors to recurrently re-experience their initial reaction to the murder, to become excessively cautious, or to avoid places, people, or events they associate with the murder. Furthermore, she writes, family members of murder victims often face unwanted media attention and may be forced to work within a justice system that offers them little influence over the prosecution of the crime. Although Asaro does not specifically address the issue of serial murder, her general insights regarding family members of murder victims certainly apply to the relatives of victims of serial killers.

There is no way to prepare for the murder of a loved one. It is one of the most catastrophic experiences that an individual or family can face in life. It has been estimated that in 1993 there were 24,526 murders in the United States. As high as this number is, it does not accurately reflect the psychological and emotional devastation that murder leaves behind. Based on her work with over 300 clients, Lula Redmond estimated that there are 7 to 10 family members, not to mention significant others, close friends, neighbors and co-workers, who are left behind to mourn each victim.

This article will discuss the impact of murder on surviving family members (termed here "homicide survivors"), contextual issues which impact the way in which homicide survivors grieve their loss, and ways in which they may be supported as they go through the process of civil litigation.

Excerpted from M. Regina Asaro, "Working with Murder Victims' Surviving Family Members," *Crime Victims' Litigation Quarterly*, vol. 2, no. 2 (May 1995). Reprinted with the permission of the National Center for Victims of Crime, a national not-for-profit organization for victims of crime and their advocates.

Loss and Grief Reactions of Homicide Survivors

When someone is murdered, the surviving family members may experience posttraumatic stress reactions in addition to the wide range of grief reactions that may result if a loved one has died from natural causes.

Homicide survivors may have lost much more than their loved one as a result of the murder. They may suffer significant loss of income, either that of the victim or their own because of inability to work; loss of the family home if mortgage payments cannot be made; or loss of dreams or expectations about how life would have been had the murder not taken place. The sense of loss may be re-experienced as, for example, parents see the friends of their murdered child graduate from high school or college, get a job or start a family.

The reactions that survivors may experience immediately after the murder may include shock and disbelief, numbness, changes in appetite or sleeping patterns, difficulty concentrating, confusion, anger, fear and anxiety. Later reactions often include feelings of depression, isolation, helplessness, fear and vulnerability, guilt or self-blame, nightmares, tremendous rage and a desire for revenge.

Redmond described many factors which may affect the course of the grieving process for homicide survivors, including the ages of the survivors and the victim at the time of the murder; survivors' physical and/or emotional state before the murder; their prior history of trauma; and the way in which their loved one died. Another important factor is the availability and utilization of social support systems. It is important to recognize that, although emotional support may have been shared between family members prior to the murder, they may each grieve their loss in unique and sometimes mutually exclusive or conflicting ways. They might find themselves emotionally withdrawn from each other after the murder, especially when issues of protectiveness, guilt, anger, or blame are present.

Studies of families of murder victims suggest that they may be particularly at risk for developing Posttraumatic Stress Disorder. . . . When a family member is murdered, the survivors often react with intense feelings of helplessness, fear and horror. The diagnosis of Posttraumatic Stress Disorder is made when symptoms persist for at least one month, the disturbance causes impairment in an important area of functioning, and criteria are met in the following three categories:

1) recurrent and intrusive re-experiencing of the traumatic event;
2) development of avoidance behaviors around places or events which serve as reminders of the murder; and
3) persistent symptoms of increased arousal such as hypervigilance or exaggerated startle reaction.

"Trigger events" which serve as reminders of the murder, such as news stories, the approach of the holidays, or the anniversary of the murder can also cause survivors to re-experience earlier stress reactions.

Reactions to the Murder

Additionally, when dealing with the loss of their loved one, family members are constantly bombarded with contextual factors which result from the violent nature of the death. These may include reactions to the murder, both their own and those of others, or "re-victimization" by contact with the media and involvement with the criminal justice system.

One of the most troublesome aspects of a murder for homicide survivors is that the murder makes no sense to them. R. Janoff-Bulman stated that people, either consciously or unconsciously, often operate on the basis of underlying assumptions about the way the world is and why things happen. These assumptions help explain or attribute blame for situations or events and may serve as a protective mechanism against the extremely uncomfortable notion that "we are not in control." Having lost the framework that helps them to feel safe and make sense of the world, homicide survivors often feel as though they are cast adrift, trying to comprehend something that cannot be explained.

It is for this reason that safety issues are often of primary concern for homicide survivors. They now know that bad things not only can, but do, happen and this brings home the reality that no one is completely safe—no one is immortal. They may become fearful and anxious when another loved one comes home late or does not call when expected. If the defendant is not incarcerated, homicide survivors may have fears which range all the way from seeing the killer on the street to being killed themselves. Family members must also deal with the reactions of others, bearing with misguided attempts at helpfulness, including such comments as, "It's been a year—you should be over this by now," "It's God's will," or "At least you still have two other children."

After a loved one is murdered, homicide survivors have little privacy; the identity and circumstances of the murder are often public knowledge. In this day and age, it is not uncommon for survivors to find a microphone thrust in their faces after a court hearing. They may learn about developments in their case for the first time on the evening news or suddenly and unexpectedly see their loved one's body on a gurney being carried past yards of yellow police tape during a "Year in Review" news special.

Helping Families of Murder Victims

Re-victimization may also result from the way in which family members are notified of the murder, whether a suspect is caught or not, the manner in which the investigation and/or prosecution are conducted, and how they are given information from the autopsy report. For instance, if the case can be prosecuted, family members find that the crime has been committed "against the state"; they further find that, if they are called as witnesses, they may not be able to stay in the courtroom during the trial. Their loved one becomes "the body," "the victim," or "the deceased" and is rarely referred to by name. This perception of injustice and lack of respect for their loved one often causes further distress for homicide survivors. The trauma may not end once the convicted murderer is sentenced; indeed, ongoing appeals and parole hearings may easily trigger later stress reactions.

Since 1970, the number of civil lawsuits brought on behalf of crime victims has steadily increased. While civil action cannot bring a loved one back, it can send the message that violent behavior will not be tolerated and that individuals must take responsibility for their actions. It can also assist homicide survivors to recover monetary losses associated with the murder; however, economic factors may not be as important to them as the notion that they are continuing to seek justice for their loved one. This may be especially true in cases where they were not satisfied with the results of criminal prosecution. . . .

The combination of grief reactions and increased vulnerability to Posttraumatic Stress Disorder often results in what Redmond called "a life sentence" for the rest of the family after a loved one is murdered. Although not always possible, practical or desirable, pursuing civil remedies against the individual who has brought so much pain into their lives can assist homicide survivors not only to recover economic losses resulting from the murder, but may hold responsible persons directly accountable to the victim's family.

LIVES FOREVER CHANGED: SURVIVING SERIAL KILLER TED BUNDY

Sabrina Rubin

In the following selection, Sabrina Rubin tells the story of Diane Cossin McCain and Susan Denton, who were college students living at the Chi Omega sorority house at Florida State University in 1978, when serial killer Ted Bundy murdered two of their sorority sisters and critically injured two others. The author not only relates the women's experience the night of the murders, but also describes the media intrusion and the frustrating judicial process that followed. For example, the author explains, the sorority sisters were asked not to discuss the case with each other and were therefore unable to offer each other much-needed support. Moreover, Rubin writes, they often discovered the gruesome details of the murders from the media rather than from counselors who could help them cope with their emotions. These experiences led both women to fight for victims' rights: Denton started a career in crime prevention and volunteered as a victims' advocate, while McCain worked to add a victims' rights amendment to the Florida constitution, which was passed in 1988. Rubin is a senior writer at *Philadelphia* magazine.

Ted Bundy haunted their dreams. Night after night, Diane Cossin McCain and Susan Denton would fall asleep to find it was January 15, 1978, all over again, and that the notorious serial killer was sneaking into their sorority house. Except in dreams, their sorority sisters didn't die, the way they had in real life; instead, Diane or Susan would step in to save them.

Haunted by a Serial Killer

But while dreams of rescue marked their nights, their days held a hard reality of grief. "I was afraid I'd never get back to normal again, that I'd never stop looking over my shoulder," Susan says now, sitting on a couch in her Orlando home. "I felt that fear of not knowing if I could ever pick up the pieces," she continues. "But that is *not* a way to live."

Reprinted from Sabrina Rubin, "They Survived a Serial Killer," *Redbook*, June 1998. Reprinted by permission of the author.

And so in the aftermath of the tragedy at Florida State University, which came to be known as the "Chi Omega Murders," and for the next 20 years, she and Diane dedicated themselves to trying to right the wrong that had been done, both to their murdered friends and to themselves as secondary victims. In a sense, they *haven't* gotten over that horrible night: It changed their lives, catapulting them into careers they had never before envisioned, molding them into people they otherwise would not have become.

"I am who I am partly because of Ted Bundy," Susan says matter-of-factly. "It's something I've learned to live with."

Waking to a Nightmare

It was a cold night in Tallahassee: January 15, 1978. Diane, a 20-year-old college junior, awoke with a start. Her roommate was coughing. Diane squinted at the clock: nearly 3 A.M. She closed her eyes with some annoyance. The Chi Omega house, where she lived with 38 other young women, was the kind of place where you learn to sleep through just about anything. The incessant coughing, though, had broken through that barrier.

"Do you want me to get something for you?" Diane asked. "No, I'll go to the kitchen and get some bread," her roommate answered. She padded out into the hall, but came back moments later. "That was quick," Diane said. "I didn't go," her roommate answered. "I had a funny feeling." Both girls drifted back to sleep. Later, Diane would recall that as her roommate had come back in, the hallway lights had gone out behind her—and her roommate hadn't touched the switch.

Minutes after Diane's roommate returned to their room, another sorority sister, Nita Neary, came home through the side door. As Nita walked through the house, she saw the silhouette of a man hurrying to the front door. Then he was gone. Something in Nita's gut told her that this wasn't simply a case of someone having sneaked a boyfriend in. She went upstairs and woke her roommate and then the sorority president. While the three young women whispered together at the top of the stairs, 20-year-old Karen Chandler stumbled out of her room down the darkened hall. Something wet was running down the front of her nightgown—she seemed to be sick or drunk. But when the girls snapped on the light, they recoiled. Karen was covered with blood.

Minutes later, Susan Denton awoke to the sound of running footsteps and the static of a police radio. She threw on a robe over her nightgown and opened her door to find the hallway full of people: sorority sisters, policemen, emergency medical technicians, and a bleeding Karen Chandler being carried down the stairs on a gurney. "Karen was attacked," somebody said. Then an EMT called from Karen's room, "Can someone come and be with this girl?" Susan floated down the hall in a trance and found Karen's roommate, Kathy

Kleiner, sitting dazed in bed, blood pouring from her face. *My God, Susan thought with horror, someone's gotten into the house.*

Diane, awakened for the second time that night, ran across the hall to Lisa Levy's room—she'll never know exactly why. She threw open the door and flipped on the light. Lisa lay in her bed amid so much spattered blood that Diane thought someone had driven by the house with a machine gun. Numb from shock, too stunned to even call for help, Diane sat on the bed and held the semiconscious Lisa. When the EMTs arrived, they had to practically tear Diane away.

Meanwhile, Susan had been asked to take a police officer around the house for an inspection. "Wake up," Susan called into each room. "There's been a problem, the police are here." When they got to Margaret Bowman's room, directly across the hall from where EMTs were furiously trying to revive Lisa, the police officer cracked the door and peered in, then asked Susan to step back. He entered the room and quietly closed the door behind him. As dawn broke, the sorority sisters were informed that Margaret Bowman had been found dead of strangulation, that Lisa Levy had died on the way to the hospital—of strangulation and blunt trauma to the head, as the girls would later discover—and that Karen Chandler and Kathy Kleiner were critically injured but would survive. The police also asked the girls to call their parents; the media was already assembling on the lawn.

Life After Murder

Many people were amazed that, in the aftermath of the crime, almost all of the Chi Omega sisters continued living in the sorority house, albeit with police officers and a private security guard stationed there. "It was our home," Susan explains simply. "I can't describe the feeling of comfort and closeness I felt, being with my sorority sisters, experiencing it together."

Television vans were camped out across the street for weeks, and reporters followed the Chi Omegas to their classes, asking, "How do you feel?" They didn't know what to feel. They didn't even truly know what had happened: After giving their statements to police, the girls had been asked not to discuss the events of that night with one another so as not to taint their recollections. Even worse, after the initial chaos—during which time police warned them not to wear their sorority letters in case the murderer had a vendetta against Chi Omega—no one called to update them with information, and they were too afraid to ask. All they knew was that two friends had been taken from their midst. Margaret, 21, had been a stunning young woman—tall, poised, and slender, with dark hair, porcelain skin, and a passion for art history. Lisa, 20, had been loved for her sweetness and exuberance. A fashion merchandising major, she'd been pleased to no end when she'd finally gotten her braces off her teeth a few months earlier. Now both young women were dead, their bedroom doors blocked by yellow crime-scene tape. And the survivors were racked with guilt, each wondering how her friends could have been so brutally victimized without anyone having heard a sound.

A couple of weeks later, the Chi Omegas found themselves at the state attorney's office, asked to give their statements yet again. But this time, a woman was waiting for them. She explained that she was a representative from the Victim Witness Unit—she was there to be a source of support, to walk them through the judicial process and to answer their questions. This added to Susan Denton's frustration. "Where have you been all this time?" she asked. "Why didn't anyone tell us about you?" That's when Susan and Diane learned that a victim's advocate is summoned only at the discretion of the police or at a victim's request; investigators hadn't thought to contact the unit until that point.

But even with the advocate, the girls found themselves no better off. When graphic information about Lisa Levy's injuries was made public—she had not only been beaten and strangled but sodomized and bitten—the girls read it in a newspaper rather than hearing it from a counselor who might have helped them deal with this new blow. And when exactly one month after the murders a suspect was apprehended in Pensacola, the Chi Omegas weren't told. Diane found out from a reporter who chased her down on her way to class. "Did you hear?" he asked her breathlessly. "There's been an arrest. A guy named Ted Bundy."

A Judicial Nightmare

Susan tried to act brave as she walked into the Leon County Jail, where Ted Bundy was waiting for her. In the months that had passed since the murders, she had read much about Bundy in the newspaper. That he was a 31-year-old law student from Seattle, described as bright, clever, and "movie-star handsome." That he was on the FBI's Ten Most Wanted list, suspected in as many as 36 murders spanning five states. That before surfacing in Florida he had escaped from a Colorado prison, where he was awaiting trial for the murder of a 23-year-old woman.

The Chi Omegas would later learn that after his Colorado escape, Bundy had chosen Tallahassee seemingly at random, after happening across a listing for Florida State University—college-age women being his victims of choice. He moved into a house on the fringes of the FSU campus. Bundy's murderous tendencies had been bottled up for the two years he had spent in jail, and once he was in Tallahassee, it took less than two weeks for him to explode into a terrifying spree: An hour and a half after the carnage at the Chi Omega House, Bundy had sneaked into another student's house six blocks away, savagely beating her. Days before his arrest one month later, he had killed a 12-year-old girl.

Bundy's arrest had not been a matter of brilliant detective work. He was actually caught for a traffic violation; police ordered him to pull over, and he fled. When the police caught up with him, they realized that the car he was driving had been reported stolen from near the Chi Omega house. He was then linked to the crime scene by Nita Neary's eyewitness, by a cast of his teeth that matched the bite marks on Lisa Levy's body, and by a length of knotted panty hose that matched those used to strangle the victims.

Meeting a Monster

In a particularly perverse turn of events, Bundy had decided to act as his own attorney, which gave him the right to depose everyone in the Chi Omega house. He called them in one by one for interviews. Diane had been called in three times, her sessions lasting an hour or more while Bundy tried to pick apart her story, chipping away at her confidence as to what she saw that night—what time she saw the hall lights go off and how she found Lisa Levy.

Now it was Susan's turn to face Ted Bundy. She took a seat next to the prosecutor and across the table from where Bundy sat. He stared directly into her eyes and asked her if, for the purposes of the deposition, she would please refer to the man indicted for the murders as "Mr. Bundy" but refer to the man questioning her from across the table as "Ted." Susan nodded.

"Have you ever met Mr. Bundy?" Bundy began.

This is so surreal, thought Susan. "Yes and no," she answered hesitantly. Bundy pressed her for an explanation.

"Well . . . not before now," she said. Ted Bundy threw his head back and laughed.

Susan gritted her teeth. The deposition felt like a mockery of justice at the end of a terrible year: Since the killings, two Chi Omegas had dropped out and one had committed suicide. As for Susan, she was finding it harder to focus and had pared down her double major to just one: criminology. The unnerving thing was, Ted Bundy knew; he had subpoenaed her records and was eager to chat about her coursework.

As it turned out, one of the next things Susan had to do was choose an internship. And although she had originally wanted to work with juvenile delinquents, she now had another idea: She would take her internship with the Victim Witness Program.

Bundy's trial was like a gruesome circus. Still acting as his own attorney, he strode around the courtroom with a cocky grin, made endless media appearances to proclaim his innocence, and actually married his girlfriend right there in the courtroom. Diane was sequestered in a hotel room, listed as one of Ted Bundy's potential witnesses. She was never called to testify and suspected that Bundy's tactic was to keep her, and the emotions she might display, out of the courtroom.

On July 24, 1979, Bundy was convicted of the first-degree murders of Lisa Levy and Margaret Bowman and of the assaults on Karen Chandler, Kathy Kleiner, and Cheryl Thomas, the young woman who lived six blocks away. On February 7, 1980, he was convicted of the first-degree murder of 12-year-old Kimberly Leach. (Because he was given the death penalty, none of the other states in which he was suspected of having committed murders tried to pursue additional charges.)

Providing Help for Victims

After the trial, both women were eager for life to make sense again but suspected it wouldn't happen so quickly. Susan dove into a career in crime prevention. She helped hatch the concept for the Florida Crime Prevention Training Institute; she helped open a battered women's shelter; she was appointed the executive director of the Orlando Crime Commission at the ripe old age of 26, and later worked for the National Safety Council. All the while, she also worked as a volunteer victim's advocate, on call all night once a week.

"It became a mission for her," says Marie Cox, a friend of Susan's since childhood. "On some level, she wanted for no one to ever have to go through what she did. But that if they did, they should never have to go through it by themselves." When Susan's beeper went off, she'd rush to crime scenes, police stations, hospitals—wherever she was needed, to meet with a victim and answer the same questions she'd wished someone had answered for her: *Why do I have to tell my story to so many different people? Why are they taking my belongings? Why do I need to be examined?* "You try to humanize the process," says Susan now. "Your role is to make sure the victim is treated like an individual rather than a piece of evidence left at a crime scene."

Helping victims was like therapy for Susan, but at the same time she was aware of how vulnerable she was. "Hardly a day went by that I didn't think about Lisa and Margaret, and being a survivor," remembers Susan. "Ted Bundy may not have physically touched me, but I was there, sleeping, at the time. It could have been me. And it was hard to get back my sense of peace and safety." She had always been outgoing but now was all but closed off to dating; whenever she was approached by a stranger, the wheels would begin turning in her head, gauging her personal space, his body language, whether people were within earshot if she needed to scream for help. More than once Susan considered writing Bundy a letter asking for a face-to-face interview much like the one they'd had years before, but this time with Susan asking the questions. She wanted to ask him just one question: *Do you confess to killing my friends?*

Susan stayed in touch with her sorority sisters the whole time Bundy was on death row. "What happened that night became a bond between us," she says quietly. But few Chi Omegas remained as close as Susan and Diane.

After graduation, Diane had begun law school at FSU, but the media glare of the trial interfered with her studies and she'd had to put her plans on hold. "It was rough on her," says Chuck Buker, an Atlanta lawyer who occasionally dated her in college and has remained her friend. "But Diane has always been a beacon of strength. Whatever she was feeling, she tried to channel it into something positive. And once she sets her mind to do something, nothing gets in her way."

Fighting for Victims' Rights

Determined to change the way victims were treated, she began talking to then–State Representative (and later Senator) Dexter Lehtinen. Together, they drafted a bill stating that every victim had certain rights: to be notified of a suspect's arrest, for instance, or to make a statement at trial. But the bill received almost no support in the Florida House of Representatives—legislators complained that it could infringe upon the rights of a defendant and, more important, would require funding. That didn't end Diane's resolve, however, and she spent the next few years gathering support for the bill.

Meanwhile, there were other battles to fight, as when she discovered NBC was filming a miniseries about Ted Bundy. "It was a terrible thing for them to glamorize our pain like that," she says now. Diane went public with her opposition, asking local networks to black out the movie (as Colorado affiliates did), mostly to no avail. In 1986, *The Deliberate Stranger* aired. The next day, Diane overheard two women discussing the film. "Can you believe those girls dressed like that?" one exclaimed. "No wonder that happened to them!" Diane had lost the battle, but the attention she received strengthened public support for the victims' rights bill. She also fought another well-publicized battle when she discovered that a class on "thrillers" was being taught at FSU—and on the reading list was a book about the Bundy murders. "And this was less than a decade after it happened!" Diane exclaims. After a protracted dispute about turning heinous crimes into entertainment, the class was canceled.

At this point, though, Diane began to hear dissent from her own sorority sisters. "Why can't you get past this?" a few asked her. "Get on with your life!" Diane was stung. "We all dealt with this thing in different ways," she insists now, "and I was only doing what I felt was right." She'd call Susan to commiserate, since Susan had been on the receiving end of the same remarks.

"I guess a small part of me wondered if maybe our friends were right," admits Susan. In the end, however, the criticism only motivated them more.

Persistence paid off. In 1988, the victims' rights amendment finally passed and was incorporated into the Florida constitution. The following year, Diane was invited to witness Ted Bundy's electric-chair execution. She declined.

Days before his execution, Bundy startled the nation by making an eleventh-hour confession, admitting to more than 30 murders in more than half a dozen states. A wide-eyed Susan Denton watched Bundy's confession on the evening news. "It made me sick, the way he was playing to the camera," she remembers. "But I kept watching, waiting for him to just come out and say what we already knew, that he had killed Lisa and Margaret."

Ted Bundy didn't give Susan the satisfaction. He took those confessions to the grave.

Finding Life After Bundy's Death

"It was a relief," Susan says of Bundy's execution. "After ten years, it was finally some closure. I mean, we can argue over whether the death penalty is a deterrent, but I know for sure that Ted Bundy is never going to kill again." That fact meant a great deal to both women: For the first time since 1978, Diane dared to sleep with her bedroom door unlocked.

In the decade since the passage of Florida's victims' rights amendment (which Diane, only half-jokingly, calls the "why-I-don't-have-two-kids-and-a-normal-life amendment"), victims' rights have increasingly become an integral part of the criminal justice system, enough that Florida State University recently sent Diane a letter to tell her how proud they are that she is an alumna. "So perceptions are changing," says Diane exuberantly. "They don't think I'm a nut anymore."

Her war having been won, Diane is finally back in law school, slowly working her way toward the degree she always wanted. She's also considering marriage.

Susan Denton now works as a neighborhood outreach supervisor for the city of Orlando and lives near her family. Like Diane, she has never been married. "But I guess you can't fault Ted Bundy for that," she says with a wry chuckle.

"We're not stuck in 1978," she adds. "We know we'll never be able to explain why that night happened. But it did. And I know it gave Diane and me the passion to do what we did."

Two decades after the crime, Susan, Diane, and their Chi Omega sisters don't get together as often. But once a year, a group of them still gather to celebrate Margaret Bowman and Lisa Levy's birthdays. It's a happy occasion, Diane says, since they're celebrating "good memories."

Executing the Murderer: A Sense of Closure

Bella Stumbo

Many people assume that the families of victims get satisfaction out of the execution of the killer of their loved ones, asserts true-crime writer Bella Stumbo, but the truth is actually more complex. In the following selection, Stumbo interviews several family members of murder victims (including a number whose loved ones were murdered by serial killers) on their feelings about this issue. These family members significantly differ in the amount of relief they received from the execution of their loved one's murderer, she reports. For example, the mother and sister of Susan Rancourt, a victim of serial killer Ted Bundy, did not rejoice when Bundy was executed, explaining that hatred only hurts survivors. However, the father of Lee Iseli, a victim of serial killer Westley Allan Dodd, tells Stumbo that he was glad that Dodd was dead but felt empty and disappointed because he no longer had a focus for his anger.

To advocates of the death penalty, executions serve as nothing less than a public service, especially for families of victims. They must surely crave execution of the murderer for revenge, for emotional closure, many people assume; those who do see the killer of their loved ones executed must experience a grim but profound satisfaction.

But do they? . . .

What follows are a few brief conversations with those who know most about capital punishment: families of victims whose killers were eventually executed. They were chosen at random, and we do not pretend that their views are representative.

But I do know that for someone like me—an average liberal who opposes capital punishment on principle but suspects that if murder ever visited her family she would probably change her tune fast—these people provided an indelible surprise. I learned that watching a loved one's murderer die doesn't provide the unqualified satisfaction those of us untouched by murder might expect it would. It's much more complicated than that.

Excerpted from Bella Stumbo, "Executing the Murderer: The Victims' Families Speak Out," *Redbook*, November 1995. Reprinted by permission of the author.

"It Was Just So Ugly"

The execution of serial killer Ted Bundy did not provide much closure for either Vivian Winters or Judy Zimmerman. The very memory of that gray January morning reduces both of them to tears.

Vivian is the mother and Judy the sister of Susan Rancourt, a 17-year-old college freshman who disappeared without a trace from Ellensburg, Washington, in 1974. Rancourt's body wasn't found until nearly a year after she vanished—in a dump site along with two other Bundy victims, all of their remains so decomposed and entangled that the families couldn't tell which was which. The next 15 years were excruciating. Bundy was arrested, only to escape and be rearrested. The legal maneuvering and media hoopla over Bundy's legal "brilliance" and good looks at times made him seem more like a cult hero than a mass murderer. To maintain their sanity, the Rancourts joined one of the country's oldest victim support groups, Seattle's Families and Friends of Victims of Violent Crime.

Most of these families were, like the Rancourts, denied the satisfaction of seeing Bundy tried for murdering their daughters. When after three stays Florida finally strapped Ted Bundy into the electric chair on January 23, 1989, he had confessed to at least 23 murders but had been convicted for only three, in Florida.

Vivian Winters and Judy Zimmerman simply went about their business that morning. Thousands of miles away and many draining years after Susan's murder, both were too numb to believe that Bundy was really about to die. They expected yet another stay. Until the media descended. "It was awful," Vivian remembers. "All the talk shows called. Reporters were everywhere." All of them assuming that these two good-hearted women were rejoicing.

Not Rejoicing; Letting Go

They weren't. Judy Zimmerman was just 21 when her sister and best friend died, and she definitely hated Ted Bundy. But, she says, her face suddenly reddening, her voice rising to a frustrated shout, "We weren't cheering! What people don't understand is that you *can't* hold on to the anger; you have to let it go whether you want to or not. If you keep it, you can't raise your children, you can't work, you can't have sex, you can't do *anything*—the hate will kill you." And no, she never wanted to attend Bundy's execution, she finishes, choking on the words as she buries her face in her arms, "because the whole thing was just so *ugly*! The way *she* died, the way *he* died—all of it was just . . . so ugly!"

For Vivian Winters, a kind-faced woman whose dark hair turned snow white soon after her daughter's disappearance, thinking of Bundy's execution also taps into memories best left forgotten. Thanks to the inventiveness of a local TV station, she spoke that morning with Ted Bundy's mother in nearby Tacoma. Mrs. Bundy told her, "I'm so sorry, I didn't want this to happen." Vivian Winters can't finish without crying, so great is her continuing pity for that poor mother. "And I told her how sorry I was too, and that none of us held her responsible."

In truth, Vivian Winters still has trouble with the death penalty. Even for Bundy. "But, speaking as a Christian," she says with a worded sigh, "I guess it's up to society to control the evil of serial killers. I mean, it does need to be tended to. . . ."

Ted Bundy's execution did provide one solid, indisputable bit of closure for these women—they could at last put away the big, thick, pitiful scrapbook they had labored over for so long. Filled with hundreds of newspaper clippings, all neatly cut and pasted and dated, it begins with the earliest bulletins from local papers about the young college student who was suddenly missing from her home. Many include photos of a pretty, smiling blond girl. Every frantic personal advertisement placed by the Rancourt family during that first year is there; every appeal for leads is there. Then come the pictures of grim-faced Seattle crews, excavating remains. And, from there, a complete chronicle of Ted Bundy's trail of victims across the United States, the manhunt, the arrest, the escape, the appeals—all of it finally ending with Seattle's banner headlines announcing the end of the Ted Bundy story.

"The Waiting Is the Worst"

Peggie Hendrickson, a Seattle legal assistant and mother of one, was 33 when her mother was murdered by a convicted rapist. By the time the killer was put to death, after all the delays, stays, and trips to the governor's office, Hendrickson was 45. During those years she went through a divorce, developed migraines, became a chain-smoker, and watched her hair fall out in clumps, leaving her with a wispy pixie. Her father's health deteriorated; he became an alcoholic. Today there is about Peggie Hendrickson an air of such solemn reserve and intelligent sadness that it makes a stranger suspect that these people truly are different from you and me.

Hendrickson's mother was murdered by Charles Campbell, as an afterthought to another, more important revenge killing that he had on his mind. The day Peggie Hendrickson's mother was murdered Campbell had actually gone to kill a neighbor who had testified against him years earlier for raping her. But as he was rummaging about the dead woman's house, her 8-year-old daughter came home from school, followed shortly by Peggie Hendrickson's mother, who dropped by to help her neighbor make dinner because the woman was ill. So Campbell slashed both of them to death. He massacred them while still serving time for the rape—he was out on an experimental daytime work-release program for well-behaved prisoners, a detail that inflamed Washington State.

"It's agony unlike anything else," says Hendrickson of the long ordeal, "because you have no control, you're just a bystander. In some ways the sustained trauma is worse than the murder. It destroys whole families because you spend so much emotional and physical energy just reacting."

And no cleansing, soothing peace descended on her the day Campbell died. Instead, she says, the opposite occurred: Awful images of her mother's senseless, bloody death came rushing back, as fresh as if the murder were yesterday. The unbearable grief and rage she had spent so long learning to control hit anew with savage force.

"All I remember is crying uncontrollably in the car as my niece drove me home. Twelve years of crap came flooding out. I guess I'd never had a chance to let it out before. But mostly, all I felt was such relief that it was all finally over, that we wouldn't have to worry about the next hearing anymore."

And maybe that was closure enough, she says with a dry smile.

Either way, she's glad Campbell is dead. "I tell myself that if God can forgive the killer, then surely he can forgive me for wanting him dead," she says. She admits she felt special satisfaction that Campbell had to be carried to the gallows. "I like to think that, in the end, maybe he finally had some inkling of the horror he caused."

But Peggie Hendrickson still smokes, her hair hasn't come back, her mother is still dead, and her personality has been forever altered.

No Regrets

Across the country, in Lumberton, North Carolina, Alice Storms hasn't had a second, unpleasant thought since the state strapped Margie Velma Barfield onto a gurney in 1984 and gave her a lethal injection. Barfield was convicted of using rat poison to murder at least four people, including her own mother and aunt, and her former fiancé, Stuart Taylor—who was Alice Storms's father.

Alice Storms's suspicions contributed to Barfield getting caught. Taylor was a healthy 56 when he suddenly became violently ill one night in 1978. After three days of retching and vomiting as doctors searched helplessly for a cause, he died. Storms pressed for tests beyond the standard autopsy; they turned up arsenic.

Velma Barfield, a sweet-faced, grandmotherly Sunday school teacher who worked as a live-in helper for the elderly, had poured rat killer into Taylor's iced tea and beer. She also confessed to doing away with her mother and two of her aging clients in similar fashion. She testified that she'd only intended to make her victims sick so they wouldn't discover she had stolen from them. She said she had been in a haze and had only done it for money to support a ten-year addiction to prescription tranquilizers and painkillers. A thick stack of pharmacy records lent some credence to the claim. But in rural Lumberton that kite didn't fly. The jury returned with a death verdict in less than an hour.

As executions go, Barfield's victims actually got fairly swift justice. Even so, it was an election season and the Barfield case drew intense media attention, not only because she looked like she belonged in a Betty Crocker ad but because she would be the first woman executed since 1962. Right up until the end, Alice Storms, then 40, circulated petitions door-to-door that called for Barfield's death.

And Storms has never regretted it, she says. "You don't get peace of mind from it, but you feel like you can finally go on with your life." Like many victims of capital crimes, she says she went through a period of feeling that it was absolutely required of her, personally, to "fix" the legal system. She became an activist in Raleigh—and a frustrated one, because nothing much changed. Now, she says, she spends her days working in the family gift shop. And for her that's growth.

Not least, Alice Storms was also thrilled to finally get the media hordes, with their everlastingly sensational approach to Barfield's impending execution, out of her life. "I used to get so angry, hearing about her day in, day out on TV, in the papers—and it was always 'this poor little grandma,'" says Storms bitterly. "Well, she wasn't sweet. She was just plain evil. I think she enjoyed seeing them suffer—just the way she killed them so slowly, and then standing by, watching it, cleaning up after the vomit and all. . . ."

Unfortunately, Storms may never be entirely free of Velma Barfield, who is still the only woman to be executed in the United States since 1962. Of the several women on death row, the next one up just may be another lady arsenic killer from North Carolina, which means the media will once again descend on Alice Storms, wanting to know all about Velma Barfield.

"Hanging Was Too Good for Him"

The complex, unresolved conflicts of Bob Iseli, a soft-spoken, sad-eyed single father, over the torture killing of his 4-year-old son are as painful as they are illuminating.

On a sunny day in 1989, Lee Iseli, a beautiful blond child, was playing at a school playground in Vancouver, Washington, across the river from Portland, when a nice young man came along. When Lee's 9-year-old brother's back was turned, the man asked Lee if he wanted to come play some games.

Instead, Westley Allan Dodd, a twisted 28-year-old with a long record of child molestation, took Lee Iseli to his apartment, where he raped and tortured him for hours, videotaping much of it. Several times, Dodd said later, he choked the boy into unconsciousness, only to revive him for more torture and rape. Finally, Dodd hanged him.

As it turned out, Dodd had earlier murdered two other young boys in the same area, but he stabbed them quickly, without the slow torture Lee Iseli endured.

Dodd was promptly convicted and, barely three years later, in early

1993, became the first person legally hanged in the United States since 1965. At his own behest. Although Washington offers lethal injection, Dodd chose hanging because, he said, he deserved to die in the same way Lee had. Dodd also expedited his own death by rejecting legal efforts in his behalf.

In short, Westley Dodd remained in control until the end—and that's part of what torments Bob Iseli. Dodd wanted to die, so he did on his own terms.

"In some ways, I really don't see the death penalty as punishment," says Iseli, a computer consultant, now 41. "It was too good for him. I mean, if you really want to punish him. . . ." His voice drifts off, the sentence unfinished. Bob Iseli is a thoughtful, civilized man with an unsettling air of calm. Which is just a front, says his vivacious fiancée, Jennifer, watching him with worded eyes. "It's a control thing. When he's asleep, he still cries."

In any case, says Iseli, ignoring her, his reaction on the night of the execution was mostly disappointment. After all the uproar, it was a letdown. "I just felt, well, nothing. Empty. I thought, Gee, is that all there is?"

Then, as time wore on, he began to realize that in some ways he actually missed Westley Dodd, "because he gave my feelings a point of focus, a place to direct my anger. Then, suddenly, that was gone, it was all over. Plus," he continues in the same measured, soft tone, "Dodd was my last real contact with Lee. . . . After he was gone, I had to, well, look at what happened to Lee in a different way, without all the distractions. . . . I mean, I'd stayed busy for so long with court, relatives, the justice system, the media. . . ."

What's more, says Iseli with refreshing candor, he enjoyed "feeling important" during that period. "Before, I was a pretty boring, ordinary guy . . . then, for the first time in my life, everybody listened to what I had to say." Finally, he says, reluctantly, he began seeing a therapist to help him deal with his anger and, perhaps even more important, with his guilt. After all, he says, he had been home watching a ball game on that terrible day—relaxing while his son was being dragged away to a terrible death. His older son, now a teenager, still blames himself too for not watching his brother. "And every time we get in an argument," says Iseli, looking away, "that always comes up."

Still, despite all Iseli has said, he doesn't want there to be any mistake about his support for capital punishment. "I hated the feeling of wanting somebody dead . . . but I am glad he's gone. And I do think it helps with closure, in a way. Now, instead of him always being in control, at least I have some control over what's going on in my life."

No Easy Answers

And just as death may have been too easy for Dodd, life in prison might have also ended up being too comfortable, Iseli thinks. "I mean, just look at Manson. He's got a fan club. And Dodd's world revolved around his mind. He would have more of a life in prison than out . . . women writing to him, big names in the media wanting interviews. . . . No, I'm glad that he doesn't go on breathing."

But it never occurred to Iseli to attend the execution. "I didn't want that to be the last picture in my mind," he says. Then, with a smile to chill the soul, "Watching people hang doesn't turn me on like it did him."

Most of these survivors agree that there is no such thing as real closure when a loved one's murderer is executed. There is only escape—escape from the endless legal delays, from the media, from their own rage, from the guilt most still feel for wanting to see another human being dead.

"What you should write," says Judy Zimmerman, "is this: that if punishment were swift and sure in this country, we probably wouldn't even need the death penalty." As it now stands, we are a schizophrenic marvel to the world, a nation unwilling to abolish capital punishment, as many Western democracies have, but also unable to embrace it fully for fear of executing an innocent person.

In the United States a sentence of life in prison is generally toothless. Susan Smith, for example, will be eligible for parole when she is only 53.

Common decency mandates an abundance of caution in dealing with the rights of accused killers. But until we find some better way to respect the humanity of the victims, our national shame remains. We need only to remember the tearful face of Ron Goldman's father speaking out at the O.J. Simpson trial to know that.

WHEN JUSTICE IS NOT SERVED

David Gelernter

Between 1978 and 1995, Theodore J. Kaczynski, known as the "Unabomber," killed three people and wounded twenty-two others with bombs he either mailed or placed at the scene. On June 24, 1993, Kaczynski mailed a package bomb to David Gelernter, whose right hand and eye were permanently damaged. In the following selection, Gelernter comments on his disappointment with the outcome of the case against Kaczynski, who pled guilty to his crimes and received a sentence of life in federal prison without parole. Gelernter argues that by allowing Kaczynski to manipulate the justice system and by failing to condemn him to death, society has blurred the distinction between good and evil. Furthermore, Gelernter believes that comparing Kaczynski's writings to those of famous political philosophers has brought Kaczynski the recognition and fame he desires, while his victims have not received the justice they deserve. Gelernter is a professor of computer science at Yale University. He is also the author of *Drawing Life: Surviving the Unabomber* (a memoir of his experiences as a victim of the Unabomber) and *Machine Beauty: Elegance and the Heart of Technology.*

There never were any group meetings among us targets of the so-called Unabomber, but we nearly had one in Sacramento, California, on the day the trial began [on January 5, 1998]. The FBI had set up a "witness room" where we could gather and get briefed, away from the press. Most of the survivors were on hand, together with other witnesses and assorted family members. I had come with my wife. Susan Mosser was there; her husband was murdered by a bomb in New Jersey. The Epsteins were there, with their son and daughter—Professor Charles J. Epstein, M.D., got blown up the same day I did. Epstein and I were among the first witnesses on the agenda. Part of the prosecution's job is to establish what happened; our assignment was to lay out for the jury what it's like when a package explodes in your face and you almost die.

The plan was to get us downstairs into the courtroom before the reporters got in. It came time for us to be escorted down in batches. There were (maybe) thirty of us, and one elevator, and a lot of after-you'ing as we arranged ourselves into elevator-sized groups. There was a bond among us after all, everyone was friendly and polite—and no one was in any hurry. The metal detector outside the courtroom is more sensitive than your standard airport model. I couldn't get through without setting off the alarm, on account of the metal in the fake thumb I wear strapped to the remainder of my right hand or, maybe, the shrapnel fragments still floating around in my chest. They tried me a few times, then waved me through.

Judge Garland E. Burrell Jr.'s courtroom is done up in mid-'60s Holiday Inn style. The furniture is austere; the walls are paneled in wood that has somehow been made to look plastic. The spectator pews are divided by an aisle down the middle. Prosecution-related people sat in front on the left, defense people on the right—"sort of like a wedding," an FBI man explained. The room lacks majesty, stateliness, bathrooms. The bathroom situation was a hot topic that morning. Rumors flew thick and fast. Some claimed that once the judge arrived, you weren't allowed out until recess. Others said that leaving was no problem, but you couldn't get back in. I never did hear the straight story.

The Faces in the Courtroom

The session was supposed to start at eight. We were seated by seven-thirtyish. The prosecutors were already there: Stephen P. Freccero, Thomas Cleary, and R. Stephen Latham. I'd got to know Freccero and Cleary, and to admire them. Cleary was the head man—tall with a trim beard and dark piercing rabbinical eyes. I once saw him, when the judge said something he didn't like, lean back in his chair and stare silently at the ceiling as if he were exasperated with God and wanted God to know it. Freccero is broader, looks and moves like a boxer, speaks in grim slow-motion, like a Gary Cooper sheriff. His features are blunt and forceful; there is suppressed tragedy in his voice. He is not humorless, but I rarely saw him smile.

Cleary and Freccero both radiate intense moral seriousness. They believed that evil had been done, and they knew who did it, and they knew what ought to be done with that man. And they were beleaguered and exhausted; they were bears at a bear-baiting. They were painfully discreet: Freccero praised the judge several times in our many long conversations, and never said a word against him. Occasionally he would criticize the defense or the press in quiet, guarded terms. The prosecution was colossally meticulous; their grids, their numbered charts, their endless roomsful of evidence could give you the queasy impression of a well with no bottom. They had dotted every *i* and crossed every *t*, but entering the funhouse of the modern U.S. justice system, you could feel them setting their jaws. When the prosecution team huddled in court, Cleary in the center, Freccero and Latham leaning sharply toward him on either side, you could picture the heat-shimmer overhead.

Preparing for Battle

A summary version of the evidence had arrived in the care of an FBI man, dozens of loose-leaf binders carefully arranged in what looked like a fancy shopping cart. The evidence had been put online too, and there was sophisticated computer equipment on hand. Amid all the grimness and high-tech: two sketch artists with neat ranks of Derwent colored pencils—such a whimsical, out-of-place touch, it made my day. One of them (I was told) made a sketch of me, and I decided that the next day I came to court I'd bring pencils and make a sketch of her. There never was a next day.

FBI agents do the legwork and handle trial logistics. They'd fetched us at the airport the night before, and they shepherded us around Sacramento in their white government-issue Chevy Luminas. The younger FBI agents are so nice it's alarming. I asked a couple of them what they thought of Director Louis Freeh, and they praised him by citing anecdotes about how much time he spends with his kids: how one child had told Janet Reno that Dad couldn't come to the phone because he was playing Nintendo; how the director had missed an official ceremony because of a boys' soccer match. In court I met a senior FBI man with a gruffer delivery and a hardboiled Tip O'Neill face, but he used the word "supportive" twice in one conversation. The whole FBI talks like a social-work agency.

We were ready. The prosecutors had prepared us well. They'd come to see me in New Haven, Connecticut, several times and showed me FBI photographs of the crime scene: my office, a bathroom where I'd stopped briefly and pointlessly to wash out my eye, the staircase I'd walked down—everything drenched in blood. In a series of long conversations in the fall of 1997 they explained their strategy and kept us informed, and the preliminaries seemed to be on course. The date approached, and (with generous help from the FBI) we planned our trip. I dreaded it, naturally; the traveling itself, the courtroom scene, the press, the testimony. I got ready by working on a series of three paintings that gradually elbowed all my other work aside, pictures of David getting set to take on Goliath; a self-aggrandizing theme, but absorbing. When I wasn't working on the paintings, I carried them around with me, studied them for hours, stayed up nights reworking them. (A painting is a form of trapped energy, like a compressed spring or a rock at the top of a hill.)

The Defendant Speaks

So we sat in court chatting about the bathroom situation, waiting for the trial to start. Towards eight, my wife asked an FBI man when the defendant would arrive. "He's already here," the answer was, "over at the defense table." The judge walked in. No one told us to rise. The first voice we heard after the judge's was the defendant's. A cool, collected voice: He and his lawyers were having a serious disagreement about how to proceed, he said. "I'm sorry I can't rise to address you," he added, "but the marshal told me to remain seated."

Bull's-eye. He'd waited till the whole cast was assembled, and we were on the verge of starting, then tossed his wrench into the works with casual arrogance and perfect aim and, sure enough, the machinery clanked to a halt. The judge adjourned to chambers, taking along the defendant and the defense lawyers and a court reporter. When the trial reconvened later that afternoon, it was only to arrange a recess. Next morning we flew home to Connecticut.

A few weeks later the prosecution made a deal, and the trial was canceled. Kaczynski would plead guilty to the crimes that were charged in Sacramento, and his other crimes too, for which he might have been tried in other states—three murders in all, plus a bunch of attempted murders. Cost to the defendant (special deal, one time only): life in federal prison without parole. Yes he had, in the great American tradition, traded up; he *used* to live in an unimproved shack in the wilderness. And if you are an ascetic bent on winning fame by preaching against society and the state, you couldn't ask for a bullier pulpit than a federal jail cell.

The prosecutors tell me they did the best they could under the circumstances. I believe them. Nonetheless, they lost.

In retrospect I wasn't David; the prosecutors played that part. The Department of Justice is a powerful institution—but the community as a whole is more powerful, as it ought to be and has to be. Elite public opinion acts on the Justice Department, the jury, and the judge. The prosecutors believed that truth and justice demanded the death penalty. But elite public opinion tends to oppose the death penalty and seemed especially prone to oppose it in this case. The defendant himself was a proven first-rate manipulator, and our legal system is wide open to manipulation. Could the prosecution win anyway, succeed in getting the murderer condemned to death? Maybe. And if an appeals court decreed a second trial, could it win again? Maybe. But in the end (my impression is) there were too many maybes for comfort—and there was the worry in the back of everyone's mind that things could somehow go horribly wrong and the murderer could walk. Every big trial in modern America is a national humiliation waiting to happen. O.J. Simpson is merely the best-known example of what is today a regular garden-variety, Mister-Rogers'-Neighborhood American type—the murderer at large. The criminologist John DiIulio estimates that there are maybe half a million of them in our big cities.

The prosecutors struggled but lost. Not because the murderer is alive and not dead. They lost—we lost—because the community was called on to condemn terrorist murder in the strongest possible terms, unambiguously, definitively—and we blew it. It was important that the man be sentenced to death, and whether the execution were ever carried out would barely have mattered. (Had he been condemned to death, apologized, and repented, I might have been inclined myself to commute the sentence.) Failure to hold the trial was a defeat in itself. We hold trials to deal justly with the accused, but that's not all; a trial is a powerful public ceremony, too, and we no longer trust ourselves to pull it off. (Ceremonies of all sorts are beyond us, from trials to political conventions to weddings.) A plea bargain in a case like this is an abrogation of the public's responsibility to face facts and come to grips with the truth.

How we dispose of the criminal doesn't matter. What matters is our communal response to the crime. Evil is easy, good is hard, temptation is a given; therefore, a healthy society talks to itself—in laws and editorials, court judgments and theater productions, public lectures, political speeches, university courses. When a criminal commits an evil act, a healthy society denounces it as such. A sustained, unanimous hiss rises from the crowd—or at least is supposed to.

Such ritual denunciations strengthen our good inclinations and help us suppress our bad ones. We need to hear them, and hear good acts praised, too. We need to hear the crowd (hear *ourselves*) praising good and denouncing evil. Not commiserating and whining and preening, not promising to be non-judgmental and always to love one another just as we are (you wish) and showering each other with ersatz forgiveness like tinsel snow at a grade-school Christmas play—those are lollipop gestures, cheap and childish, sticky-sweet and without moral substance—but *praising good; denouncing evil*. Goodness is unnatural, and we need to cheer one another on.

But ever since the intelligentsia took over the cultural elite, moral leadership is hard to find. The crowd babbles and sulks, and no one can understand it. What to expect of a society that no longer roots for its own best instincts? No longer talks intelligently to itself? Moral chaos. A third of babies born out of wedlock; half a million murderers at large. Children learning about sex instead of morality. Power and money ranking higher than childrearing on our moral scale. A president who grows more popular the worse he behaves. A terrorist murderer who is rewarded instead of punished.

Rewarding a Killer for His Crimes

Which is exactly what happened to the murderer Theodore J. Kaczynski. Up at Harvard last term in Lit 129, "Reading the 18th Century Through 20th Century Eyes," the reading list included Pierre Augustin De Beaumarchais, Denis Diderot, Immanuel Kant, Jean-Jacques Rousseau, Michel Foucault, Milan Kundera, and "Unabomber," among other distinguished thinkers. (I'm grateful to Thomas Lipscomb for pointing this out to me.) The same thing could have happened nearly (though not *quite*) anywhere in modern academia. I'd bet money that Harvard is not the only college with this particular terrorist on its reading lists.

And so what? Bad men can be good writers. Norman Mailer once stabbed his wife, and I've written about him myself and praised his books.

Trouble is, Kaczynski made the Harvard reading list not despite his vicious crimes but because of them. Some thinkers (I don't deny) agree with his anti-technology ideas. But no serious person ever claimed that his thoughts were new, or that his manifesto was well argued or well written. Kaczynski made that Harvard reading list on the basis of our shattered hands and shattered eyes, permanent injury and permanent pain—ours, the lucky ones who survived. Three unlucky men died to make Kaczynski's name at Harvard. He attacked us with bombs for exactly this purpose: to get famous, win attention for his ideas. Harvard rewarded his hard work with the thing he wanted most.

Should we decorate Harvard for guts at least, pin a medal on its chest for courting public outrage in defense of depravity? Of course not. Harvard risked nothing. Harvard knew perfectly well that, by and large, its faculty, students, and moneyed supporters wouldn't give a damn. (There are a few honorable exceptions, which are precious to those of us with a personal stake in the thing.)

Paris, 1893: A terrorist bomb explodes in the Chamber of Deputies. No one is killed but forty-seven people are hurt. The anarchist intellectual Laurent Tailhade is asked to comment. He speaks prophetically for the 20th-century intelligentsia and for Harvard University circa 1998: *"Qu'importe les victimes si le geste est beau?"* What difference do the victims make if the gesture is beautiful?

A Moral Failure

When a terrorist murders a man, it is a meaningless act. There are evil men in every society, and they do evil things; that's all. It's up to the community to redeem the evil and collectively transcend it, by responding with dignity, assurance, and absolute clarity. But nowadays we disdain to do that, and we are haunted as a nation by unresolved evil—we dine at Macbeth's every night, and pretend not to see Banquo's ghost. I wrote a book in which, some people claimed, I blamed the intelligentsia for Kaczynski's crimes. Such an accusation would have been ludicrous, and I didn't make it. What I blamed on the intelligentsia was our morally bankrupt response—especially the press's response. We can't hold society accountable for failing to prevent every evil act. We can and must hold it responsible for failing to condemn every evil act.

Harvard's course makes no difference in itself. There's a lot worse going on in academia today. But it is a perfect crystallization of the credo we have learned to associate with intellectuals—not all of them, but too many: *"Si le geste est beau . . ."* Lit 129 speaks loudly in its own small way. My guess is that, two generations ago, a large majority of Americans would have condemned such a course as disgusting, and most intellectuals would have shrugged it off. And my guess is that, today, a bare majority of the public would still find it disgusting and a large majority of intellectuals would still shrug it off. Just a guess.

In police terms, which are important, our communal response to Kaczynski's crimes succeeded. We found the man and put him away. In moral terms, which are even more important, our response was a failure. Which leaves us today with a new responsibility: to respond to the response. Public life is a conversation forever, year to year, generation to generation. With the right communal response, we can redeem the prosecutors' bargain. The way to do it is by telling them, "You lost, no question—but we honor you for fighting." The community will either seal the defeat by shrugging it off or, by admitting that it *was* a defeat, and a painful one, turn it into a kind of victory: a reaffirmation that evil will always exist but we will never accept it; we will always fight it. For myself, I'm left with three painted Davids, one per prosecutor. You can't put everything in words; that's why we have paint too.

Keeping Promises

On that day I met her in the witness room, Susan Mosser was dignified and beautiful and dressed in black. She wouldn't have testified in Sacramento; the murder of her husband would have been tried separately in New Jersey. She had come to register support and see what happened. I'd written the Justice Department when it was pondering whether to seek the death penalty in this case; I pointed out that the Mossers' youngest child was 15 months old when her father was murdered, that no one remembers life at that age, and that the crime of erasing a father from his child's memory is the evilest crime I can imagine.

But when I met Mrs. Mosser I wasn't thinking about children; what came to mind for some reason was a promise I'd made my wife a long time ago, that someday I would buy her a house by the shore. Such houses don't come cheap, and I still haven't delivered; but someday I believe I will. When it's 3 A.M. and I can't sleep, I don't think, ever, about the evil coward who worked hard, burned the midnight oil, and made that Harvard reading list at last—an American success story; a dream come true. But I do wonder sometimes what promises Thomas Mosser made and will never keep. A famous passage in the Mishnah, tractate Sanhedrin, lays down that to murder a man is to destroy a whole world. We have come a long way since then. For sophisticates like us, destroying worlds is no big deal anymore.

DISCOVERING A SERIAL KILLER IN THE FAMILY

Richard Jerome and Fannie Weinstein

In the following selection, Richard Jerome and Fannie Weinstein relate the story of Julie Baumeister, who discovered that her husband Herb had led a secret life as a homosexual serial killer. Describing her life with Herb from when they met at Indiana University, Julie maintains that he was a devoted family man but reveals that he had a history of emotional problems. Julie depicts her shock when she discovered that while she and the children were away from home, Herb would cruise the gay bars of Indianapolis, pick up gay men, and later dispose of their bodies. Shortly after the police uncovered the remains of missing gay men at the Baumeisters' farm, the authors report, Herb was found dead from a self-inflicted gunshot wound. In 1998, Indiana investigators closed the case, concluding that Herb Baumeister had indeed been a serial killer, having murdered at least sixteen men. At the time this article was written, Richard Jerome wrote for *People Weekly*. Fannie Weinstein is a true-crime writer and author of the book *Where the Bodies Are Buried*, an account of the life and crimes of Herb Baumeister.

Julie Baumeister was troubled that day in the fall of 1994 when Erich, her 13-year-old, brought home a human skull. He'd found it in the woods of Fox Hollow Farm, the family's $1 million estate in the Indianapolis suburb of Westfield. Julie was even more unsettled when Erich led her to the site of his ghoulish discovery. There, among the fallen leaves, lay a cluster of bones.

That night, Herb Baumeister, Julie's husband of 23 years, dispelled her anxiety: The bones, he said, were from a medical school skeleton once owned by his late father, an anesthesiologist.

Uncovering a Secret Life

What they were doing in the backyard Herb didn't say; days later Julie noticed they had vanished, carried off by an animal, she assumed. She

Reprinted from Richard Jerome and Fannie Weinstein, "While Julie Was Away: Family Man Herb Baumeister Led a Secret Life. Was He Indiana's Worst Serial Murderer?" *People Weekly*, December 23, 1996, by permission of *People Weekly*. Copyright ©1996 Time Inc.

quickly forgot the episode. "It wasn't like I was sitting at home with nothing else to think about," she says.

In fact there was much Julie Baumeister, now 48, didn't know about Herb. Every summer, Julie usually left town for part of each month, taking Erich, now 15, and daughters Marne, 17, and Emily, 12, to stay at a lakeside condo 100 miles to the north, owned by Herb's mother, Elizabeth. Herb stayed home during the workweek. By day he would mind the couple's business, a chain of local thrift stores called Sav-A-Lot. By night, Julie later learned, he would cruise the gay bars of Indianapolis.

Herb's other secrets, police believe, were chilling and deadly. In June 1996, while he was visiting the condo, officers found hundreds of bones at Fox Hollow Farm, adding up to the remains of seven people. Four have been identified: Roger Alan Goodlet, 33, Steven Hale, 26, and Richard Hamilton, 20, all of Indianapolis, and Manuel Resendez, 31, of Lafayette, Ind. All frequented the same bars that Baumeister did—and all went missing on days when his wife and kids were away. For now, says Sgt. Ken Whisman of the Hamilton County (Ind.) sheriff's department, Baumeister is merely a prime suspect "in the disappearance" of the four identified men, who won't be ruled homicide victims until forensic specialists determine a cause of death. But officials believe that when the bodies are vetted (six Indianapolis men who fit the profile of the victims are missing), Herb Baumeister may emerge as the most prolific serial killer in Indiana history.

If so, he is beyond earthly justice. The day after police began searching his property, the 49-year-old Baumeister disappeared. He had been missing for eight days when campers discovered his body July 3, 1996, lying beside his car in Ontario's Pinery Provincial Park, shot through the forehead with a .357 Magnum. He left behind a rambling, three-page suicide note, apologizing for his family's finan-cial woes (the business was nearly bankrupt) but not mentioning the hideous crimes he is now thought to have committed. His widow was stunned. True, she and Herb had grown apart and were contemplat-ing divorce. But Julie had blamed the tensions on their precarious finances. "The police came to me and said, 'We are investigating your husband in relation to homosexual homicide,'" Julie says, recalling her first contact with detectives. "I remember saying to them, 'Can you tell me what homosexual homicide is?'"

Examining the Past

For Julie Baumeister the shock was all the more jarring because of the close-knit, even cloistered, family life she and Herb had tried to build at Fox Hollow Farm. The Baumeisters, who had few friends, showered their attention on their children. Herb, Julie recalls, was a dedicated parent, involved in all aspects of their children's upbringing, whether it was choosing their preschool, buying their Christmas toys or making their peanut-butter-and-jelly sandwiches.

Perhaps he was trying to re-create what had seemed to be his own happy childhood. Julie says Herb grew up in a Beaver Cleaver kind of home in Indianapolis, the eldest child of Herbert and Elizabeth Baumeister. He entered Indiana University in 1965 but left after one semester. For a time he worked as a copy boy for the *Indianapolis Star.* Garry Donna, then an ad representative at the paper, recalls him as eager to please but eccentric. For one thing, he and a friend co-owned a secondhand hearse. "I remember [friends] saying, 'What's the deal with this guy?'" Donna says. "I just said, 'Well, Herb's just Herb.'"

Herb returned to IU in the fall of 1967 and met Julie, also a student there. "He was nice, fun to be with and good-looking," she recalls. "We both liked cars, and we were both Young Republicans." They married in 1971 and soon bought a house in Indianapolis. Herb began clerking at the State Bureau of Motor Vehicles, where he would work his way up to supervisor. Julie taught high school English. "We did everything together," she says. "He would push the mower, and I would trim the bushes." But in the early '70s Herb became so depressed that his physician father had him committed for over a month to a psychiatric hospital. Julie did not dispute the decision. He was "hurting and needed help," she says now. In fact, ex-colleagues at the motor vehicle agency say he was a perfectionist given to sudden, unprovoked rages.

Trying to Hold on to a Dream

After Herb left his job in 1985, he worked at a local thrift store. The experience inspired him to pursue what Julie calls their "joint vision." In 1989, after borrowing $350,000 in seed money from Herb's mother, they opened the first of three Sav-A-Lots, where they sold used clothing, giving some $50,000 of their profits annually to a charity benefiting neglected children. Attorney John Egloff, who represented their business, says both partners were intelligent and "socially conscious," though Herb was domineering. "Julie deferred to Herb," he says, "but wasn't very happy about it." Oddly, Sav-A-Lot employees note, Baumeister would often disappear during the workday, sometimes for hours at a time.

After initial success, the Baumeisters' business began to fail—as did their marriage. As Julie tells it, the long hours they put in at the stores, the pressures of parenting and, later, the financial strain, led to a kind of burnout. Herb moved out in February 1991 and filed for divorce. The couple soon reconciled, though, and that November, in spite of their business problems, bought Fox Hollow Farm. Purchased with a small down payment, the estate boasted a four-bedroom house and an indoor pool. Julie says they saw it as a "utopia" where their children "could Rollerblade without having to worry about cars coming around the corner."

Though she didn't know it, by then Herb was also involved—perhaps uneasily—in the gay nightlife scene. "Some people, when they come into a gay bar, act like they're afraid of being here," says Jim Brown, owner of the upscale Metropolitan Restaurant and Nightclub, which caters to gay professionals. "He didn't seem like he was comfortable."

Looking for a Killer

It was in May 1993 that gay men began disappearing in the area—10 would vanish in a little over two years. Police scoured gay Indianapolis, interviewing bar-goers and posting flyers. But leads were scarce. Then, in the fall of 1994, a man told them of a strange tryst he had had that summer with someone named Brian: They had gone to Brian's sprawling estate and, at Brian's behest, had engaged in autoerotic asphyxia, a sexual practice involving suffocation, often to the brink of death. The informant remained shaken by the encounter. In the fall of 1995, he had spotted Brian again and, aware of the rash of disappearances, had taken down his license-plate number. It turned out to be the missing link: Brian was Herb Baumeister.

In November 1995, detectives showed up at Fox Hollow Farm asking to search the estate. When Herb refused, police, lacking sufficient evidence for a warrant, went to work on Julie. Approaching her at a Sav-A-Lot, they told her about Herb's cruising—and that he was a suspect in the disappearances. "I was angry," Julie says. "I said, 'You're wrong. That can't be true.'" When she confronted Herb with the charges, he dismissed them; Julie pressed no further.

With nothing to go on but one man's brief and bizarre encounter, police made little headway for five months. When they approached Julie a second time, she rebuffed them again. Still, her apparent loyalty to Herb belied their escalating marital problems—by June 1996, the couple were no longer speaking. Moreover, Julie, now haunted by the skull Erich had found, had become increasingly suspicious. "What if the police are right and I'm wrong?" she recalls thinking. On June 24, 1996, when Herb was away, she finally allowed police to inspect the property. Remembering the two-week search that followed, she says she clung to her children as if "huddling all my puppies together." Herb's eight-day disappearance before his suicide added to the agony. "I kept saying, 'Where is he?'" Julie recalls. "But no one knew."

The months since Herb's death have been particularly wrenching for Marne, Erich and Emily, who, Julie says, idolized a father now portrayed by police and local media as a monster. Still, she insists, "nothing can take away the love these kids had for their dad." Late in the summer of 1996, she and the children moved from Fox Hollow Farm back to the house in Indianapolis where she had begun her life with Herb nearly 25 years ago. "Our biggest question now is how he could have loved us and done this," she says of Herb's alleged atrocities. "Happiness as we knew it is never going to return."

CHAPTER 5

PUBLIC REACTIONS TO SERIAL KILLERS

PUBLIC REACTIONS TO SERIAL MURDER: AN OVERVIEW

Joseph C. Fisher

Although serial murder is actually an infrequent occurrence, the public fear of serial killers is extremely high. Joseph C. Fisher explains that this intense fear has its roots in the random and inexplicable nature of serial killers' crimes. Fisher examines the progression of public reactions that occur when a serial killer is loose in the community. When a pattern of serial murder is first discovered, he writes, the public looks for rational explanations and believes that the experts will soon solve the crimes. However, if these experts are unable to resolve the case, the public begins to believe that a supernatural force is at work and often appeal to paranormal assistance such as psychics. If these methods fail, the public comes to believe that the serial killer may have superhuman characteristics that explain why he can continue to evade detection. Furthermore, the author maintains, these reactions are heightened by a media that is eager to satisfy the public's desire for news of the crimes. Fisher is a sociologist and the president of the research firm InterData. He has written several books and articles on advertising and criminology, including *Killer Among Us: Public Reactions to Serial Murder*, from which the following selection is taken.

Homicide is a fixture in contemporary American life. Every year more than 20,000 individuals die at the hands of their fellow citizens, and of these, two-thirds will be killed by a family member or someone they know. Yet, over time the public has become inured to this staggering figure. So many violent deaths provoke no outrage or embarrassment. They cause no outward expressions of fear, and little is done to modify the conduct of everyday life in response.

By comparison, serial murder is a truly rare phenomenon. Although estimates vary widely, perhaps only 10 serial murderers are active in the United States every year, and they may account for just 100 murders annually, or less than 1 percent of the total homicide count. A person in the United States is as likely to be struck and killed by lightning as to die at the hands of a serial killer. Whether by a serial murderer or an act of God, the odds of death for the average American are below one in two million.

Fascination and Fear

Despite its scarcity, serial murder receives inordinate attention in the media, having been the subject of innumerable movies, books, television plots, and news reports. Serial murder fascinates. It is so premeditated, methodical, vicious, and uncommon that we cannot escape its allure, its capacity to astonish and horrify, its power to instill fear. But beyond fascination, serial murder touches a more basic, primal level. It intrudes on the most protected and inviolable areas of experience and beliefs, expectations about life that are so fundamental they seem to have been genetically imprinted from birth. As such, serial murder has the ability to instill fear far in excess of the true risk it represents.

Serial murder strikes foremost at expectations that one is safe and free from personal harm. Victims selected by chance vividly illustrate an inherent vulnerability to personal violence. Serial murder conjures up images not only of painful destruction but, what is worse, also of death at the hands of a stranger with whom one could not expect to reason and from whom one could expect no mercy. In this regard, reactions to serial murder are similar to public perceptions of crime generally. Without question, the crimes that people fear most, such as murder and rape, happen the least often. Moreover, death and injury from crime are secondary to the fact that it is associated with strangers, mysterious and threatening individuals whose motives are unknown and hence whose attacks are unpredictable and indiscriminate. Thus, reactions to serial murder emanate from the same sources as fear of other crimes—personal vulnerability, defenselessness, risk of death and injury, and most of all, fear and mistrust of strangers.

While reactions to serial murder and other forms of personal violence have much in common, serial murder is indeed unique. It has the capacity to activate fears and keep them alive like no other crime can. A single homicide, though tragic, has an element of finality to it. The deed is done, the killer has been caught, and the threat is over. The event is quick and isolated, and the risk to others does not extend beyond the victim. With serial murder, the risk is wider, the threat continues, and fear is ubiquitous and increases with time.

A Fear of the Unknown

The number of deaths and the length of time involved act as accelerators to the buildup of fear. Elapsed time permits the body count to grow, emphasizes the futility of police efforts, and generally contributes to feelings of personal helplessness and collective risk. The sense of vulnerability increases with each new body discovered, while anticipation of the next murder becomes as much a source of dread as the discovery itself. As a result, public passions intensify the longer a killer is free, causing fear to grow exponentially. . . .

At the core of the fear caused by serial murder is the incomprehensibility of what is happening. The killer's motivations and actions are beyond the experience of daily life and impossible to understand. In this way, serial murder differs fundamentally from the everyday violence that is tolerated with such sangfroid; as one specialist on serial murder noted:

> Homicidal crimes of passion, though reprehensible, can at least be understood and dealt with rationally. Thus, given the cultural context of this society, most adults can "understand" that volatile interpersonal relations sometimes end in a homicidal act. Even in felony homicides and "classical" murder, it is possible in a grim sort of fashion to make sense of the homicide in terms of patterns of relations, between the killer and victim. But this cannot be said of serial killings, where an innocent person is slain, sometimes after inhuman torture and degradation by a stranger.

The killer's motives are unknown, and the unknown is feared most of all.

Often serial murders can display a considerable degree of planning and thoughtful execution. It is especially difficult to appreciate how such irrational behavior can be committed so rationally. The fact that the killer is within the community only compounds the sense of unreality. How is it possible that a killer can function sanely, rationally, and normally on most occasions but viciously attack on other occasions? . . .

The Power of Reason

The initial response to the killer among us is to find refuge in the rational. An attempt is made to find reasons for events that lie within the domain of normal behavior. Consequently, even suspiciously abnormal occurrences are interpreted as representing the most likely, ordinary, and commonplace eventualities. When teenagers disappeared in the Richard Valenti case, [which involved the kidnap and murder of several young women in Folly Beach, South Carolina, in 1973 and 1974], the first interpretation given was the most obvious: they ran away. This explanation was given rather than the highly unlikely one: they came to lethal harm.

In the early phases of an investigation, especially before bodies are discovered, explaining behavior in everyday terms is equivalent to denying that a crime has occurred. As such, it constitutes a collective defense mechanism against the awful potential of what might have happened. It serves a similar function for authorities, allowing them at once to deny the crime by denying the victims and hence providing a basis for inaction. At some point, however, bodies are discovered, and it is clear that the logic of everyday experience has been suspended. What one has come to know and expect no longer provides reference points to navigate in the unknown.

For the public the shared features of the murders and victims, the common denominators, provide the basis for a rational understanding of the crimes. Even inherently irrational actions are made comprehensible if they have an internally consistent order or pattern. The paradox of serial murder is that the characteristic that makes it most beyond our capacity to understand, repetition, at the same time provides the key to the public's ability to apprehend it. Thus, it is the repeated killing that cannot be grasped. Yet if the murders are connected in some fashion, they have a logic which, however abnormal, the public can discern and use to explain the crimes.

From the point of view of investigators, rationality translates into a reliance on logical, scientific means to catch the killer. When their own efforts fall short, police appeal to experts whose specialized knowledge and proprietary methods of discovery are expected to solve the case. All manner of specialists are consulted—psychiatrists, psychologists, criminologists, forensic pathologists, hypnotists, handwriting analysts, lie detector specialists, computer scientists, to name a few. There is an implicit respect for the authority of learned men and faith that they will outsmart the killer. The experts' special knowledge is expected to illuminate what appears on the surface to be irrational action and to decode the encrypted motives in the evidence left by the killer. . . .

Ultimately, experts, academic research, and scientific methods are almost never instrumental in apprehending a serial killer, or as one criminologist specializing in the study of serial murder noted, "A review of serial murders occurring over the last few years reveals that most serial murders are caught by chance or coincidence and not by ratiocination or scientific investigation." As time passes without a successful resolution to the case, faith in rational processes, experts, and the scientific method diminish. In its place the police and public will turn to supernatural explanations for the crimes and superhuman methods of finding the killer.

Supernatural Appeals

Coexisting in the public's imagination with rational explanations of serial murder are a set of interconnected beliefs whose foundation is the assumed role of supernatural forces in daily occurrences. From the standpoint of collective reactions to serial murder, belief in the supernatural is expressed in three ways: (1) that the killer's behavior is caused by otherworldly, especially demonic or satanic, forces, (2) that the killer possesses superhuman powers, and (3) that the case will be solved by miraculous means. Hence, events are thought to be determined by extraordinary forces that are inherently mysterious, unknowable, or explainable only by faith.

Concepts such as evil, monsters, and demonic possession are ancient and culturally universal, forming something of an archetypical imprint on the collective psyche. As one expert on serial murder pointed out, "In the past, explanations for mass and serial murders were often derived from demonology or the belief that events were controlled by external forces or spirits. The notion that life on earth was primarily controlled by forces of good and evil has its origins in the belief in the existences of gods and devils." While science has illuminated many of the unknowns that give rise to superstitions and phantasmagoric images, belief in supernatural causation remains widespread. Indeed, responses to serial killers demonstrate how thin the veneer of rationality is and how quickly people revert to atavistic ways of thinking.

Inhuman Behavior

The extreme inhuman actions of the killer often reinforce and substantiate belief in the supernatural. Excessively cruel torture or brutal slayings, what experts call "overkill," completely divorce serial murder from normal behavior and even from routine homicide. The killer clearly gains something more from the process than just the end result, the death of the victim. Concentration on the process of murdering, the fact that it is a source of enjoyment, entertainment, and satisfaction for the killer, is taken as proof of malevolence.

Other aspects of the murders lend further credence to the belief that serial killers are immanently evil. Killers who dismember corpses, cannibalize, drink blood, or have sex with the dead evoke antediluvian images of vampires and werewolves. Even the popular lexicon used to describe the killers as fiends, ghouls, and monsters and the names given to describe them such as Richard Chase "The Vampire Killer," Albert Fish "The Cannibalistic Killer," or Richard Ramirez "The Night Stalker" recall ancient myths and fears. The fact that many murders are committed in a ritualistic fashion, repeated over and over, and that some serial killers have dabbled in the occult, been involved in covens or satanistic cults, or leave satanic symbols at the crime site provide the final proof of supernatural influence, if any more were needed.

Added to the pantheistic notions of demons, witches, and vampires is the good-evil duality embedded in religious teachings. If God is the agent of creation and can perform miracles, then a devil destroyer exists who is equally powerful. And if divine presence can take human-saintly form, the devil must have disciples who are evil incarnate. The undercurrent of the supernatural, and particularly religious beliefs, in responses to serial murder also explains some seemingly anomalous behavior after the killer is caught. A presumption exists that no person, no matter how evil, is beyond redemption. Killers and the public alike can hold this view. As a consequence, it is not uncommon for convicted killers to embrace religion and repent their past sins, and they can do so with an obsessive fervor that once characterized their murders. Also not uncommon are attempts to convert or save the convicted killer.

Supernatural Intervention

Supernatural causes imply supernatural remedies and spiritual cures. At times the public may appeal for divine intervention and deliverance from the crime spree. Or they may see the hand of Providence in the fortuitous circumstances that lead to a killer's arrest. As an example, Tracy Edwards, who narrowly escaped death at the hand of Jeffrey Dahmer and subsequently led police to the killer's apartment, saw himself as an agent of God's will. He thought his life had a larger meaning as a result; in his own words, "God sent me there to take care of the situation."

When the murders are committed in a single place, the site itself can assume an evil aura, forever tainted by what took place there. As in the case of John Wayne Gacy whose house was leveled and now is a vacant lot, the building may be razed; its eradication is viewed as a necessary step in the healing process. In Milwaukee, families of the victims initially performed an exorcism outside Jeffrey Dahmer's apartment to rid the building of evil spirits. Eventually, a community group bought the entire apartment complex for the sole purpose of destroying it.

Perhaps the most common appeal for supernatural assistance during a serial murder investigation involves the introduction and use of psychics. In virtually every serial murder case that goes unsolved for any length of time, at least one psychic will become a key player in the drama. Some well-known psychics such as Gerard Croiset, Jr., who was involved in the Valenti case, are consulted regularly. More high-profile psychics such as Peter Hurkos even make something of a part-time career out of assisting serial murder investigations.

The use of psychics, like other supernatural elements in the public's response to serial murderers, has deep historic and cultural roots. Myths and literature are filled with stories of heroes who consult oracles, seers, and soothsayers for a vision of the future and insight into how to achieve specific goals. Interestingly, predictions are often given in obscure and cryptic form such that a number of interpretations could be supported. Common among these legends is an appeal to a person or persons whose clairvoyance enables them to foresee the future and aid men who are not so gifted.

Psychics used in serial murder cases follow this paradigm precisely. They are assumed to have special powers of clairvoyance that are innate or gained by an accident of fate. Furthermore, while the insight psychics provide into past events can be stunningly accurate, descriptions of the likely killer are often couched in terms of characteristics that could apply to many individuals. The net result is enough valid information for the police and public to marvel at the psychic's power and maintain their faith in the supernatural but not enough concrete information to solve the case. Unfortunately, psychic powers are no better than scientific means of profiling in finding the killer.

Serial Killers with Superhuman Powers

If the police cannot catch the killer with their normal investigative methods and the superhuman powers of psychics are also ineffective, in the public's mind there must be another reason why the killer can continue to escape. The only remaining explanation is the killer himself. It must be something the killer does or some ability he possesses that enables him to murder at will. It is this logic train, arising after all rational and supernatural methods of investigation have failed, that begins the process of transference. The defining feature of this stage of public reaction is reached, therefore, when the qualities of omniscience and omnipotence that were once reserved for those pursuing the murder are gradually ascribed to the killer. . . .

Transference is expressed in a variety of ways. The killer can be seen as exceptionally intelligent, carefully planning the next crime. The fact that many serial killers, in fact, do have above-average intelligence and do dwell on and perfect their modus operandi lends credence to this belief. The killer might also be described as having special physical abilities; the hands of a watchmaker and the ability to scale the sides of buildings were skills attributed to the Boston Strangler. And of course, supernatural powers once thought vested in psychics are ultimately attributed to the killer; they can anticipate every move the police make, or they can spellbind their victims, ensuring they will be trusting and compliant before their death. The cumulative effect of transference results in the killer taking on larger than life dimensions in the public mind.

Much of the official and community response to the serial killer is driven by his seemingly uncanny ability to evade the police. One aspect of the evasion is the killer's ability to abscond with a victim, sometimes in broad daylight and in public, without causing a commotion or tipping anyone off to what lies ahead. More than any other factor, the ability of serial killers to get victims to cooperate in their own capture gives rise to the belief in their superhuman powers. And yet, although appeals to the supernatural and transference form the basis for a large portion of the public reaction to serial murder, the reality is much more mundane. Far from being omnipotent, serial murderers are uncommonly ordinary, and their ability to evade the police is more a function of their anonymity and external social forces than their supernatural powers.

In every serial murder case then, a dynamic tension develops between the rational and supernatural. Both investigators and the public vacillate between the two. When dealing with events rationally, the police will appeal to experts to help solve the crimes, while the public will seek the inner logic of common denominators that connect the murders or the victims. When rational explanations and solutions are abandoned in favor of the supernatural, the killer is seen as immanently evil, a slave to demonic forces, while resolution of the terror is sought by appealing to those with otherworldly power. If the murderer remains at large long enough, the belief in superhuman power is transferred from those seeking to catch the killer to the killer himself. The killer assumes an aura of omniscience in the public consciousness and is thought to possess superhuman powers that help him avoid capture. . . .

Social Impact

The social consequences of a killer at large within the community can be seen then as a three part process. First, the causative factor, chronic fear, originates in the constant threat posed by the killer and the failure of the investigation to remove the threat, the reasons for which are found in the composition of human consciousness and collective behavior. Second, operating according to their own economic demands, the media constantly remind the public of the threat, intensify popular sentiments, and may inadvertently add to the gratification the killer receives from the crimes. Third, the end result is a breakdown in collective solidarity and social order due to defensive changes in patterns of behavior by numberless individuals, disintegration of social structure, and self-defeating conflict along political, ethnic, economic, and lifestyle lines.

Ordinary Obscurity

One of the abiding mysteries of serial murder investigations is why it is so difficult to apprehend the killer. Despite the efforts of legions of police, special task forces, the services of experts, and the intervention of individuals with supernatural powers, killers routinely escape detection. If the killer is ever captured, it is usually not quickly and not often as a result of official activities.

It is even more puzzling that in many cases, the killer is a suspect and frequently one of the earliest to be picked up and questioned by investigators. For any one of a myriad of reasons, different for each case, the killer is released by the police and inadvertently allowed to continue killing. Perhaps the most well-known example occurred when police found a naked Asian youth, handcuffed and bleeding, staggering in the street. Unsuspecting, they turned him over to a man they thought was his homosexual lover, Jeffrey Dahmer, who killed him within in hours. . . .

Even when police are proactively trying to find a criminal, the barriers to an arrest are daunting. The problem is not a paucity of good leads. Quite the contrary, there are too many, and every bit of investigative work just adds to the total. In the typical serial murder investigation the police are inundated with leads, tips, evidence, and good suspects. The logistical difficulty in managing so much information can create insuperable problems. For example, in the Yorkshire Ripper investigation "the paper records at one point weighed 24 tons, requiring a move within the building in which they were housed because of concerns over the building's structural integrity."

The police strategy used to deal with this ocean of information and sea of suspects is both natural and effective. They proceed by a process of exclusion rather than inclusion. As a consequence, the police attempt to find reasons to eliminate a person as a suspect rather than to continue to keep that person under suspicion. The goal is to whittle down the list of suspects, and to this end reasons are found to rule them out, not in. So in the end, one contrary piece of evidence can invalidate and supersede all indications of guilt.

Even when the killer comes face-to-face with authorities, sometimes with bodies in tow, the killer is allowed to escape. Police, like all humans, tend to explain events in terms of experiences that they encounter daily. When ruling out suspects, then, they are most apt to find a normal, everyday reason for suspicious behavior, and hence they ignore what may seem obvious in retrospect. It was more natural to think Jeffrey Dahmer was a homosexual having a domestic quarrel with his lover than it was to suspect him of being a serial killer and sometime cannibal.

The killer, in turn, does nothing to make investigators wary or suspicious. Unencumbered by the guilt and remorse most murderers feel, they fall back on a disarmingly genial manner and easily talk their way out of trouble. Hidden by a false mask of sanity, then, their behavior seems to be too normal to be that of a person capable of atrocities.

Finding a serial killer is, on balance, then an extraordinarily difficult endeavor. The obstacles to apprehension are encountered at every turn—in the structure of the political system, in the competition between police forces, in the accumulation and management of mountains of investigative data, in the psychology of the investigators, and in the behavior of the killers. It is not surprising that a man like John Wayne Gacy can stay in place and kill for years. With all the advantages on their side, the truly remarkable fact is not that killers evade arrest so easily but that they are ever apprehended at all.

Any channel of information that makes the public aware of the murders or sustains interest in them will increase public response. At times, the public's insatiable desire for news, the media's commercial interests in providing it, and the killer's need to publicize his invincibility can create a synergistic situation that spirals out of control. Even in less extreme cases, the media can play an enabling and perpetuating role in community reaction.

Of course, the public is not an innocent bystander in the process. Just the opposite: people have a limitless desire, even need, for information, and the more outrageous and abhorrent the crimes, the greater the public fascination. Something tantamount to a self-fueling engine of public opinion is created. Fear, uncertainty, and morbid curiosity lead to a demand for more news, delivery of which generates a higher level of anxiety and interest. The intensity of public feeling is ratcheted ever upward.

Competition between news agencies only exacerbates the potentiating impact of the media. Simply having multiple sources provide the same information increases the amount of exposure given the crimes, and therefore increases the likelihood that a person will learn about or be reminded of the murders. In addition, professional and financial rewards accrue to the reporters and services that can provide fresh and ever more detailed information. Not surprisingly, the more lurid the details provided, the greater the public interest and acclaim for investigative reporting.

Everyone it seems who is remotely involved with the murders becomes a celebrity, and reporters are no less immune to publicity's siren-song than others. Anne Schwartz, the *Milwaukee Journal* reporter who broke the Dahmer story, provides a vivid description of what it was like to be a reporter covering the case.

> As the news spread, the paper received calls from around the country. We found our stories all over the world, and they ran in the *Los Angeles Times*, the *New York Times*, and the *International Herald Tribune*. We saw our bylines in French, Spanish and German. Reporters from out-of-town papers called the newsroom and spoke to whoever picked up the phone, as if he or she were an expert on the case. If you worked for the *Journal* you must know something about Jeffrey Dahmer.

> Who wants to do "Larry King"? a secretary yelled out. Reporters lunged for their phones. We got calls from *People* magazine, a producer from "Geraldo," a Canadian radio talk show, and a publishing company looking for someone to write a book in a month.

> We were celebrities. We were dizzy with it.

Having access to information about the case, or for that matter proximity to information, became a saleable commodity. Reporters became the story, and the media became the news.

Just the process of reporting the news can shape and change it. Witnesses to the Dahmer tragedy continually modified and embellished their stories under the glare of media attention. Tracy Edwards, whose escape led directly to Dahmer's arrest, became an instant celebrity and the darling of the talk show circuit. On the night of Dahmer's capture, Edwards was a humble near-victim who was thankful for police support. On the talk shows he became a self-styled Houdini who brought Dahmer to justice. Predictably, he eventually sued the police for their alleged lack of assistance on the fateful night.

The media have even been implicated in a more insidious form of influence, encouraging others to commit murder. Evidence for this presumed effect are the frequent occurrence of copy-cat murders and the hysteria surrounding product-tampering cases. Indeed, during the Boston panic, police were convinced that several murders were disguised to appear as if they had been committed by the Strangler, while in Milwaukee, one man was heard to say he was "going to do a Dahmer thing" just before he bit off his lover's lip during a violent argument.

Media Relationships with Serial Killers

The killer, equally, can be caught up in the media vortex and influenced by it. But unlike reporters and witnesses who are passive observers of events, the killer can determine them. In fact, the psychology of some serial killers is such that media attention is inextricably bound up with their pathology. For them media attention becomes a means through which they can extract great psychic gratification from the murders. News stories are not only watched carefully, savored, and even kept as souvenirs, but in some cases the press is manipulated, becoming at times almost a public relations agent for the murderer.

The apotheosis of media involvement comes when the media become directly involved with the killer. The killer leaves notes at the scene and eventually begins to communicate directly with prominent media figures. Editorial writers address their columns to the killer, speculate on his motives, and write impassioned pleas for the killer to surrender to them personally. A self-serving reciprocity is established between the killer's need for attention and the media's need for a story. In the interest of both the killer and the press, public emotions are whipped into a frenzy.

In summary then, the media have a multidimensional impact on a serial murder case. Media reports make the population aware of the murders and help maintain their preoccupation with the killings. Those involved with the case and even those who report it become instant celebrities in constant demand by a news-hungry public. Notoriety, in turn, influences the actions and interpretations of those involved in the case so that in the end media attention can shape and potentially make news. For a particular type of serial killer, news reports can be a source of extended gratification and can help propel the murderer to further killings. For those killers who have a special perspicacity into the workings and impact of the media, it can be a means to dominate and control the popular imagination.

Fear experienced on a personal level is manifest in individual actions. Typically, people act in accordance with their expectations, even if the expectations do not accurately reflect reality. When presented with a real or perceived threat, personal behavior is modified accordingly. Taken on a collective basis, changes in countless numbers of social contacts and interactions, no matter how brief or seemingly inconsequential, have enormous impact on social cohesion and grave consequences for community solidarity. . . .

Not only does the murderer force everyone to be vigilant when dealing with others, but also a level of suspicion is created that destroys social bonds. . . . Suspicion, in turn, breeds isolation. All forms of social contact are avoided, including those with neighbors, friends, and family. People restrict their movements, go out less often, and are unwilling to venture into areas that are unfamiliar or places where strangers may be encountered. In the end, social solidarity is as much a causality of the serial killer as the unfortunate victims.

With the breakdown in social cohesion comes a breakdown in social control and, most importantly, in the informal mechanisms of crime prevention, which, as one criminologist points out, are "probably more effective in preventing crime than formal methods of social control such as the police." Fear of crime restricts contact and social interaction, one of the primary deterrents of crime. One of the deleterious aspects of fear of crime is that it feeds on itself. In some respects, the serial murderer inadvertently helps himself by engendering mass fear in the populace.

Ultimately, the feeling of suspicion generalizes to social institutions. Faith in public officials and law enforcement agencies diminishes rapidly and finally evaporates entirely. The outcry is particularly pronounced after the killer is captured, often by chance alone, and it is learned that numerous opportunities were missed to stop the killings earlier.

Fear of the serial killer also magnifies the divisions that exist within the community. Since the killer is viewed as an outsider and a stranger, all those who are different are categorized as a threat. Intolerance, bigotry, and scapegoating increase, as does the use of racial and ethnic stereotypes. A common byproduct of a serial murderer at large is an upswing in anti-Semitism, racial conflict, and gay bashing.

Identifying the offender with another social group contains the threat. It allows people to distance themselves from personal risk by simply avoiding contact with the outsiders. In so doing, a sense of psychological comfort is produced that enables people to continue to work and function in the regions in which they feel secure. Not coincidentally, it enables them to react more strongly, express outrage more openly, and demand retribution more vehemently than would be possible if the killer were viewed as a member of their own social group.

A reciprocal process can occur among minority groups. They may react defensively to the anger directed at them from the wider community. More often, the killer selects victims from their ranks. This fact at once gives foundation to the majority belief that the killer is a member of the group. The minority group is doubly maligned, first to be the focal point of community rage while at the same time being the most at risk. In response, the minority group may question how willing and able the community is to protect them. The police and city officials, as representatives of the majority population, are most apt to take the brunt of minority reaction.

The net result of the cycle of mutual distrust is a reinforcement of traditional boundaries and stereotypes. Old wounds are open, and long-simmering disputes and affronts come to the surface. The murders polarize the community along social, ethnic, and lifestyle lines and exacerbate extant political tensions. The resultant social damage long outlives the killer's murderous career.

On a community level, the killer among us isolates individuals and causes them to question those in authority. These symptoms of community dissolution take on a more active, virulent form when emotional release is directed at minority segments of the society. The killer may be seen as being part of a particular social group, the group may be blamed for allowing the killer to go undetected, or they may be just a convenient scapegoat for the fear and guilt that are more generally felt. For any of a number of reasons then, specific social groups may become the outlet for the tension of the general population.

IMAGES OF THE SERIAL KILLER IN POPULAR CULTURE

Philip Jenkins

Philip Jenkins is a professor of history and religious studies at Pennsylvania State University in University Park. He is also the author of Using Murder: The Social Construction of Serial Homicide, *from which the following selection is taken. Jenkins traces the changes in the way serial killers have been portrayed in popular culture from the 1950s to the present. In the 1950s and 1960s, films and books portrayed serial killers as psychologically disturbed individuals who were influenced by their upbringing and environment, Jenkins explains. This image changed beginning in the 1970s, the author writes, when serial killers began to be portrayed in popular culture as inhuman monsters. Jenkins argues that the manner in which serial killers are portrayed in popular culture influences the way the public reacts to actual serial killers. In particular, he maintains, the current trend of presenting serial killers as subhuman has created an increase in public fear of the threat of serial murder and widespread approval of federal law enforcement involvement in serial homicide cases.*

There is abundant evidence that serial killers and similar figures have long played a significant role in popular culture. The idea of using a serial killer as a fictional villain is by no means a recent innovation, but the volume of such depictions has expanded enormously over the last two decades. Publishers and filmmakers clearly believe that there is a vast market for stories on this theme, and the continuing success of these works suggests that their perceptions are quite correct. The scale of this interest is unprecedented, and so perhaps is the complexity of the images presented.

Tracing Images of the Serial Killer

This selection will trace the development of these cultural images, and especially the steady shift away from the portrayal of multiple killers as creatures of individual psychopathology ("psychos"), and toward more moralistic and even supernatural interpretations of ever more terrifying and dehumanized monsters. This transition occurred in both cinema and the novel, and it profoundly influenced media coverage of the topic. The growing tendency to view serial killers as exemplifying supernatural evil reflected trends in contemporary debate and investigation.

It is difficult to know whether the bureaucratic law enforcement attitudes toward serial murder preceded or followed changes in popular culture, and whether the specific image of the "monster" developed in the media before it was popularized by police agencies. It has been noted that in coverage of serial murder, the boundaries between fiction and real life were often blurred to the point of nonexistence. However, both true-crime and fictional depictions rendered great service to the Justice Department by promoting its orthodoxy in the interpretation of the offense. . . .

Psycho and Afterwards: 1960–1978

During the 1950s, Robert Bloch developed in several short stories the idea of the killer as psychotic or multiple personality. The Ed Gein case provided the basis for an ambitious treatment of the theme, and Bloch's novel *Psycho* was the source of Alfred Hitchcock's 1960 film of the same name. The commercial and critical success of *Psycho* indicated the immense potential of the issue, and a boom began in films depicting multiple murder. Most were based on real-life cases, although with considerable fictional license being taken. The career of Ed Gein [who killed at least fifteen women between 1954 and 1957, using their skin and body parts for clothing, utensils, and furniture] provided the basis for *Psycho* and *Deranged*, while later pictures followed the careers of Albert De Salvo (*The Strangler*, 1964; and *The Boston Strangler*, 1968) and Charlie Starkweather (*Badlands*, 1973). *Dirty Harry* (1971) freely synthesized the stories of novelist Gary Krist and Zodiac, [who is suspected of killing at least thirty-seven people between 1966 and 1971 and who has never been apprehended]. Hitchcock's *Frenzy* (1972) [was] derived from the Jack the Ripper story, though in modern-day guise. There were in addition numerous other treatments of the original Jack the Ripper case, which continued steadily from the 1950s through the 1980s (see, for example, *A Study in Terror*, 1966; *Hands of the Ripper*, 1971; *The Ruling Class*, 1972; *Murder by Decree*, 1979; *Time After Time*, 1980; or U.S. television movies like *Jack the Ripper* and *Jack's Back*, both 1988). . . .

In 1972, *Last House on the Left* drew to some extent on the Manson murders. [Charles Manson, along with three of his female followers, known as "The Manson Family," was convicted in 1971 of seven murders, including actress Sharon Tate, who was eight months pregnant at the time.] The film was of particular significance because it established the reputation of filmmakers later important in the horror genre: Its producer, Sean Cunningham, went on to direct *Friday the Thirteenth*, while director Wes Craven was the maker of *Nightmare on Elm Street* and *The Hills Have Eyes*. Also influential was *Texas Chainsaw Massacre* (1974), which was inspired by the Gein case. This latter was a low-budget work that enjoyed great international popularity. It was *Texas Chainsaw Massacre* that introduced the idea of the killer as a deranged monster wielding bizarre weapons and thoroughly depersonalized by his use of a mask. *Stranger in the House* (1975) provided other influential themes: a college sorority setting that allowed the killer to stalk attractive young women, and the timing of the murders around a major holiday, in this case Christmas.

The Slasher Film and the Thriller Novel

These themes coalesced in 1978 in John Carpenter's much-imitated *Halloween*, which tells the story of the fictional killer Michael Myers. Michael first appears as a child, when he kills his sister. After many years in a hospital for the criminally insane, he escapes and (masked) begins a spree in which he murders several teenagers now living in his former neighborhood. Finally, he is outwitted and defeated by the heroine, but on each occasion when he is apparently killed, it transpires that he survives to kill again (the resurrection is a device derived from Brian De Palma's 1976 film, *Carrie*). Michael Myers appears in the film as a thoroughly inhuman monster, voiceless and literally faceless, whose only function is to serve as a relentless killing machine. The film was not directly based on any specific case, but the concept of the multiple murders of young women over a single night may have owed something to Ted Bundy's rampage in a Florida sorority house earlier that year.

The influence of *Halloween* was soon seen in a wave of derivative films, which came to be known as *slasher* (or "slice and dice") movies. These were at their height in 1980 and 1981, at exactly the time when media attention was so focused on real-life cases of multiple sexual homicide, above all the cases of Ted Bundy, John Wayne Gacy, and the Atlanta Child Murders. . . .

Cinematic treatments alone ensured that serial murder would enjoy a prominent role in popular culture during the 1980s. However, the boom in slasher movies at the end of the 1970s coincided with a revival of interest in horror themes in the popular novel. The horror genre was resuscitated by the work of authors like Stephen King and Peter Straub, who employed both secular and supernatural themes, and who often made use of extreme and violent images. The success of such writing encouraged many imitators in search of new themes, especially as traditional villains like vampires and werewolves had become so hackneyed, implausible, and even humorous. Moreover, the new generation of writers was addressing an audience accustomed to the graphic violence of the gore films, which was far beyond what had been normal for traditional horror. It is not therefore surprising that several authors were attracted by the serial murder stories then occupying such a prominent role in the media, and King himself used a campus serial killer as the basis for his 1978 novella *Strawberry Spring*.

There were several important novels from this era. In 1979, Shane Stevens's best-selling *By Reason of Insanity* used the case of Richard Speck as a model for the killer's planned rampage in a women's hostel, while the fictional villain himself was obsessed by his supposed relationship with 1950s rapist Caryl Chessman. In 1981, Stuart Woods's *Chiefs* portrayed a multiple killer attacking boys and young men, and burying their remains in a secret cemetery, a concept that owed much to the cases of both Dean Corll and John Wayne Gacy. Also in 1981, Lawrence Sanders's *Third Deadly Sin* explored the theme of the female serial killer. The same year, Thomas Harris's *Red Dragon* was influenced by several true-life incidents that he studied with the advice and assistance of the FBI's Behavioral Sciences Unit (BSU).

Red Dragon was by far the most influential book of its kind from this period, but all these works contributed to shaping an emerging genre. Serial murder books generally differ from mainstream murder mysteries in that the interest of the study does not lie in the quest to identify the killer. In fact, this information is usually provided at a very early stage, and the book focuses on the career of the criminal and the means used to catch him or her. The book often tells the story at least in part from the point of view of the killer, a key element of *Red Dragon, By Reason of Insanity*, and the 1979 book *The Face That Must Die*, by the British horror author Ramsey Campbell.

The ideas presented in *Red Dragon* enjoyed a resurgence in 1988 with the publication of Harris's *The Silence of the Lambs*, which is to some extent a sequel. This book was an enormous best-seller, and among other distinctions it became a main choice of the Book of the Month Club. Harris draws on real life cases in both books, especially in the portrayal of Hannibal Lecter, "Hannibal the Cannibal," who is presented as an evil sadistic genius rather than a confused inadequate like *Psycho*'s Norman Bates. This shift of perceptions reflects the influence of real offenders, chiefly Ted Bundy, but also the intelligent and articulate Edmund Kemper, who had provided Robert Ressler with some of his most valuable interviews. The Buffalo Bill killer of *Silence of the Lambs* is based on a synthesis of Ed Gein and Gary Heidnik, but the killer also employs tactics pioneered by Bundy to entrap his victims.

The influence of Harris's work was vastly enhanced by the release of film versions. *Red Dragon* attracted a little attention under the title of *Manhunter* in 1986, but the film version of *The Silence of the Lambs* (1991) was an international sensation, with Anthony Hopkins offering a terrifying portrayal of Hannibal. This success attracted imitators, and there was soon a wave of both fact and fiction books with covers boasting their serial murder theme. Some novels claimed to be in the tradition of *The Silence of the Lambs*, or to have villains in the tradition of Hannibal Lecter, while a number came close to imitating the butterfly motif of Harris's best-seller. Robert L. Duncan's *The Serpent's Mark* (1989) depicted a behavioral scientist nicknamed "the Monster Catcher," while Joe Monninger's *Razor's Song* (1991) asserted that its villain could be compared to both Hannibal Lecter and Ted Bundy.

The overlap between fact and fiction is especially blatant (and problematic) in the true-crime literature, where case studies of serial killers frequently refer to Harris's work as if it were the definitive account of the true-life phenomenon. The fictional Hannibal became a villain as well known as any authentic offender, and was even cited in journalistic accounts as if he were a real figure. On the cover of a 1992 paperback studying Randy Kraft (by Dennis McDougal) describes the book as "the true story of a real-life Hannibal Lecter." Child killer Charlie Hatcher was described by writer Terry Ganey as "the real-life embodiment of Hannibal Lecter."

Harris's work also established a precedent in using a Quantico setting, and focusing on the mind-hunting endeavors of the FBI's behavioral scientists. Van Arman's *Just Killing Time* was typical in including a scene at Quantico, in which the head of the agency VICAT [*sic*] is lecturing about the vast scale of the serial murder problem:

> In 1985, there were 14,516 murders in America classified as without motive. . . . [F]rom this group of killers, only sixteen suspects have been captured. . . . [T]hat number does not include an additional five thousand bodies that simply turn up each year in the category of unidentified. . . . If you are a middle or upper middle class family of four, the chances are 37 percent that you will meet a serial killer in your lifetime. . . . [L]ess than one percent of all motiveless homicides were ever solved.

David Lindsey's *Mercy* (1990) was one of many novels to popularize the characteristic BSU terminology and worldview, while there was even a series of thriller novels under the generic VICAP title. [VICAP is the FBI's acronym for the Violent Criminal Apprehension Program.] . . .

The New Boom: 1991–1994

The film *The Silence of the Lambs* further stimulated popular fascination with this topic. In the *New York Times*, "a fiction editor at a major publishing house" was quoted as saying that 1989 appeared to be "the year of the serial killer." The theme attracted the interest of some of the best-selling contemporary authors, such as P.D. James, Robert B. Parker, Jonathan Kellerman, and Ed McBain. Over the next three years there was an upsurge of novels on serial killers, works such as David Lindsey's *Mercy*, James Neal Harvey's *By Reason of Insanity* (1989), and Herbert Lieberman's *Shadow Dancers* (1989). The most commercially successful books from these years included Ridley Pearson's *Undercurrents* (1988), Peter Straub's *Koko* (1988), and John Sandford's *Rules of Prey* (1989), all of which were followed by multiple sequels. In different forms, the serial murder theme came to occupy a prominent role in several related genres, in mystery and detective novels no less than in horror and suspense. The theme also appeared in "serious" literary works, in novels by Peter Ackroyd, Paul West, Philip Kerr, and Carol DeChellis Hill. . . .

The new stereotype achieved a quirky culmination in the television series Twin Peaks (1989–1991), which features an FBI agent of awesome forensic and investigative powers summoned to investigate a serial murder in a small rural community. Perhaps parodying the excessive media claims for the mind-hunters, the fictional agent Cooper receives his most significant clues in dreams and visions.

True Crime

The issue was covered as extensively in the news media and other "factual" sources as in fiction. There was a spate of news reports during the early 1990s. On television, serial murder stories became a staple of semidocumentary shows about police and crime investigation, which often used sensationalized dramatic reconstructions of crimes and other incidents in the career of the offender; and multiple murder was the theme of many talk shows hosted by celebrities like Geraldo Rivera or Phil Donahue. These programs often tried to involve the viewing audience to the point of encouraging the fantasies that the public itself was helping to solve the crimes.

On December 7, 1988, there was a two-hour prime-time television special entitled *Manhunt Live!*, which reported on current serial murder investigations with particular emphasis on the Green River case. Viewers were urged to call a special telephone hot line with possible leads, a pioneering idea that became the basis of the popular "America's Most Wanted" series, hosted by John Walsh. A book on the same case included an appeal for information to the Green River telephone hot line, offering a publisher's reward of fifty thousand dollars for evidence leading to the killer's conviction. Recently, a number of books have been sold with accompanying audiocassettes, so that readers can place themselves in the imaginary position of investigators interrogating Arthur Shawcross or Henry Lee Lucas. Court TV allows viewers to "attend" serial murder trials, and the channel has sought to broadcast every available case, including quite obscure events like the Alejandro Henriquez trial in New York City.

The interest in factual true-crime accounts was especially apparent in published accounts of real-life cases, and there is now a True Crime Book Club. Of course, multiple homicide is by no means the only theme of true-crime books, and in recent years, other topics that have enjoyed considerable attention include organized crime, tales of family murders among the rich and famous, and sensational crimes of passion like the Amy Fisher case of the early 1990s. However, serial murder stories usually account for between a third and a half of the output of such books.

Moreover, the volume of multiple-murder accounts has expanded significantly in recent years. In 1974, the Corll and Kemper cases led to a then unusual spate of at least seven books in a single year, and major cases like that of Gacy and Bundy were also widely discussed in the early 1980s. The genre thrived during the following decade. In 1990, *Publisher's Weekly* remarked on the growing spate of serial murder books, and the pace at which books appeared accelerated to unprecedented heights in the aftermath of *The Silence of the Lambs*. There is some evidence that the true-crime flood was beginning to abate by the end of 1993, but the theme remained in vogue in the thriller novels.

In the four-year period from the start of 1990 to the end of 1993, over forty book-length studies of individual cases appeared, in addition to general accounts of the serial murder phenomenon, and at least twenty collections of briefer studies, often drawn from the true-detective magazines. . . .

Images of Disturbed Individuals

Portrayals of serial killers grew sharply in number [during the latter part of the twentieth century], but they also changed fundamentally in character. In the middle years of the century, there had been a wide range of available images and stereotypes, from the monstrous lunatics of the comic books or detective magazines to the far more complex images of some of the films. However, the prevailing image in the more serious works tended to emphasize the individual pathology of the killer, who is usually depicted as sick and inadequate rather than evil. This is certainly true of [the film] *M*, and the midcentury cinema was heavily influenced by Freudian interpretations of the roots of crime. In Bloch's [novel] *The Scarf*, the killer David Morley is clearly motivated by feelings of revenge against a brutal and sexually repressive mother, emotions reinforced by a disastrous early sexual experience with a middle-aged teacher.

This psychoanalytic approach reached its apogee in *The Sniper* (1952), which addressed the topic of serial murder with a sophisticated and sympathetic awareness of contemporary criminological theories. The film is heavily Freudian in nature, depicting a disturbed young man constantly seeking revenge against his mother. The compulsive nature of the sniper's violence also bears an explicit resemblance to the William Heirens case, which formed the basis of *While the City Sleeps* (1956). This tradition continued in Hitchcock's 1960 film *Psycho*, in the conclusion to which a psychiatrist interprets Norman Bates's violence in terms of his relationship to his mother, and in effect suggests that Norman should not be blamed for his crimes. In the British *Peeping Tom* (1960), similarly, the killer is presented as a severely disturbed psychiatric case. Other 1960's films like *The Boston Strangler* and *In Cold Blood* reinforced the image of the killer as an inadequate who was the slave of his upbringing and environment. In fiction, broadly psychoanalytic (and mother-oriented) themes predominated in ripper books of the 1950s like Georges Simenon's *Maigret Sets a Trap* and Colin Wilson's *Ritual in the Dark*.

Images of Depraved Monsters

From the early 1970s, the complex psychological analyses of the earlier films began to give way to new attitudes and emphases, and the changes often reflected shifts in more general public attitudes toward the etiology of crime. Above all, the more therapeutic views of the 1950s were transformed into law and order perspectives, which emphasized the guilt and moral depravity of the individual offender. One of the most successful instances was *Dirty Harry*, which returned to the basic plot of *Sniper*, reproduced the original San Francisco setting, and used many of the same visual images, but with a radically different ideological twist. In the later film, the killer is depicted as a creature of pure evil, who cynically takes shelter behind psychiatric diagnoses of his alleged sickness. Moreover, the film criticizes the gullible and soft-hearted courts and media that permit such imposture. The same theme emerged in other hard-boiled thrillers like Charles Bronson's *Ten to Midnight* (1983), in which a Bundy-influenced killer announces that he will escape punishment by feigning an insanity defense. The audience is clearly meant to support the Bronson character's instant decision to kill him without trial.

In terms of the causation of serial murder, the films of the 1980s offered explanations that often verged on the supernatural, or overtly portrayed superhuman monsters, representatives of total, incomprehensible evil. It is instructive to contrast the psychoanalytic approach of *Sniper* or *Psycho* with a film like *Halloween*, in which no serious attempt is made to explain Michael Myers's wrongdoing in secular or psychological terms. In contrast to *Psycho,* in *Halloween* it is the psychiatrist character who agrees that Michael Myers is, in fact, the bogeyman.

As in so much else, *Halloween* shaped the genre, and serial killers were increasingly portrayed as monsters. This derived partly from the common device of the villain's resurrection after apparent death. In commercial terms, this near invincibility left open the possibility of future sequels; but it also reflected crossover from the supernaturally oriented gore genre to which these films were so closely related. In the context of the slasher films, such resurrections tended to promote increasingly inhuman interpretations of the killer's origin and powers.

Supernatural Serial Killers

In 1978, Michael Myers was certainly intended to represent a human villain, and so initially was the derivative Jason of *Friday the Thirteenth*; but by the mid-1980s, Jason had become so immune to normal rules of human behavior to be brought back from the dead by a lightning bolt, in a manner reminiscent of older Frankenstein or Dracula films. This trend reached its height with the *Nightmare on Elm Street* series, which began in 1984, in which the serial child killer Freddie Krueger appears only as a supernatural figure seeking revenge on the families of those responsible for his death, and kills his teenage victims in their dreams. By the late 1980s, Jason and Freddie had firmly established themselves among the more traditional figures of supernatural evil who provided themes for Halloween costumes, characters such as Dracula and the Mummy.

The theme of the serial killer as possessed by supernatural evil also occurred in Stanley Kubrick's *The Shining*, another 1980 film, which can scarcely be placed in the same category as the slasher movies. After the Gainesville murders of 1990, the media speculated that the crime scenes included features copied from the recent film *Exorcist III*, which depicts a demonically possessed serial killer. The same year, the television series *Twin Peaks* used a parody of such a possession theme to explain the serial murders at the heart of the plot, involving a demonic figure known as Bob.

A similar transition to the superhuman occurred in literature, most notably in the work of Thomas Harris, who drew so heavily on real-life cases. However, he takes considerable artistic license with these characters, especially in portraying killers like Hannibal Lecter as uncontrollable monsters little different from the most savage wild animals, who must at all times be restrained in captivity to prevent them from making savage attacks on guards or visitors. In reality, serial killers appear much more able to restrain their violent instincts. However, this portrait of the multiple killer as a monster in human form was influential on subsequent depictions. Similar stereotypes also occur frequently in the emerging genre of *splatterpunk*, short stories of extreme graphic horror strongly influenced by the gore films. Inevitably in such a context, serial killers are depicted in the most monstrous and nonhuman guise, reflecting trends in both the novel and the cinema.

Cultural Images Shape Policy

It is scarcely too much to describe multiple murder in the 1980s and 1990s as a cultural industry in its own right, with serial killers as a pervasive theme in television, the cinema, and the publishing world. Fictional and true-crime depictions also had a clear impact on changing perceptions of real world offenders, which would be significant for shaping debates over policy, and in every case the emerging view reflected the ideas proposed by federal law enforcement agencies in the early 1980s. This affected the popular view of the scale of the crime, the nature of the offender, and the appropriate antidote to the evil.

First, the intensity of the coverage clearly supported charges that serial murder was a vast menace. The popular books and articles on the topic naturally tended to report inflated statistics, but there was also the impressionistic effect based on the sheer volume of easily available serial murder books. Multiple murder therefore acquired high public visibility, which in turn increase the likelihood that the news media would report on relevant stories. In terms of law enforcement priorities, the prominence of serial murder made it likely that prestige and rewards would be won by successful interventions in this area, and therefore the offense would attract resources.

Moreover, the specific type of multiple murder that gained visibility was very much that of the extreme sexual sadist or psychopath. There was a cyclical effect, in which the media tended to focus on crimes that most resembled available public stereotypes: sex killers like Bundy, cannibals like Hannibal. In turn, reporting of those specific cases reinforced awareness of these stereotypes. This reinforced the idea that the real serial killer was a ripper or sexual killer, rather than a medical murderer or a woman killing members of her family or intimate circle.

Finally, the popular culture depictions of the problem placed massive emphasis on the heroic role of the (federal) mind-hunters, rather than the ordinary police officers and detectives from local agencies, who are virtually always responsible when serial killers are apprehended. Derek Van Arman's *Just Killing Time* features as hero "the head of the federal agency that hunts the most dangerous criminal alive—the serial killer." The unit was needed because serial killings were "types of assault local enforcement had little chance of solving without help." In *Fair Game*, Bernard Du Clos claims that murderer Robert Hansen was pursued and arrested with the assistance of "VICAP, the FBI unit made famous in *The Silence of the Lambs*."

Taken together, these cultural trends established a public expectation that the federal experts in fact possessed the highest expertise in such cases, and that it was normal or even essential to seek their advice when murders were not solved rapidly. This tended to promote the view that serial murder cases were almost ipso facto federal in nature, exactly the view that the Justice Department had been at such pains to cultivate in the early 1980s.

CENSORING A SERIAL-KILLER WEBSITE

Charles Levendosky

Charles Levendosky writes on First Amendment issues for the *Casper Star-Tribune*, a Casper, Wyoming, newspaper. He is also the creator of their website, First Amendment Cyber-Tribune (FACT). In the following selection, Levendosky relates the controversy that began in September 1997 when Wyoming governor Jim Geringer and South Carolina governor David Beasley pressured America Online to drop Sondra London's website, which featured the writings of serial killers Danny Rolling and Keith Hunter Jesperson. According to Levendosky, the First Amendment was designed to protect citizens from censorship by the government, including even the writings of serial killers. Furthermore, he argues, people who visit the website should be able to choose whether or not they want to view the writings of serial killers without interference by political figures. Shortly after this article was written, Sondra London's website was picked up by a different provider and was once again available on the Internet.

The Internet has survived attempts by state legislatures and by Congress to restrict or control its content. The First Amendment proved to be an effective shield in those cases. But a new kind of attack against freedom of speech on the Internet lunges for the jugular vein of online service providers—to cut off their economic blood.

Fortunately, a little Internet jujitsu can throw the attacker and make the speech more available.

Reactions to a Serial Killer Web Site

On Sept. 4, 1997, Wyoming Gov. Jim Geringer wrote a letter to Steve Case, chairman of America Online, to protest a Web site posted through AOL services. Geringer criticized AOL for providing Internet access to journalist-writer Sondra London of Florida who created a Web site that put the writings and ramblings of serial killers Dan Rolling and Keith Hunter Jesperson online.

Reprinted from Charles Levendosky, "Web Censorship Turns into Million Dollar Forum," *Casper (Wyo.) Star-Tribune*, September 14, 1997, by permission of the author.

Jesperson killed a woman in Wyoming and Geringer wants to extradite him from an Oregon prison where he is serving two life sentences for other murders. In the letter, Geringer claimed the Jesperson Web pages promote violence.

He wrote, "I am disgusted that the AOL services allow this subhuman to mock his victims and flaunt his crimes."

The governor concludes his letter: "This is not about censorship. It is about moral responsibility. It is about the duty of the nation's largest internet provider to stand up for decency and say there are some things—no matter how legal—that you should choose not to embrace and not to promote.

"I call on America Online today to review this website and to adjust its policy against the promotion of violence. You should drop this website immediately."

The governor was reacting to a series of Web pages entitled "The Self-Start Serial Killer Kit!" authored by Jesperson. It contained statements like "Now you can be the only serial killer on your block!" and "See what works and what doesn't!" and other twisted imaginings.

In an interview on Sept. 6, 1997, London, who has written two books on serial killers and one on death row inmates, responded to Geringer's criticism saying that her intention is to educate the public about the thought processes of serial killers.

A week after Geringer sent his letter to AOL, South Carolina Gov. David Beasley joined the effort to pressure AOL into dropping the serial killer Web site.

That same day at a governor's press conference in Cheyenne, Marc Klaas, the founder of the Klaas Foundation for Children, called for a boycott of AOL. Klaas' 12-year-old daughter Polly was abducted and killed in California in 1993.

Geringer said he supported the boycott and noted that several people had contacted his office to say they had cancelled their AOL service. He called their actions "very encouraging."

Three hours after the news conference, AOL capitulated. And on Sept. 12, 1997, AOL removed London's Web site.

Certainly, Geringer has a right to criticize America Online. And America Online has the right to offer its services to whomever it pleases, and within the limits of its vague contract may cancel those services for practically any reason it pleases.

However, London's Web site did not violate the First Amendment—no matter how many people were offended. And despite Geringer's uninformed contention that Jesperson no longer has any free speech rights because of what he did, Jesperson does indeed still have the right to speak about his crimes.

In 1996, the Barnes & Noble bookstore in Wyoming's state capital, Cheyenne, stocked the book that London wrote with serial killer Danny Rolling, *The Making of a Serial Killer.* Gov. Geringer didn't call for a boycott of the local store or demand for "moral reasons" that the store get rid of the book. Yet accessing a Web site is a lot like selecting a book in a store. You look at the book and based upon the title or the author, you choose to open the book or not.

The reader, the viewer makes a personal choice. You have to select a Web site and go to it. The governor would take that choice away from the public.

Censorship Can Backfire

It is troubling when a head of state uses the power and prestige of his position to attempt to censor protected speech. It violates the spirit of the First Amendment, at least. The First Amendment was created to protect the citizenry from the censorship powers of government.

Imagine a governors' conference in which 15 or 20 governors decided to pressure an online service provider to cancel a Web site. While no legislative action is taken, the effect could be substantial—depending on the response from the Internet world.

In this case, Internet citizens used the combined Geringer-Beasley-Klaas weight of influence against the would-be censors. Internet jujit-su flipped an obscure Web site into the light for many viewers—and will keep it online.

In the days that followed, London had 14 offers for free hosting of her serial killer Web site and to mirror the site.

In an interview on September 13, 1997, London said, "It is very gratifying to me the way the free speech contingent of the world has leapt to life here. I've never had so many friends. . . . People who aren't particularly interested in serial killers, all of a sudden care because they're like me—they don't want anyone interfering with the right for anyone to speak.

"I've been trudging along on this beat for quite awhile. That Web site has been up there for a long time. All of a sudden I'm the great Satan. Why, because the governor is involved? . . . It's a mechanism to conjure up some hypothetical enemy that you can demonize and then portray yourself as there to save the people from this threat.

"I'm very gratified at the way this has turned around." The traditional response to speech you don't like, she said, is to ignore it—and any other response only serves to invigorate speech.

"Those who hate my speech, need to know that I have never had more attention in my life. This is way beyond my wildest dreams. There is no way I could have contrived a million dollar ad campaign that would bring this kind of attention and give me the forum to stand up and say what it is I am trying to say."

London says she can't get to all the requests from producers to be on their shows. She already has had a number of radio and television interviews since Geringer started the controversy.

This time the Internet censors lost. This time. . . .

ROMANCING A SERIAL KILLER: TRUE LOVE OR EXPLOITATION?

Ian Katz

Some notorious serial killers attract admirers and have even become engaged and married while in prison. In the following selection, Ian Katz examines journalist Sondra London's relationships with serial killers and discusses her possible motives, particularly concerning her fiancé Danny Rolling, who is awaiting execution for the murder of five people in Gainesville, Florida. Katz reports that several years after London discovered she had once dated convicted serial killer Gerard Schaefer, she made an agreement with Schaefer to be the sole channel of his fiction and other writings. Soon, the author explains, other killers sought London out to tell their story, which is how she met Rolling. London publishes Rolling's artwork and writings, from which she has received a great deal of publicity, Katz writes. Although it often appears that London's relationship with Rolling is nothing more than mutual exploitation, Katz reveals a side of London that indicates her relationship with Rolling is more intimate. Katz is a columnist for the *Guardian*, a British daily newspaper.

Sondra London is not, to judge from her colourful use of language, the kind of person who would object on principle to sex before marriage. But she has most definitely not slept with the man whom she has pledged to make her fourth husband. In fact, she has never even touched him.

Engaged to a Serial Killer

London's fiance is Danny Rolling, dubbed the Gainesville Slasher long before he pleaded guilty early in 1994 to killing five students in the small Florida university town. Even by the demanding standards of serial killers, the murders were unusually gruesome: each of his victims was terribly mutilated and the head of one of the four women he killed was found on a shelf.

But that doesn't bother London, a 47-year-old freelance journalist

Reprinted from Ian Katz, "Marriage Most Foul," *The Guardian*, June 19, 1995, by permission. Copyright ©1995 by The Guardian News Service Ltd.

with square, weather-beaten features and tired brown eyes. London says she fell in love with Rolling the moment she saw him through the thick glass of a prison visiting room. Rolling, who refers to himself and London as "the Romeo and Juliet of crime", evidently felt the same way. According to London, their proposals crossed in the mail a few weeks later.

The couple never met outside prison and, since Rolling received five death sentences for his crimes, they almost certainly never will. If Florida authorities ever allow them to marry, they may get to touch briefly at the austere ceremony. (The prison provides a plastic bouquet.) . . .

Not that people are overflowing with sympathy for the couple's sad story of frustrated love. To many, she is just another death row groupie, one of a distressingly large number of women drawn inexplicably to the perpetrators of appalling crimes.

But London is intelligent and articulate, not at all the picture of a typical death row groupie. So others attribute to her a more cynical motive: they suggest the union is purely a marriage of convenience. London is a journalist desperate for a story, they say. And prepared to go to any lengths to get it.

Certainly it is true that she penned a series of articles purporting to be Rolling's confessions in a supermarket tabloid, and also that she has compiled a collection of his memoirs which she is currently trying to get published. But she argues cogently against the suggestion that her relationship with Rolling is little more than a business transaction. "Danny Rolling wrote to me and in his first letter he gave me the exclusive rights. I had the story already, so there was no need for artifice. If I don't care for him, why am I still writing to him every day?"

It is only fair to point out that the idea of falling in love with a serial killer may not have seemed quite as outlandish to London as it might have done to you or me. Back in the 1970s, she was amazed to read that a deputy-sheriff called Gerard Schaefer had been convicted of two appalling sex murders and was suspected of involvement in more than 30 others. Amazed because she had dated him at high school.

A Voice for Serial Killers

A few years later, she had the idea of exploiting her unique personal knowledge of Schaefer, just as the crime writer Anne Rule had turned her friendship with Ted Bundy into a blockbuster. She got in touch with him and struck an agreement under which she acted as the sole conduit of his pornographic "killer fiction" and other writing.

Word quickly got round. Soon her mailbox was filled with letters from killers, and she sprinkles her conversation with matter-of-fact references to them. Poor so-and-so who killed "to prevent earthquakes". Bobby Lewis, "a pimp, but a pimp by nature and actually a pimp too". Larry Lonchar, who's asked her to take his last statement before he is executed.

It was through Lewis that Rolling contacted her and asked her to tell his story. It was just business, she says, until she read that he had sung in court while facing robbery charges. "I thought, what is this guy? He must be interesting." After corresponding for a while, they eventually met in February of 1994.

London giggles childishly and flutters her eyelids as she describes the moment they first saw each other.

"I was so excited and he was so excited and I was just like so. . . . One of us would be talking and the other would be just looking. It was hot, it was hot, it was real hot."

They were not allowed to meet again but they have kept up a daily correspondence, professing and re-professing their mutual adoration. "I want the whole bloomin' bloody world to know . . . I love Sondra with all my heart," wrote Rolling in one letter readily made available by London. She describes herself as a kind of mirror on the killer's soul. "He can't see himself," she explains, "but he can reveal himself to me and I can tell him what I see and who he is and what he's all about."

Though she denied it at the time, London says she knew from the beginning that Rolling was guilty of the crimes with which he had been charged. But her horror at the killings could be reconciled with her growing affection for him because serial killers, she believes, have "multiple personalities". Danny had three or four. The one that prompted him to kill was "Gemini . . . absolute evil". Why could she not be in love with the others?

"Serial killers have a whole personality that is functional, with a front and a back and a middle and no pathology in it, and that's why they can become serial killers. Actually, I have a different relationship with each of the Dannys."

Rolling's personalities have all "stabilised" now, she says, and he has even banished Gemini. "But he still loves rape and he's unrepentant about that. He's appalled by the murders but rape is a part of Danny."

That could be a problem, since London was twice a rape victim herself. Sometimes she tries to explain to him the pain of rape but it doesn't do much good.

Doesn't she ever worry that he dreams of raping her? Or worse? Certainly not. "If someone really is a serial killer and you're their friend, you're safe. They want to carry on killing, so they don't want to get into trouble and if they kill someone they know, they know they'll get caught."

In 1995, London published the first issue of *Dan's Fans*, billed as "the Danny Rolling Fanzine". She says it is a way for the killer to reply to the many people who write to him in prison, but the professionally produced newsletter ($3 per issue, $10 for four) looks as though it were born of more commercial considerations. The cover features one of Rolling's Gothic "artworks", depicting a naked woman and a dragon: "The raven-haired Gypsey Enchantress represents my fair Lady

Sondra," it explains inside, "and I the Dragon, the Possessed Prince, swooned by her charms." Another picture shows a werewolf holding up the severed head of a woman.

Between re-affirming his love for his "sugar babydoll" and the exclusivity of London's access to his "Thought Generator", Rolling offers his pensees on subjects from The Destiny of Man to his favourite weapons, movies, drugs. There is even a "safety tips" section: "Take it from one who knows: It pays to be paranoid!"

Another Side to Sondra

After a few glasses of wine, London talks less about love. "I'm a writer who wants a big story, who dated a serial killer and is left with a lifetime fascination with serial killers, and here comes this prime example of a serial killer and says: 'I'm giving myself to you on a silver platter'."

But just when you have decided that the Rolling-London relationship is about nothing more than mutual exploitation, you encounter the jealousy. It explodes to the surface the moment you bring up Debbie Huber, the New Orleans "murderabilia" collector who London claims tricked Rolling into sending her a self-portrait and a letter professing his love. "The woman wants to be me. She wants my boyfriend, she actually wants to be me."

It's there too in the regular feature in *Dan's Fans* in which London promises to reveal the depths to which journalists have gone in their attempts to secure an interview with Rolling. In issue one, her target is an Orlando reporter who dropped, in a letter to her beau, that "coincidentally, I'm a petite brunette—for what that's worth". Those were precisely the words used most often to describe Rolling's female victims.

London's possessiveness, however, stops at the prison gates. Would their relationship work if he were ever released? "I don't think so. I might try but I don't think it would last. He's too disturbed, his behaviour's too bad. Guys don't treat me that way and get away with that shit."

ENSURING THAT CRIME WILL NOT PAY

Charles S. Clark

In the following selection, Charles S. Clark discusses the controversy over legislation that prevents notorious criminals such as
serial killers from profiting from their notoriety. These "Son of
Sam" laws, Clark explains, were named after serial killer David
Berkowitz, who called himself the "Son of Sam" in notes he left
at his crime scenes. The author relates that when Berkowitz sold
his story for $250,000, an outraged New York assemblyman
introduced legislation to put the profits in an account for the
families of the killer's victims. While victims' rights activists
argue that crime should not pay, Clark reports, others claim that
"Son of Sam" laws violate the right to a free press, asserting that
one purpose of the First Amendment is to keep the public
informed about crime and criminals. Clark is a staff writer for the
weekly periodical *CQ Researcher*.

The rock group Guns N' Roses tucked a macabre surprise inside its
compact disc release, *The Spaghetti Incident*. Listeners were treated,
with nary a mention on the album cover, to a song called "Look at
Your Game, Girl," written in the 1960s by California mass murderer
Charles M. Manson.

Victims' Advocates Speak Out

Crime victims' advocates were appalled, and the Sacramento-based
Doris Tate Crime Victims Bureau launched a boycott against the
group's Hollywood label, Geffen Records Inc.

The controversy comes at a time when the imprisoned Manson is
already accumulating royalties from a contract with a Newport Beach,
Calif., T-shirt manufacturer, which sells shirts bearing Manson's eerie
portrait to young surfers. Equally galling to many crime victims was
the report that Chicago serial killer John Wayne Gacy, before his execution in 1994, had found a market for sales of his clown paintings.

"It's a travesty," says victims' rights activist John Walsh, host of the
Fox Network TV show *America's Most Wanted*. Walsh, whose 6-year-

Reprinted from Charles S. Clark, "Laws That Make Sure Crime Doesn't Pay," *CQ
Researcher*, July 22, 1994, with permission.

old son Adam was murdered in the 1980s, deplores the way tabloid news shows pay criminals for interviews. "Any money made through victimization should go for compensation, therapy and rebuilding the lives of victims. No other society allows criminals to profit from crimes," he says.

The idea that criminals can become media stars and profit from their crimes is "a symbolic, gut issue that instantly outrages anyone," says David Beatty, director of public affairs for the Arlington, Va.–based National Victim Center. "It's the ultimate insult from the victim's perspective, and it calls into question the basic notion that crime doesn't pay."

Laws against profiteering from notoriety are known informally as "Son of Sam" laws. They are named for serial killer David Berkowitz, the postal worker who terrorized New York City with random shootings in 1977, and who left notes at the crime scenes signed "Son of Sam."

The crimes of Berkowitz, who eventually sold his story for $250,000, prompted an outraged New York assemblyman to introduce legislation to put such profits in an escrow account to be tapped by victims' survivors. Some 40 states imitated the New York law, and in 1984 the Federal Victims of Crime Act empowered federal judges to order the "literary profits" of criminals diverted to the Crime Victims Fund.

Challenging "Son of Sam" Laws

The New York law, however, was challenged by publisher Simon & Schuster, among others, which called it a violation of the right to a free press. "The First Amendment has a broader social purpose, which is to serve as a counterbalance for the public to understand such issues as crime," says R. Bruce Rich, First Amendment counsel to the Association of American Publishers, which filed a friend-of-the-court brief in the case. Under the original New York law, Rich says, profits from a book could be seized even if "one page in a 500-page book recounted a youthful offense that was never prosecuted, like stealing a pen from a store.

"So who is to play God and decide how much of a chilling effect the law should have on publishing? It's an unpopular position. But our society incarcerates more people than any in the world, and therefore writings about the criminal mind and the criminal experience are deeply relevant."

In December 1992, the U.S. Supreme Court struck down the law, sending state and federal legislators back for creative ways to redraft it. "The Court didn't strike down the whole idea, just the way it was drafted," says Washington attorney Deborah Kelly, who chairs the Victims Committee for the American Bar Association. The goal is to say that "it's OK to write the book, just that criminals can't then get rich and retire to Beverly Hills."

Revised in 1993, the New York law is "an improvement, but still doesn't get around our constitutional problems," says Rich. He says a number of the revised state laws appear to avoid singling out the criminals' media contracts and take the more evenhanded approach of confiscating all his assets.

Sentencing judges, meanwhile, are using disincentives to discourage defendants from writing books. When former student radical Katherine Ann Powers was sentenced in 1993 for her role in the 1970 slaying of a Boston policeman, Suffolk Superior Court Judge Robert W. Banks forbade her from profiting from the killing by selling her story while in prison and while on probation for 20 years after her release.

In California, the Legislature is considering a bill to expand the state Son of Sam law to prohibit even indirect profits from notoriety, which would halt Manson's profits from T-shirts. And the Doris Tate bureau continues to canvass music stores to discourage purchases of Guns N' Roses albums or any Geffen products.

At one point, the record company offered a donation to settle the matter but backed out when it learned the money wouldn't be tax deductible, according to Kelly Rudiger, executive director of the Tate center.

"We've told them that we're not legally able to remove the track because Guns N' Roses has creative freedom in their contract," says Bryn Bridenthal, Geffen's vice president for media and artist relations. She points out that under California's law, all of Manson's royalties go to the surviving son of one of his murder ring's victims, the only one to file a claim.

"Guns N' Roses didn't know it was a Manson song when they chose it," she says, "but they later decided it was preferable to leave it in so that the victim's son gets some money. Everyone was comfortable that Manson wouldn't get a dime."

ORGANIZATIONS TO CONTACT

The editors have compiled the following list of organizations concerned with the issues presented in this book. The descriptions are derived from materials provided by the organizations. All have publications or information available for interested readers. The list was compiled on the date of publication of the present volume; the information provided here may change. Be aware that many organizations take several weeks or longer to respond to inquiries, so allow as much time as possible.

Crime Victims United of California (CVUC)
1121 L St., Suite 406, Sacramento, CA 95814
(916) 448-3291
e-mail: cvu-pac@cvu-ca.org • website: http://www.cvu-ca.org

Organized by the surviving family members of murder victims, CVUC endeavors to enhance public safety, promote effective crime-reduction measures, and strengthen the rights of crime victims. CVUC endorses political candidates who are pro–law enforcement and pro–victims' rights. It also sponsors educational forums, meetings, and mailings on victim-related issues.

Justice for Murder Victims (JMV)
PO Box 16670, San Francisco, CA 94116-6670
(415) 731-9880
e-mail: vocal@vocal-jmv.org • website: http://www.vocal-jmv.org

A project of the Catina Rose Victims of Crime Assistance League (VOCAL), JMV works within the legal system to ensure that current laws are enforced and promotes new legislation in the interest of public safety. JMV monitors parole hearings and offers support to the surviving family of murder victims by providing assistance in procuring benefits and understanding judicial procedures. On its website, JMV publishes current and past issues of its bimonthly newsletter, which gives updates on current cases and contains articles on victims' rights issues.

National Center for the Analysis of Violent Crime (NCAVC)
Federal Bureau of Investigation, Critical Incident Response Group,
FBI Academy, Quantico, VA 22135
website: http://www.fbi.gov/vicap/vicap.htm

Created by the FBI, the NCAVC is a law enforcement–oriented resource center that provides assistance to law enforcement agencies confronted with unusual, high-risk, vicious, or repetitive crimes. Among its many research topics, NCAVC studies violent serial crimes, including serial homicide and rape. The center also offers investigative support through its Violent Criminal Apprehension Program (VICAP), which alerts law enforcement agencies in different jurisdictions to the possibility that a single serial killer may be operating in their area. These "VICAP Alert" notices are also published in the monthly *FBI Law Enforcement Bulletin*.

National Center for Victims of Crime (NCVC)
2111 Wilson Blvd., Suite 300, Arlington, VA 22201
(703) 276-2880 • fax: (703) 276-2889
e-mail: victimservice@ncvc.org • website: http://www.ncvc.org

NCVC focuses on providing training and technical assistance to lawyers, social services workers, and other professionals who deal with victims of crimes, including survivors of serial killers or family members of their victims. The center also works to protect victims' legal rights through its public policy division. It maintains a resource library and publishes the *Crime Victims' Litigation Quarterly*.

National Coalition Against Censorship (NCAC)

275 Seventh Ave., New York, NY 10001
(212) 807-6222 • fax: (212) 807-6245
e-mail: ncac@ncac.org • website: http://www.ncac.org

NCAC is an alliance of organizations committed to defending freedom of thought, inquiry, and expression by engaging in public education and advocacy at the national and local level. It believes censorship of violent materials is dangerous because it represses intellectual and artistic freedom. NCAC maintains a library of information dealing with First Amendment issues and publishes the quarterly *Censorship News*.

National Criminal Justice Reference Service (NCJRS)

PO Box 6000, Rockville, MD 20849-6000
(800) 851-3420 • (301) 519-5500
e-mail: askncrs@ncrs.org (for questions) •
e-mail: puborder@ncjrs.org (for publications) • website: http://www.ncjrs.org

An international clearinghouse, NCJRS is one of the most extensive sources of information on criminal and juvenile justice in the world. NCJRS supports all bureaus of the U.S. Department of Justice and maintains specialized information centers for Office of Justice Program agencies, including the Office for Victims of Crime (OVC), the Bureau of Justice Statistics (BJS), and the Bureau of Justice Assistance (BJA). The NCJRS collection contains the latest research findings, statistical reports, program descriptions, and evaluations on victim issues published by public and private sources, including the federal government.

National Organization for Victim Assistance (NOVA)

1757 Park Rd. NW, Washington, DC 20010
(202) 232-6682 • fax: (202) 462-2255
e-mail: nova@try-nova.org • website: http://www.try-nova.org

This organization consists of victims' activists, researchers, and criminal justice professionals who monitor legislation, offer support programs, and provide information on victims' rights. NOVA sends multidisciplinary teams to the scenes of major crimes and provides training to professionals in such fields as law enforcement, mental health, social work, and community services. On its website, NOVA publishes articles by victims and professionals and provides access to other publications on violent crime and victim assistance.

National Organization of Parents of Murdered Children (NOPMC)

100 E. Eighth St., B-41, Cincinnati, OH 45202
(888) 818-POMC • fax: (513) 345-4489
e-mail: NatlPOMC@aol.com • website: http://www.pomc.com

NOPMC is a self-help group that provides support and education to the families and friends of homicide victims. It works to prevent the early parole and release of convicted murderers and to stop the entertainment industry's marketing of violence. The organization publishes the booklet *Path Through the Criminal Justice System*.

BIBLIOGRAPHY

Books

John E. Douglas, Ann W. Burgess, and Robert K. Ressler	*Sexual Homicide: Patterns and Motives*. Old Tappan, NJ: Simon & Schuster, 1995.
John E. Douglas and Mark Olshaker	*Journey into Darkness*. New York: Pocket Books, 1997.
John E. Douglas and Mark Olshaker	*Obsession*. New York: Pocket Books, 1998.
Stephen J. Giannangelo	*The Psychopathology of Serial Murder: A Theory of Violence*. Westport, CT: Praeger, 1996.
Eric W. Hickey	*Serial Murderers and Their Victims*. Florence, KY: Brooks/Cole, 1996.
David Lester	*Serial Killers: The Insatiable Passion*. Philadelphia: Charles Press, 1995.
Terry Manners	*Deadlier than the Male: Stories of Female Serial Killers*. North Pomfret, VT: Trafalgar Square, 1997.
Robert K. Ressler and Tom Shachtman	*I Have Lived in the Monster: A Report from the Abyss*. New York: St. Martin's Press, 1998.
Harold Schechter and David Everitt	*The A–Z Encyclopedia of Serial Killers*. New York: Pocket Books, 1997.
Mark Seltzer	*Serial Killers: Death and Life in America's Wound Culture*. New York: Routledge, 1998.
Richard Tithecott	*Of Men and Monsters: Jeffrey Dahmer and the Construction of the Serial Killer*. Madison: University of Wisconsin Press, 1997.
Russell Vorpagel and Joseph Harrington	*Profiles in Murder*. New York: Plenum, 1998.
Colin Wilson and Damon Wilson	*The Killers Among Us: Motives Behind Their Murders*. Waltham, MA: Warner Books, 1996.

Periodicals

Jane Caputi	"American Psychos: The Serial Killer in Contemporary Fiction," *Journal of American Culture*, Winter 1993. Available from Popular Press, Bowling Green University, Bowling Green, OH 43403.
Kevin Clarke	"Waiting for Gacy," *U.S. Catholic*, November 1994.
Jackson Devon	"Serial Killers and the People Who Love Them," *Village Voice*, March 22, 1994. Available from 36 Cooper Square, New York, NY 10003.
Thomas Evan and Daniel Klaidman	"Blood Brothers," *Newsweek*, April 22, 1996.

Anne C. Gresham   "The Insanity Plea: A Futile Defense for Serial Killers,"
                              Law and Psychology Review, Spring 1993.

Joseph Grixti   "Consuming Cannibals: Psychopathic Killers as
                              Archetypes and Cultural Icons," *Journal of American
                              Culture*, Spring 1995.

Mark Hansen   "What Price Gory?" *ABA Journal,* August 1996.

Bill Hewlett and   "Smooth Operator," *People Weekly*, December 4, 1995.
Fannie Weinstein

David Kempler   "One Man's Summer of Sam," *New York Times*, August
                              23, 1998.

Pam Lambert   "Nightmare Alley," *People Weekly*, February 16, 1998.

John Leo   "The Unabomber Is a Killer, That's All," *Conservative
                              Chronicle*, May 29, 1996. Available from PO Box
                              37077, Boone, IA 50037-0077.

Eugene H. Methvin   "The Face of Evil," *National Review*, January 23, 1995.

Diana Lambdin Meyer   "Animal Abusers More Likely to Abuse People,"
                              Horizons, Fall 1996. Available from PO Box 128,
                              Winnipeg, Manitoba, R362G1 Canada.

Patricia Pearson   "Murder on Her Mind," *Saturday Night*, June 1994.

Mark Seltzer   "Serial Killers (II): The Pathological Public Sphere,"
                              Critical Inquiry, Autumn 1995. Available from The
                              University of Chicago Press, Journals Division, PO Box
                              37005, Chicago, IL 60637.

Kathleen M. Timmons   "Natural Born Writers: The Law's Continued
                              Annoyance with Criminal Authors," *Georgia Law
                              Review*, Summer 1995.

Wayne Wilson   "Modus Operandi of Female Serial Killers,"
and Tonya Hilton   *Psychological Reports*, April 1998.

INDEX